CROSSROAD

SELECTED BOOKS BY DAVID KIRBY

Poetry

Sarah Bernhardt's Leg
Saving the Young Men of Vienna
Big-Leg Music
The House of Blue Light
The Ha-Ha
I Think I Am Going to Call My Wife Paraguay: Selected Early Poems
The House on Boulevard St.: New and Selected Poems
The Temple Gate Called Beautiful
Talking About Movies With Jesus
The Biscuit Joint
A Wilderness of Monkeys

Anthology

Seriously Funny: Poems About Love, Death, Religion, Art, Politics, Sex, and Everything Else, co-edited with Barbara Hamby

Non-Fiction

What Is a Book?
Ultra-Talk: Johnny Cash, The Mafia, Shakespeare, Drum Music, St. Teresa Of Avila, And 17 Other Colossal Topics of Conversation
Little Richard: The Birth of Rock 'n' Roll

CROSSROAD

ARTIST, AUDIENCE, AND THE MAKING OF AMERICAN MUSIC

DAVID KIRBY

newamericanpress

Milwaukee, Wis. • Urbana, Ill.

newamericanpress

www.NewAmericanPress.com

© 2015 by David Kirby

Printed in the United States of America

ISBN 978-1-941561-02-7

Book design by David Bowen

Cover image courtesy of DWS / Bigstock.com

For ordering information, please contact:
Ingram Book Group
One Ingram Blvd.
La Vergne, TN 37086
(800) 937-8000
orders@ingrambook.com

TABLE OF CONTENTS

To Newton Collier, soul man

I'm a theatrical performer. I'm whispering in your ear, and you're dreaming my dreams, and then I'm getting a feeling for yours. I've been doing that for forty years.

— Bruce Springsteen

The Hot Potato Theory

JACK WHITE, BEST KNOWN AS A FOUNDING MEMBER of the White Stripes, has chewed out many a passive audience for its torpor—" for not participating in the two-way experience of rock & roll," as writer and fan William Giraldi says. In contrast to European audiences, White thinks that, in Giraldi's words, "American audiences are so pampered, feel so entitled, that a concert for them is like a night at the movies," as though they are saying, "'I bought my ticket, juggler, now entertain me as I repose.'"

On the night Giraldi is writing about, Jack mocks the crowd just that way, asking if they think they're at the movies. Most people are seated except for a teenager in the cheap seats who is on his feet and digging it. The musician singles the kid out and praises him for being the exception to the general indolence. Then he tells his stage manager to give the kid every piece of White Stripes merchandise he can lay his hands on; minutes later, the manager can be seen hauling a Santa's sack of presents up to the first tier.

If you look at the footage of most concerts or see a photo of some kids losing their minds at a club, you might get the idea that the artist-audience transaction is a one-way street, that a more or less indifferent group of musicians gets up on stage, and a pack of idol worshippers appear out of nowhere to howl, mosh, and spill beer. From Beethoven to the Beatles, the gods are in the footlights, and we fallen mortals in the pit.

But if you talk to people who write songs and play in bands, you get a totally different picture. Every band I've ever talked to (and the one I was in) proceeds by trial and error; they try out songs, musical styles, shoes and shirts, and personnel, and they adjust as they go, just as Dostoevsky wrote timeless novels by adapting them to the reading public of 19th-century St. Petersburg. The Great Man Theory, which argues that history is changed mainly by figures

< 11 >

like Caesar and Napoleon, has been viewed skeptically for years in every field—except music.

There is in the exchange between artist and audience another meaning of the phrase "shock of recognition," because the audience looks at the artist and sees what it can be, just as the artist looks out at the throng of ecstatic faces and thinks, "As you are, so I was—who am I now?" And in the exchange that takes place between artist and audience, both agree, not to answer these questions, but to ask them.

In *Crossroad*, I'm taking a closer look at that intersection described in the subtitle. There are artists, and there are audiences, and the two come together thanks to a lot of behind-the-scenes activity by songwriters, producers, and other unsung heroes of the industry; music is the result. A lot of these pieces began with my picking up a book about somebody whose music I loved, and one problem with a lot of music books is that they aren't about music—they're about musicians. And while it can be fleetingly entertaining to read about your favorite rock star's addictions and sexual conquests, you find that you're left with the question you began with, namely, where'd the music come from?

Crossroad begins before the golden age of rock 'n' roll and ends a couple of decades after. A lot of books that cover that period look exclusively at the artists, but I widen the focus here. As Montaigne says, raisins are the best part of a cake, but raisins are not as good as a cake. Sure, the spotlight's on the stars, but let's take a look at the whole house—the whole cake, as Montaigne would say. I want to take a broader view of how the music world works, how the moving parts link up (or not), how carefully worked-out systems collide with unforeseen accidents, how geniuses and stumblebums somehow manage to make the music that rewires our brains, electrifies our very souls, and keeps us young forever.

Of course we want the singers who stir our very souls to be Great Men and Women, to be larger than life. How else can they move us? And of course we want our music to come from heaven rather than slither across the sidewalks and lawns that ring our humdrum lives. But the musicians I know, and certainly the best among them, say something like this: I started by following my

< 12 >

passion, but then I started paying attention to what people wanted, even if they themselves didn't know what that was.

IN A WAY, WHAT I'M WRITING about in *Crossroad* is what academics call "reception theory," which looks at ways in which the significance of a text is not in the text itself but in the relationship between the text and its audience.

But that's the last time you'll see the phrase "reception theory" in these pages.

Then again, you shouldn't expect to come across any old-school moralizing here, or anything on pastoralism and redemption. It's not that those themes are outdated. All music is intrinsically humanistic, even religious. In *Black Song*, John Lovell, Jr. writes: "Every folk song is religious in the sense that it is concerned about the origins, ends, and deepest manifestations of life, as experienced by some more or less unified community. It tends to probe, usually without nailing down definite answers, the puzzles of life at their roots."

And isn't that true of all music? Doesn't every song, be it pop or punk or rap or a Christmas carol, deal with the "deepest manifestations of life"? To put it the other way around, doesn't every song come from and go back to the people who make and consume it—isn't every song a folk song?

The Church of Music has never been bigger, and they're adding new pews every day.

And as in scripture, music makes its point through parables. Key to all art, even the most abstract or experimental, is the presence of story. Tell stories, said Motown's Berry Gordy, Jr. to his song writers. And tell them in the present tense: not "my girl broke up with me" but "my girl is breaking up with me." If I tell you what I see as a truth, you may or may not buy it, because the answer is coming from me. But if I tell you a story worth listening to, the answer will come from you.

It's this exchange between speaker and listener, between writer and reader, between singer and audience that is at the heart of *Crossroad*. Bob Mould of Husker Dü espouses what he calls the hot potato theory: "It's like inspiration

< 13 >

is a hot potato you pull out of the oven and then toss to someone else. So we listen, we become fans, we become inspired, we create, and somehow the work we create eventually finds its way back to the ones who inspired us."

What is an audience? Here's a story that tells exactly what an audience does. Producer Butch Vig played a tape of his latest find to a group of friends; it would become an album called *Nevermind* by a little-known group called Nirvana. Vig's tiny audience didn't know that the album would go on to sell 30 million copies, introduce alternative rock to a mainstream audience, and be named by *Rolling Stone* as one of the most influential albums of all time. They just liked the rawness and intimacy of Kurt Cobain's voice, Dave Grohl's thunderous drumming, the amateurish passion of the guitars, the catchy hooks.

When the tape ended, there was silence. And then someone said, "Play it again."

That's what an audience is. That's all it has to be. On the one hand, the whole concept of audience has changed radically since I began to listen to rock and pop in the fifties; as I say in my chapter on soul reviver Sharon Jones, where once there was a single audience for pop music, now there are countless smaller ones.

On the other hand, the concept of audience has never changed and never will. The first time a couple of cavemen beat rocks together while a long-haired cave mama shouted her version of the hunter-gatherer blues, either her listeners shrugged and crept back into the shadows or said, "Play it again."

Music critic Jon Pareles says that the golden age of rock music is easy to define: it's whatever you were listening to between ages 16 and 23. Before that, you had to do what the grownups said; afterward, you were a grownup yourself. Between, you saw your life filling with freedom and pleasure, but responsibility hadn't really arrived. And the music told you that. It told you that you could change the world, and by changing it, you could make a place for yourself it.

And the music said that at lightning speed: listen to the first line Barrett Strong sings in "Money (That's What I Want)," says Greil Marcus, and then the last. You won't think it's the same person, because it isn't, because a desperate, sweaty guy starts the song, but a happy, fulfilled one ends it.

< 14 >

For sheer transformation, though, there's no more dazzling spell than that cast by the Drifter's "Dance with Me," which made it to #2 on the r 'n' b singles chart in 1959. What happens to the singer in this song is nothing short of a "magic moment," to name another Drifters classic. What's more, whereas Barrett Strong is shouting to the world about the money lust we all have, in "Dance with Me," there's an audience within the song itself.

In the words of Bruce Springsteen, a boy walking across a gym floor toward a waiting girl isn't just asking her to dance—he's putting his life in her hands. That's what it sounds like here: as a string section lays down a base coat of syrupy emotions, the Drifters minus lead singer Ben E. King sing "Dance with me" four times, almost faintly, yet on a rising scale, as you might if you were talking to yourself and working up your courage.

Then Ben E. King bursts out with "Dance with me!" He's too loud, and his voice is a little high. It's an awkward moment, but maybe that's for the best. He has caught the girl off guard, and before she can recover, he's pressing his program: "Hold me closer," he says, "closer and closer."

This is going well! Or at least she hasn't said no. In fact, he's feeling so bold now that he moves in for a kiss in the song's bridge, and then he says something extraordinary, something so deal-breaking that it can only work: "We're no longer strangers," says the young man, "now we're more than friends."

Wait a second—what happened to the friend stage? How do you go from being strangers to "more than friends"? There's only one answer: through magic, that's how.

And while we're waving our arms in the air and making the impossible occur right there on the gym floor, let's take it all the way and say "we'll be lovers / when the music ends."

Or nearly all the way. From Adam to Prometheus to Goethe's Faust, the history of magicians is a story of overreach and tragic consequences. So the actual line in the song is not "we'll be lovers" but "maybe we'll be lovers." Maybe.

Some high-speed conquest, huh? Actually, here's the best thing about what happens in "Dance with Me": *it happened and it didn't.* The song is only two

< 15 >

minutes and twenty-one seconds long. We never hear from the girl. Was there a girl at all? Maybe the guy is just singing to himself in the bathroom mirror as his dad yells at him to hurry up in there.

Which is the great thing about a pop song, that it is what its audience wants it to be. To guys, the song is a training manual. To girls, it says, you are desirable. To both, it says that there is someone out there for you, someone to go through life with, to take the sting out of your journey through this world—all you have to do is get your courage up.

The singer in "Dance with Me" is a shy, frightened boy when the song begins and a happy, confident man by the end. Listen to him shout! "A-whoa-ho!" he cries, over and over. The music is so hypnotic that we don't even notice the transformation.

But on some level, you know. If it can happen to him, it can happen to you.

CERTAINLY THE WORLD CHANGED FOR ME in 1955, when the air waves were dominated by Patti Page singing "How Much is That Doggie in the Window?" and Mitch Miller's "Yellow Rose of Texas."

One day, I turned on my little green plastic Westinghouse radio and heard a voice say, "A-wop-bop-a-loo-mop, a-lop-bam-boom!" It was as though electricity had shot through my body; my shoulders shook, and my arms rose in the air as though they belonged to somebody else. "Tutti Frutti" wasn't just a song. It was a switch on history's circuit breaker, and when Little Richard flipped that switch, in an instant, as Keith Richards said, the world changed from monochrome to Technicolor.

As fast as I could, I peddled into town to the record shop and bought the 45 of "Tutti Frutti," though to cover my tracks I got the Penguins' "Earth Angel" as well. My mother wasn't too keen on this whole rock 'n' roll fad, so I'd play her "Earth Angel," which is closer to a lullaby than anything else. She'd listen, smile, say, "Now that's what I call music," and go out to look at her rose garden, which is when I'd unleash Little Richard's hellfire.

I didn't know I was putting money in Little Richard's pocket—not much,

< 16 >

as it turns out; it wasn't till later that I found out he was making half a cent per record.

I also didn't know that, when I bought that little vinyl record, I'd become part of an audience, one to which, even if you just bought a CD recently or listened to Pandora, you belong as well. I thought Little Richard was talking to me alone, telling me everything I needed to know about love, desire, and, mainly, the importance of being silly. He was talking about freedom, really, and in doing so, he multiplied exponentially the audience for a type of music so audacious that it had grown folks shaking with terror.

And for good reason: the new audience was not only bigger but scarier. "Anarchy had moved in," writes Nik Cohn of the first days of rock'n' roll. Prior to that time in the music business, "for thirty years, you couldn't possibly make it unless you were white, sleek, nicely spoken and phony to your toenails—suddenly now you could be black, purple, moronic, delinquent, diseased, or almost anything on earth, and you could still clean up."

In the 1991 film *The Commitments*, a group of working-class Dubliners form a band devoted to the soul music they love, and after one grueling rehearsal, the musicians form a circle so they can pat each other on the back. Every audience should do that, in my view. You and I might not be able to carry a tune in a bucket, but those artists need us, and we need each other.

Which artists, you say? In *Crossroad* I write mostly about rockers and mostly American ones, though it's my feeling that if you rock, you are American, which is how bands like the Beatles and Led Zeppelin sneak into this book. Lenny Bruce said all New Yorkers are Jews, whereas if you're a Jew, you can't be Jewish if you live in, say, Idaho, and the same principle applies to music: if you rock, it doesn't matter if you live in Estonia—you're Elvis's cousin. And while the term "rock 'n' roll" shows up here than any other, I'm really writing about the tradition of roots music in which folk becomes country and blues which become rock, hip-hop, dance music, and so on. "Rock 'n' roll" is a term of convenience, then, but it's also the broadest swath I'm writing about as well as the great body into which the other categories flow and emerge.

So there are chapters here on anonymously-authored songs ("John Henry," "The House of the Rising Son"), rhythm 'n' blues pioneers (Fats Domino, Otis

< 17 >

Redding, Little Richard), pure pop stars (Cyndi Lauper, Neil Diamond), cross-ing over and not (Big Bill Broonzy), how geography shapes music (the chitlin' circuit), segregation and integration (and the re-segregation of contemporary pop music), don't-give-a-damn geniuses (Bob Dylan, Townes Van Zandt), tribes (punk, grunge, and so on), songwriters (the Brill Building gang, Doc Po-mus), tortured souls (Brian Wilson, Mary Wells), and more. There's a chapter on technological changes in music and one on a group that never gets enough credit, the producers who connect artists with audiences.

Which audiences? There are audiences that love to lean in and listen to crooners like Sam Cooke and Peggy Lee, ones that want to be dominated (by Queen, say, or Led Zeppelin) and even repelled (fans of the Doors and the Velvet Underground). Some audiences and artists, like the majority of late twentieth-century Detroit bands and the grunge crowd, mirror each other so intensely as to appear seamless. Most artists entice their audiences with some-thing familiar before moving on to newer and more challenging work, both in concert and over the length of a career. The Beatles' first songs were Little Richard covers; would we even know who they are today if their first single had been "Eleanor Rigby"? And when the connection between audience and artist is at its most intimate, every listener, whether on a tinny farmhouse radio or in a stadium so big it has its own zip code, thinks the singer is singing to him or her alone, the way Martha and the Vandellas seem to do.

On a given night, a given band will try some version of all these approach-es, and if the band knows what it's doing, the audience will shoot sparks like a fallen power line.

The dance-music master Bassnectar said of his 2011 release *Divergent Spec-trum* that "this is a collection of songs I have created for maximum impact in large settings on massive sound systems for groups of people who want to get wild."

Isn't that what audience is about? Take out the phrase "massive sound sys-tems," and it's what's always been there. If girls just wanna have fun, audiences just want to get wild, and when they do, the artists do, and the cycle keeps feeding on itself.

< 18 >

The first time Jerry Lee Lewis kicked his piano stool over, it was an accident, but his fans screamed the roof off, so that little move became part of every show. And, yes, the lyrics say, "'Scuse me, while I kiss the sky," but when I saw Jimi Hendrix perform "Purple Haze" live, he pointed to his guitarist and said, "'Scuse me, while I kiss this guy" because the audience liked that better.

How artist and audience connect is best described by the Kinks' Ray Davies as he talks about their hit "You Really Got Me." As Bob Stanley points out in *Yeah! Yeah! Yeah!: The Story of Pop Music from Bill Haley to Beyoncé*, his encyclopedic study of pop music, that song is the first one ever to shift key twice during each verse. In Ray Davies' words, "it's just like chatting up a girl." You start by getting her attention—*da-nana-da-na!*—and "when she gets bored, you change the key."

Well, in theory. If only it were that easy! Just about every artist flies by the seat of his pants and then looks back to tell you how the flight was planned. As it turns out, Davies is right, even if retrospectively.

The best thing about art is its delicious messiness. One of the chapters that was the most fun to write is about the self-sabotaging songwriter Will Hodgkinson, who, despite his contacts with the best people in the music industry, writes a song of which his own wife says, "I just can't bear it any more . . . if you keep playing that song, I think I might cry."

As Bob Stanley points out, calculated copying doesn't work as well as spontaneous leaps in musical DNA. One of the first successful R&B groups from the fifties was the Orioles, who spawned the vast number of bird groups who didn't do nearly as well: the Larks, the Penguins, the Robins, the Crows, the Flamingos.

And In 1956, when Frankie Lymon and the Teenagers sold two million copies of "Why Do Fools Fall in Love," it was largely because of Lymon's youthful, exuberant, almost girlish voice, so "within a year, there were over seventy groups who featured a black male lead on the edge of puberty."

The group's real impact isn't seen until years later, though: "it's hard to

< 19 >

imagine the Jackson Five without the Teenagers," says Stanley, and "the entire sixties girl-group is based on their sound." All of which simply reminds us, in Standley's words, that "the interdependence of living musical forms is essential."

For that reason, there is no system behind *Crossroad* other than chronology, and even that's pretty loose. Marcus quotes Neil Young as saying the most astonishing thing, which is that if you look at it in the right way, rock 'n' roll actually predates its sources: "Rock & roll is reckless abandon. Rock & roll is the *cause* of country and blues. Country and blues came first, but somehow rock & roll's place in the course of events is dispersed."

What does that even mean? It's just as inexplicable as the lyrics to many a Neil Young song, and just as true. Bob Dylan hints at a meaning when he says he was so much older then, and now he's younger. I know I'm sixteen again when Buddy Holly or the Drifters come on the radio, and if the deejay doesn't play the records I want soon or fast enough, I just pop in a CD and start time traveling—don't you? We gotta get out of this place, said the Animals, and there's no ticket more sure than a two-minute rock song.

Rock 'n' roll appeals to an audience with no sense of history. Teenagers don't know where their music comes from, and they don't care. Nor should they. As long as it's new, different, and not something their parents like, that's what counts. As amorphous as audiences are, especially young ones, one thing we can say is that each seeks a heightening of emotions fueled by desire, fear, anticipation.

When you throw history out the window, everything else goes, too. That's why the Pilgrims came to America, and that's why rock 'n' roll was invented here. And that's why, to understand history, we need to remember that, when everybody's running toward the dance floor, the music is all that counts.

There is no how-to to the making of music that touches the hearts and souls of other, just trial and error, just listening to others and going back to the drawing board again and again. Here I write about artists I've learned from and artists I love. I write as well about the audiences I've been part of even as I dream of the ones to come. Mainly, I write about how artist and audience come together. Sure, I was in a band once, but I know my place in the great chain

< 20 >

of things. Jack White will never have a quarrel with me: I'm right there in the front row, shouting myself hoarse. I'm a kid again, I'm the age I am now, I'm long gone and looking back on a life whose soundtrack is the most electrifying music anybody ever listened to. There's no better place to be.

< 21 >

Steel Drivin' Man:
The Story Behind "John Henry"

THE FIRST THING TO KNOW ABOUT HISTORIANS is that they don't trust history: people and power tend to mess with the truth. Scott Reynolds Nelson, himself a historian, says "each generation comes up with simple narratives that cover over a complicated, contested past." The problem is, when you try to erase something, your smudges always betray you. The legend of John Henry is the story of just such an erasure, and a restoration of the actual portrait unveils the likeness not only of a dead man but also of the world that murdered him.

The public picture of John Henry shows a strapping African-American man with bulging muscles who traveled around the South making good money with a nine-pound hammer and a work ethic to match; it's true that he died after beating the newfangled steam drill in a contest, but he lived large before that and, according to the most popular variant, even had the love of a good woman named Polly Ann.

No wonder there are almost two hundred versions of "John Henry," a song among the first to be called a blues song and one of the first to be recorded as "country."

Only nobody working on a railroad in the nineteenth century had a life remotely like John Henry's. Among documents that researchers have uncovered are the papers of a railroad carpenter named Henry Grady who couldn't spell worth a lick and had terrible penmanship; since he often wrote from a moving boxcar and used the purple crayon that carpenters marked lumber with, the letters Grady wrote his sister are all but impossible to read.

Patiently deciphered, though, they tell a story that is terrible to hear. In Grady's story, accidents are frequent and disfiguring, and the mangled bodies begin to pile up. Far from being folk heroes, railway workers are treated like

< 23 >

pariahs by the townspeople they encountered. Worse, many of them worked as slaves even after the Civil War. Grady mentions that a contractor was using "several hundred state convicts" to build railbeds, and the practice seems to unsettle him.

In the archives of the Virginia State Penitentiary, there is an 1872 report that says forty-eight black convicts died that year, nearly ten per cent of the prison population. What killed the black convicts?

In most instances, the answer is railroad work, but that's like saying Lincoln was killed by a piece of lead rather than John Wilkes Booth. The real John Henry was killed by a slower process that had many authors, but he was murdered just as surely as the president was.

Far from being a giant, the real John William Henry was a little over five feet, one inch tall. He was received into the prison in 1866, having been sentenced to ten years, an unusually long term for a young man of nineteen who had been charged with the relatively minor crime of housebreaking and larceny.

The man who arrested him literally had a hole in his head: he was Charles H. Burd, an inept former Union lieutenant who may have been shot by one of his own men. At any rate, the musket ball went four inches deep into his skull and not only left him with an ugly wound but most likely the full range of symptoms that result from lead poisoning: joint pain, irritability, loss of memory and concentration.

Burd took John Henry into custody following a daytime theft from a grocery store, and an equally unsympathetic judge put him in prison for ten years—a death sentence, given that the convicts who labored on railroads had no say about job conditions and were often worked to death.

Usually they died of silicosis: when the charge went off, the sandstone mountains that the dynamiters blasted through filled the air with silica, microscopic particles that scarred the air sacs of the men who cleared the rubble and eventually caused them to die of tuberculosis and pneumonia. The paid workers could protest these conditions and did bring about meaningful changes; the convicts, of course, could not.

< 24 >

Forensic anthropologists from the Smithsonian who examined the nearly three hundred corpses discovered in 1992 on the grounds of the Virginia Penitentiary noted that roughly eighty per cent of the bodies were black men in their early twenties. Talk about a hole in history: prison records said nothing about the buried men. (And you can forget about Polly Ann as well; in their race to the lowest rung of humanity, the convicts enjoyed only the sorry consolations of rape and masturbation.)

The individual bodies were not identified, but one of them was surely that of John Henry. Cruelly treated in life, the contract workers were at least given a burial of sorts, but even that act was stained by the profit motive. Contractors had to post a bond guaranteeing that every prisoner would be returned or else they would forfeit a hundred dollars per man. The catch is that, to prevent contractors from saying that a prisoner had died rather than escaped, even the dead prisoners had to be returned. And so the real John William Henry, a few years into his twenties and a little over five feet tall, after a few hard years of freedom and a fatal descent into the hell of the prison system, disappears for more than a hundred years, sleeping unquietly beneath the Virginia soil as he waits for present-day researchers to dig him up.

Meanwhile, John Henry the folk hero was popping up all over the place. He appeared at first in the songs of trackliners (also known as gandy dancers), the army of perhaps forty thousand black men who built and rebuilt the South's railroads following the Civil War. Few trackliners were literate, but their songs weren't meant as art objects or even songs per se so much as tools, part of the workingman's kit as much as any maul or pick or shovel: the crew shoving heavy iron rails into place would sing a few syllables and then a *huh!* as they lifted together.

That being said, these songs-as-tools nonetheless contained their authors' dreams and frustrations as much as the lyrics of Cole Porter or Johnny Mercer do. In this particular case, says Scott Reynolds Nelson, "while the ballad of John Henry has been forged, reshaped, and recycled by people who feel an uncontrollable urge to change it, the song is still a document, a kind of black box in an age before jet engines: it carries a message from the supposedly voiceless,

< 25 >

illiterate railway workers of the nineteenth century whom no one expected to leave a trace."

THROUGHOUT HISTORY, AS POEMS AND SONGS are composed and revised until they reach a peak of popularity, the troubling social issues at their base have always been smoothed over and prettified, as Chris Roberts has shown in *Heavy Words Lightly Thrown: The Reason Behind the Rhyme*, his study of the connection between the charming nursery rhymes of our youth and the often bloody politics that underlie them. Thus "Little Jack Horner" is about a real estate swindle (Thomas Horner, steward to the last Abbot of Glastonbury, managed to "pull out a plum" when he reserved a choice manor for himself during Henry VIII's dissolution of the monasteries), and "Baa Baa Black Sheep" is a protest against unfair taxation, since two thirds of the wool go to the "master" or temporal lord and "dame" (a slang term for the church) and only one third to "the little boy who lives down the lane."

So how did John William Henry the convict become John Henry the folk hero? First, there must have been some basis in fact. A compact figure with all the energy of youth, perhaps John Henry really did wield that hammer with an uncommon zeal; too, it's easy to imagine the older men taking an interest in a young fellow who reminded them of their own children or themselves when they were just out of boyhood.

Second, no art succeeds without craft at its base, and "John Henry" allied itself musically with centuries-old ballads, songs that had been popular enough to make the journey from England to America and take new form here. Thus the tune of the most familiar version derives from "Earl Brand," which dates from the 1560s, and the line "Darlin' who gonna buy your slippers (yes)" is a borrowing from "The Lass of Loch Royal" ("Oh, who will shoe your pretty little feet?"), written down by English ballad hawkers four centuries earlier.

Then there's that ingredient essential to the success of any popular song. It has to have a firm anchor in the culture of the times: in a word, audience appeal. "John Henry" was first recorded by Fiddlin' John Carson, a self-pro-

< 26 >

claimed man of the people who was secretly a member of the Ku Klux Klan and therefore an unlikely advocate of populist virtues. But in the 1920s, the song hit a chord with textile mill workers who were threatened by the machines that, like the steam drill in the song, made more money for the owners while it eliminated jobs and turned the work environment unhealthy for those who still had them; the mill workers even suffered from lung disease the way the railroad men did, the microscopic cotton fibers kicked up by the machines clogging their air sacs as surely as the pulverized rock of the mountains choked the men who laid track.

As time went on, the big man just got bigger. He's a brother to Pecos Bill and Paul Bunyan as well as Samson (another doomed strong man) and, in some versions of the song, Ulysses (a wanderer). John Henry became a rallying figure on socialist posters and murals, several of which are reproduced in these pages. And while it may sound farfetched to link John Henry with Superman, in some song versions, the muscular superhero punishes capitalists who sent miners to their deaths, war profiteers, and fascists who tried to corrupt children's minds. Thus did the Steel Drivin' Man become the Man of Steel.

Musically, "John Henry" wasn't just a rock tossed into the pond. It was a boulder, and the ripples haven't stopped rippling yet. Versions have been recorded by roots musicians like Furry Lewis, Leadbelly, Bill Monroe, and Mississippi John Hurt. Johnny Cash recorded "John Henry," and among the best is the version by Bruce Springsteen.

Such contemporaries as Van Morrison, the Drive-By Truckers, and Gillian Welch covered either the song itself or another about the John Henry legend. Since ripples create ripples, there are no doubt countless musicians today who were set afire by someone who was set afire by "John Henry," who was part of that numberless audience of American schoolkids and camp-goers who sang spirited, off-key versions of the song and tossed it like a hot potato to a future audience.

Because that's the way a song like "John Henry" works. Greil Marcus writes of "the twists and tangles folk songs take as they emerge from real life, live on in the imaginative life of singers and dancers, and then as the songs are pulled

< 27 >

back into real, lived life, until you can't the song from the events behind it and in front of it, the real from the imaginative—when you can't tell if an event caused the song or the song caused the event."

The story of John Henry is as great and as terrible as any, and no book tells it better than Scott Reynolds Nelson's *Steel Drivin' Man: John Henry, The Untold Story of an American Legend*. (A gifted writer as well as an academic, Scott Reynolds Nelson is also the author of *Ain't Nothing but a Man: My Quest to Find the Real John Henry*, an engrossing memoir written for young readers that should turn some of them into historians.) *Steel Drivin' Man* ends on a note of high rhetoric, speculating how the men who condemned John William Henry and thousands of others like him to an early, wasting death may have been motivated by a sense of shame. The Confederacy has gone into the Civil War certain of a quick victory, and that arrogance was crushed in one humiliating defeat after another. White Virginians had wept like children on Civil War battlefields. Somebody had to pay.

There was no chance to take revenge on the people of the North, so vengeful Southerners turned their rage on the most vulnerable among them. Thus the story of "John Henry" is, in Nelson's words,

> the story of a murder, and of the unnamed dead buried in the sand without gravestones. It is the story of the rage of a Yankee soldier with a terrible wound who consigned a black man to his death. It is a story of state laws that appeared just but let Virginia's assemblymen cuff and slap down the black men who strode about them like conquerors, let them hurt the John Henrys who had seen haughty planters run away from the ramparts of Petersburg, had seen the planters surrender, had watched them beg for mercy. . . . It is a story of a man robbed of his dignity and his life, who in death claimed victory. It is a story of an octopus built and sustained by forty thousand aching hands, and arms, and backs, an octopus whose origins are remembered in the breath of forty thousand men.

< 28 >

A song authored by a people rather than just one person, "John Henry" articulates the desires and fears of working people, lovers, even parents: like the baby Jesus except that he's "sittin' on his daddy's knee" instead of his mother's, John Henry foresees his own death. And it stands out among the thousands of song of its type by having created an academic audience of its own: folklorists at the Library of Congress say "John Henry" is the most researched song in the U.S., perhaps the world.

< 29 >

Did Georgia Turner Write
"The House of the Rising Sun"?

ON A FALL DAY IN 1937, sixteen year-old Georgia Turner leaves her family's log cabin in Middlesboro, Kentucky, and makes her way to a house where Library of Congress researcher Alan Lomax has set up his 350-pound Presto "portable" reproducer, a needle-driven recording machine that captures songs on heavy, fragile acetate disks. After warming up with a standard called "Married Life Blues," Turner sings her favorite, a song about a house in New Orleans they call the Rising Sun.

Twenty-seven years later, a provincial English band called the Animals is asked to join the British tour of Chuck Berry and Jerry Lee Lewis. The musicians know this is their chance to make it big, so they look for a song that will make an impact—"I realized one thing," said lead singer Eric Burdon, which is "you can't outrock Chuck Berry."

They'd heard versions of a song that by now had been covered by Josh White, Bob Dylan, Nina Simone, and others, so organist Alan Price, one of the unsung geniuses of twentieth-century pop music, writes a new arrangement that opens with boiling arpeggios instead of the traditional gentle strum and goes on to churn like a hurricane, its center shot through with Eric Burdon's hellfire cries of a soul trapped in pain and anger.

The Animals' version is so infectious that many listeners think that the English band wrote "The House of the Rising Sun." But scholarship suggests that no one person wrote it, even the Georgia Turner whom Alan Lomax credited (along with Bert Martin, who contributed "other stanzas") as the author of the greatest blues anthem of all time.

Because some of the songs that get under our skin the most aren't written so much as assembled; if ever a song was written by its audience, it's this one.

< 31 >

Cultural historian Greil Marcus has written that so many songs that emerged from what he calls "the old, weird America" are made out of "verbal fragments that had no direct or logical relationship to each other, but were drawn from a floating pool of thousands of disconnected verses, couplets, one-liners" that eventually achieved "a kind of critical mass."

And journalist Ted Anthony writes of what he calls the "floating lyric," that is, one that occurs originally in one song but then migrates to another where it might be more appropriate. The result is what he calls "handmade music" on one page and "mongrel music" on another. The latter isn't a negative description, as Anthony uses it; our mix of "heritages and experiences and outlooks and travails makes us stronger and healthier," he writes, "both in our culture and in the music. . . . We come from what we believe is a single world, but it is so many, all existing at once."

SO WHAT ARE THE WORLDS that flow into the single matrix that is "The House of the Rising Sun"? For starters, there's New Orleans, the forbidden city, the home of Mardi Gras, the festival of masks. There's the house itself, most likely not a mere bordello but an all-purpose sin palace, a temple of gambling and drink and dope and the pleasures of the flesh. There's family: the mother who sews for a living, the father who is never there, the brother (or sister, depending on the version) who must be protected from the life of "sheer misery" from which the singer can't escape.

If you look at the lyrics on a page, your best guess might be that the singer is a prostitute who realizes she can't escape the only life she knows. Evidence of this (and of the song's staying power) can be seen in performances like the recent one by 84 year-old Barbara Cook, about which *New York Times* critic Stephen Holden said this:

> For her new show, she learned eleven songs she has never before performed. The most daring choice on Wednesday was a version of "House of the Rising Sun," sung a cappella, that was steeped in resignation, joined to "Bye Bye Blackbird." Researching "Bye Bye

< 32 >

Blackbird" on the Internet, [Cook] said, she read that it was about a prostitute leaving the city to go home to her mother. Put together, the songs portrayed one woman returning to a brothel, the other woman fleeing one.

Thanks to the Animals, though, it's hard not to think of the singer as an angry young man. In some versions of the song, the House of the Rising Sun seems like a prison. But the real jail here is the one the singer has built for himself. The verse that haunts the most is one that occurs late in the song, the one that says:

> One foot is on the platform
> and the other one on the train.
> I'm going back to New Orleans
> to wear that ball and chain.

These lines shake with horror. The singer has escaped—he's not even in New Orleans any more—yet he can't stay away. He knows he should stay in Cleveland or Detroit or wherever he is; he's got enough scratch for a train ticket, so he can just keep moving, if he wants to, can join the tide of drifters and grifters and low-lifes that ebb and flow along the rail lines, in and out of cities great and small, just in reach of a handout or a day of backbreaking labor, just out of sight of the law.

Instead, he's already got one foot on the step of that train car. He's going back to New Orleans, to the thing that will kill him, the thing can't resist. Most of us will never face such a choice. Yet each of us is to some degree a slave to the poison in our own veins, to the darkness that we fear and despise and that makes us human.

Of the hundreds of versions of the song that have been recorded, it's no wonder that the Animals' version of "The House of the Rising Sun" is that one that most people know. We all have emotions we can't rid ourselves of and that make us angry, and no one expresses that anger better musically than the boys from Newcastle-on Tyne.

In *Chasing the Sun: The Journey of an American Song*, the closest Ted

< 33 >

Anthony comes to identifying the song's origin is when he doubles back to Kentucky and interviews a man named Ed Hunter who played harmonica on Georgia Turner's 1937 version. Hunter is sipping from a beer in a foam-rubber sleeve that says "Jesus is Coming—Everyone Look Busy" and has little interest in where the song came from or what it means; as for Georgia and her family, "they left," he says, "and I never did see her no more."

It turns out that the Turners followed others from Appalachia and sought work in the industrial Midwest, ending up in Monroe, Michigan. There she raised eight children, some of whom Anthony locates and interviews. She also developed a smoking habit and died of emphysema, but not before Alan Lomax located her and made sure she got at least few royalty checks before her hard life ended.

And she did get credit, or at least partial credit, for writing "The House of the Raising Sun." In real sense, though, she didn't write that song, and neither did the Animals. Nobody did, or maybe it's better to say that we all did.

< 34 >

The Chitlin' Circuit, or
Is Hitler the Father of Rock 'n' Roll?

IT'S 1951, AND A GROUP OF TEENAGERS who call themselves the Kings of Rhythm are motoring up Highway 61 from the Mississippi Delta, their instruments tied to the top of the car. A nineteen year-old named Ike Turner is driving, and he and the band are on their way to Memphis when they hit a bump that sends their equipment flying. Turner and the others hale from Clarksdale, where poor folks make instruments out of wire and broomsticks, so when they discover a fracture in their amplifier, they just patch it and shoulder on.

Multiply this scene a thousand times and you'd have the raw material for a documentary on the chitlin' circuit, that string of venues where black entertainers not only made a decent living in a segregated time but also honed their chops and got ready to raise the curtain on a new sound called rock 'n' roll. A lot of musical biopics have told parts of the story by showing how artists as different as Ray Charles, Etta James, and Ike & Tina Turner went from one club to another, learning how to "dump house," that is, turn the joint upside down with their seething rhythms and surefire stagecraft. But no single film tells the whole story.

THAT STORY BEGINS WITH A MUSICIAN and entrepreneur named Walter Barnes, a mover and shaker who crossed racial lines to buddy up with the Al Capone who taught him how to organize. In the Jazz Age, so-called territory bands played out of hotel ballrooms and broadcast over low-watt radio stations but also traveled as far as their reputations (and broadcasts) carried them. Barnes contacted dance-hall operators, promoters, colored-friendly hotels and restaurants, and took the territory band to a whole new level; like Capone's Italian ancestors, he fused a bunch of separate city-states into a cohesive whole.

< 35 >

Barnes was followed by the Ferguson brothers, Denver and Sam, who not only sent around the eight to ten piece orchestras of the earlier era but also booked smaller blues acts. Knowing, like Barnes, that the mob controlled the big northern cities, the Fergusons put the black audience first. In a sense, they profited from segregation, because their audiences were demographically concentrated in every town of any size; for that very reason, they were thirsty for the footstomping entertainment that the brothers specialized in.

The key to the chitlin' circuit was "the stroll," the main thoroughfare of the black part of town, the street with the barber shops, dental clinics, drugstores, cab companies, restaurants, lodgings, and dance halls. In Monroe, Louisiana, that would have been Desiard Street; in Jacksonville, Florida, West Ashley Street; in Macon, Georgia, Fifth Street; and in my town of Tallahassee, the stroll would have been Macomb Street, where, when I came in 1969, the Red Bird Club was still in business.

Business was definitely done old-school style on the stroll. Music writer Preston Lauterbach paints a comical yet menacing portrait of Houston promoter Don Robey counting up the take at the Bronze Peacock club in the dark hours of the morning, loading a fresh clip into a .45 caliber pistol, snapping two shells into a double-barreled twelve gauge shotgun, then tugging the piled-up cash into the bank in a little red wagon, the shotgun over his shoulder and the .45 in the hand of the associate who had his back. "More than one startled bank guard fumbled for his own holster," writes Lauterbach, "before he realized what was happening."

Just before and during World War II, entertainers like Louis Jordan and the Tympany Five showed that a handful of musicians could make just as make noise as an entire orchestra. As men and resources went into the war effort, Jordan became the model for every black pop group for the next fifteen years, from Little Richard and Fats Domino to B. B. King and James Brown. These entertainers roughed up Jordan's svelte style as swing became rhythm 'n' blues and the word "rock" began to appear in one form or another in song lyrics, like Roy Brown's 1947 "Good Rockin' Tonight," as well as newspaper write-ups that described audiences as "rockin'" to the new sound.

In fact, when they finally got to Memphis in 1951, Ike Turner and his Kings

< 36 >

of Rhthym recorded a song called "Rocket 88," thought by many to be the first rock 'n' roll song. In truth, there's no such thing, since many songs can make the same claim. But all of the songs that do come from the chitlin' circuit. It's also impossible to say that Fats Domino, Jerry Lee Lewis. Chuck Berry, or any other oft-cited figure is the single father of rock 'n' roll. But given the effect of the war on the rise of the four- and five-person combo that had to be outrageous to make up for its small size, can we not add to the list that ultimate square Adolf Hitler? If you were part of the audience in those days, you weren't just a music lover—you were a patriot.

WHEREAS EARLIER A TALENTED BLACK MUSICIAN in the South would have to head to New York or Chicago and compete with others for a place in a big-name orchestra, now it was easy to find work in one of the lively Southern cities where club work abounded along with recording opportunities as well as the chance to strut one's stuff for the national talent agencies that were starting to take notice. Segregation was still the law of the land, and a cruel irony may have contributed to the musicians' profits, since they couldn't spend what they had earned in largely white-owned hotels and restaurants. Like many others, Little Richard kept his group's earnings in an attaché case he carried with him everywhere, the thousands piling up as the entertainers slept in their cars and dined on sardines and crackers.

And since they made the same rounds again and again, the musicians also profited by repeatedly encountering, playing with, and learning from each other. A Memphis hustler named Andrew "Sunbeam" Mitchell set up a club over a drugstore on the corner of Beale and Hernando Streets where the house band mixed with talented locals as well as visiting stars, thus creating a sort of musical academy "that was both highly competitive and carefully nurturing," an environment that generated both "a quantity and quality of lessons that were simply not available anywhere else."

Like a lot of characters on the circuit, Sunbeam was a mixture of kindness and mayhem; he kept a pot of chili on the stove for musicians who were temporarily without funds, but he was known to be handy with a six-shooter, too.

< 37 >

"Sunbeam was a nice man," recalled a drummer named Howard Grimes, "but dangerous." He sold bootleg whiskey and ran an illegal gambling operation, which meant that he paid off local law enforcement as well. One time the sheriff dropped by for his payoff, but it hadn't been a good week at the club, so he and Sunbeam got into an argument. Suddenly shots rang out, and someone shouted, "Lord have mercy, Sunbeam done shot the sheriff!" Business is business, though; the sheriff survived, no charges were pressed, and the musicians came and went.

As the music changed, the bands' names did, too, and in a way that suggests the difference between the start of the chitlin' circuit and its end. In the beginning, the road was ruled by Dittybo Hill and His Eleven Clouds of Joy, Herman Curtis and His Chocolate Vagabonds, Belton's Society Syncopators, and Smiling Billy Stewart and His Celery City Serenaders. Later, these groups were replaced by the Chickenshackers, the Mighty Mighty Men, the Tempo Toppers, and the Famous Flames.

But even combos as macho-sounding as these couldn't stand up to the forces of urban renewal. The combined effect of racial integration, a new moral push in municipal government, and the federal Housing Act of 1949 meant that slums would be purchased so that civic blight could be replaced with vibrancy. At least that was the idea; what this often meant in practical terms was that functioning black neighborhoods were replaced with high-rise projects that quickly turned into crime factories. And following the 1956 Federal Aid Highway Act, even more black-owned homes and businesses gave ground to the first interstate highways, and the chitlin' circuit effectively disappeared.

IN TALLAHASSEE, THE RED BIRD CLUB has long since vanished. Where once stood a ramshackle wooden building that churned out rhythm 'n' blues is now a foreign car repair shop that services Mercedes Benzes and Porsches. But I've heard that Duke Ellington played there when the chitlin' circuit was young, and it's a fact that, just before it passed into history, Ray Charles played at the Red Bird as well.

< 38 >

I remember walking around the club when I first got to town. I can't say that the roof flapped up and down like the lid on a steam vent while quarter notes cartwheeled through the air the way they did in the old Merrie Melodies cartoons, but I do remember that the wooden slats seemed to vibrate as the cats on the bandstand wailed and the dancers threw down.

Segregation was no longer *de jure* then, but it sure was *de facto*. One Saturday night, though, finally I got the nerve to walk in. People turned, stared, then smiled and found a seat for me. I was in heaven—for about fifteen minutes. This was a community, but it wasn't mine. I could go to the Red Bird, but the merrymakers there couldn't go to any club I went to. So I finished my beer, shook a few hands, and left.

Within a few years, of course, everybody was partying together. The Red Bird's not there any more, but there are plenty of other clubs. And the reasons to get on the dance floor and act the fool haven't changed. Because you can pull the building down board by board, but the music? That's indestructible.

< 39 >

Walking to New Orleans:
The Man Behind the World's
Most Popular Music

IN THE FIRST DAYS OF HURRICANE KATRINA, a friend in Los Angeles told me the catastrophe seemed "like something that's happening in another country." True enough: images of grandmothers floating face down in the water and of babies screaming into the camera because they are hungry are ones we associate with third world countries, not ours.

And then rumor put a face on the tragedy. Word got out that Fats Domino was dead. Rescue workers had found the body of an elderly male in the ruins of the seminal rocker's home in New Orleans' Ninth Ward, and for a day, thoughts of a frightened old man trying to escape the rising water brought many a music lover to the brink of tears and beyond. Not to worry, as it turned out: while countless fans no doubt got out their scratchy 45s of "Blueberry Hill" and "Ain't That a Shame," Fats was eighty miles away in Baton Rouge, snoozing on the couch of Louisiana State quarterback JaMarcus Russell, who had only met the singer once before.

Then again, the Fat Man has always had a knack for landing on his feet. His French-speaking Creole ancestors were a tight-knit clan; from them he gained pride, confidence, and a social fluency that kept him afloat during the turbulent days before civil rights became the law of the land. Of course, he also gained a musical sense so organic it may as well have been hard-wired into his nervous system; even before the Civil War, Creoles gathered in New Orleans' Congo Square with slaves and the free alike to perform hip-shaking African dances that prompted one Northern visitor to invoke witch-hunting Puritans when he said, "Oh, where are our select men of Salem?"

The young Antoine Domino loved music so much that, instead of playing after school with other children, he hurried home to pound the keys of the

< 41 >

family piano. By the fourth grade, school itself had become an afterthought, and the boy who would be the man called Fats dropped out to become an iceman's helper, and if the customer of the moment also happened to have a piano, he slipped in sometimes to bang out a few bars of boogie-woogie. Desperately poor and mocked by others for his ragged overalls and tangled curls, Domino later draped himself in fine suits and stacked his hair into a trademark cube that he maintained with liberal applications of Murray's Pomade.

An early producer, Lew Chudd, bought him a maroon Studebaker Champion that rhythm 'n' blues scholar Rick Coleman describes as "half-automobile, half-rocketship," and not long thereafter, Domino started acquiring a new Cadillac every year.

These outward signs of showbiz success notwithstanding, Domino has always come across as modest and soft-spoken and thus the opposite of such rock 'n' roll wild men as Little Richard. A more militant generation would accuse the smiling Domino of being an Uncle Tom, but everything in this thorough, readable biography suggests a simpler truth: Fats Domino is probably just a happy guy.

NOT THAT HE COULDN'T HAVE FOUND plenty to be unhappy about, if he'd wanted. The story of rock's high-jacking by profit-minded promoters is well-known, though it's hardly the most engaging part of Fats' history. Far more interesting is the New Orleans angle and how a musical community gave birth to one of the greats, who, in turn, gave back. Thanks to Coleman and other researchers, we know now, for example, how, in typical New Orleans street bands, bass, keyboard, horn, and drums fit together in a kind of jigsaw pattern, the parts creating a whole greater than their sum in a way that later influenced Phil Spector's "wall of sound" effect.

Too, New Orleans is the home of the nonsense syllables that are thought to stand in for traditional African drum patterns. Little Richard's "A-wop-bob-a-loo-bop-a-lop-bam-boo!" at the start of "Tutti Frutti" is the best-known example. Tuneful rather than merely rhythmic, these cries keep time like drum beats, but they also express joy and, what is more, appetite.

< 42 >

To follow Fats as he changes from a shy youngster ashamed to wear overalls to school into a world-famous performer is to relive the birth of the music that changed the world. Typically, Domino is modest about his invention: "Well, I wouldn't want to say that I started it," he recalls, but I don't remember anyone else before me playing that kind of stuff." Of course, Elvis Presley is the bridge between Domino and the white teenagers who embraced rock as a lifestyle, but Elvis knew he was only the middle man: "A lot of people seem to think I started this business," he said as early as 1957. "But rock 'n' roll was here a long time before I came along. Nobody can sing that kind of music like colored people. Let's face it: I can't sing it like Fats Domino can. I know that."

In *Blue Monday: Fats Domino and the Lost Dawn of Rock 'n' Roll*, Rick Coleman writes that "Presley's unprecedented fame obscured black pioneers like a supernova obliterating neighboring stars, making him the unwilling figurehead of white denial, even as he insisted that rock 'n' roll began as rhythm and blues" and quotes cultural theorist Joseph Roach on "the staggering erasures required by the invention of whiteness." Elvis has been unfairly accused of high-jacking rhythm and blues, but Coleman views him rightly as "unwilling," as no more willful than a supernova (literally, according to the dictionary, "an extremely bright, short-lived object that emits vast amounts of energy").

My friends and I who grew up on Fats, Chuck Berry, and Little Richard sneered at the naive who thought Elvis "started this business," and, in doing so, we overlooked Elvis's single most significant cultural contribution. Elvis gave white people back their bodies. The moves may have come from Congo Square, but if Elvis hadn't wriggled his hips on television (everybody, or at least the teenaged viewers, knew what Ed Sullivan was hiding when he had his cameramen shoot the singer from the waist up), we'd all still be doing the foxtrot.

IN ADDITION TO THE IMPLICIT RACISM of the recording industry, Fats could have found plenty to get hot about in the explicit racism of the live performance end of music. Incidents from the day range from the ridiculous to the sublime, an example of the former being the 1956 show in Houston where blacks where allowed to dance but not whites, though when white teenagers hit the dance

< 43 >

floor, it was decided that only whites could dance.

Seeing his audience spliced and diced like a Sunday chicken, the Fat Man, in a rare outspoken moment, said, "I won't play if Negroes can't dance." Teens of every shade began to bop together, though, and in that way defined the very word "audience." It's a singular noun filled with plurality; people don't storm gyms to be alone. Finally, police stopped the show, provoking a riot. On a happier occasion, the sheriff in a Mississippi town tried to put back up a rope that segregated dancers had knocked down, but the mayor stopped him, saying, "Everybody here knows each other."

Incidents like these took place against the larger backdrop of American racism, where Ed Sullivan presented Domino at the piano but hid his band behind a curtain (presumably the trombone player stood well back) so white TV viewers wouldn't have to deal with too many black faces at once, an act of erasure exceeded only by the 1954 CBS production of *The Adventures of Huckleberry Finn* that showed Huck alone on his raft, having excised the slave Jim, whose quest for freedom is the book's driving force. The cause and effect relationship between the success of "race music"and the rise of civil rights is emphasized again and again in Coleman's book, as in the two epigraphs, both newspaper headlines from the day, that begin one chapter: "TEENAGERS DE-MAND MUSIC WITH A BEAT, SPUR RHYTHM & BLUES" and "SUPREME COURT OUTLAWS SEGREGATION."

If, in later years, the hits didn't keep coming as they did at first, Domino never became an oldies act, as many performers from rock's early days have done. His ability to continue as a productive artist can be explained in part by a lifelong openness to music from others.

One early hit, "I'm Gonna Be a Wheel Someday," made its way to Domino from an unpromising source: Roy Hayes, a Cajun clerk who worked for a drug wholesaler in Baton Rouge, wrote the title on a packing slip as a rebuke to his boss.

Regarding the insufficiently acknowledged connection between rhythm and blues and country music, Gerald Early writes in *One Nation Under a Groove* that "what made Motown possible was not that Elvis Presley covered r & b but that Fats Domino, in the end a more significant artist, not only crossed

< 44 >

over with r & b hits in 1955 but with a Country and Western tune, "Blueberry Hill." Domino was upset when Hank Williams died, saying, "That country music tells a story; that's just like rhythm and blues. Look at Hank Williams—he was twenty-nine when he died, and the songs he wrote, man!" He went on to record three of Williams's songs, including his signature "Jambalaya."

IN 1986, DOMINO BECAME ONE OF THE ORIGINAL ten members of the Rock and Roll Hall of Fame; the others are Elvis, Chuck Berry, Little Richard, Jerry Lee Lewis, Sam Cooke, James Brown, the Everly Brothers, Buddy Holly, and Ray Charles. Musician Dave Bartholomew, who produced many of Domino's hits, said "He's just like the cornerstone—you build a new church, and lay the cornerstone, and if the church burns down, the cornerstone is still there. I think Fats Domino will be here till the end of time."

In the end, Domino survived poverty, racism, and the hard-living lifestyle that saw many of his musicians succumb to drink, drugs, stroke, heart attack, and late-night car crashes; an associate used to joke that Fats had "killed two or three bands." He even survived the hurricane that killed more than 1400 people; characteristically, after surveying his destroyed neighborhood, Domino moved to a new home across the river, observing, "Whatever goes up gotta come down some kinda way."

So maybe all those smiles weren't intended just to reassure white audiences. It could be that the chubby fellow really is happy. If you had given the world rock 'n' roll, wouldn't you be? And if you'd knocked down the rope that kept the white and the black communities from dancing together and becoming one, you'd be happier still.

A Tallahassee friend recalls that, in 1964, some do-gooders decided to have a Coke party for black and white teenagers. "We eyed each other suspiciously," he said, "and then somebody dropped a needle on a Fats Domino record, and we just started dancing." All the politicians in the world couldn't have done a better job than the Fat Man with the funky piano.

< 45 >

< 46 >

The Ghost in Rock Music: Big Bill Broonzy

LIKE MANY AN ITINERANT BLUESMAN, Big Bill Broonzy scattered more than musical notes as he traveled. At one point, biographer Bob Riesman throws up his hands and declares that "a full reckoning of the the number and identities of Big Bill Broonzy's children . . . remains, for now, an unfinished task." Perhaps because he made so many of them, Big Bill was notably good with children; patient and kind, he always made time to sing to them when he played at a party or stayed overnight at someone's home during his ceaseless travels at a time when no blacks, much less a blues singer, were welcome at most hotels. The kids liked Bill, too. At a time when they were expected to hover silently on the edges of adult activities, the little folks were licensed to whoop and shake their fannies when Big Bill began to shout the blues.

In lives as busy as Bill's, often a tiny detail casts more light than a dramatic event, and one such moment here tells more about the musician's character and work ethic than any account of his groundbreaking concerts. In 1955, Big Bill stayed with seminal English blues musician and TV personality Alexis Korner and his wife Bobbie in London, and, as was his wont, he sang to the couple's three and a half year-old daughter at bedtime. What astonished Korner was not the gesture itself but the fact that Bill rehearsed before each performance. "He would never, ever go in without practicing first," said Korner. "He would sit in his room and he'd practice the two songs he was going to sing for her. And what's more, he would practice alternate verses, in case he forgot the right ones."

By this time in his career, Big Bill Broonzy had played all over the world at rent parties and Saturday night fish fries and in venues as swank as Carnegie Hall and the Salle Pleyel in Paris, and he was known for the planning he put into every appearance. Few who knew him, though, would have imagined

< 47 >

he'd put so much work into a performance of lullabies for an audience of a single child.

Yet a scene like this tells only part of the story of a man who came and went in life, floating in like a mist off a lake and leaving the same way. Born Lee Conly Bradley, he became William Lee Conley Broonzy in adult life. And that's not all: as Riesman points out, Big Bill "specified incorrect marriage dates to wives whose names he changed in the telling, heaped praise on a favorite uncle who is absent from all family records and memories, relocated his own birth to a different state and set it in a different decade, and gave himself different first and last names."

Why this "misdirection," as Riesman calls it, referring to the fuss a magician makes to distract an audience from a trick's crucial action? He speculates that behind Bill's sleight of hand lie the usual reasons: avoiding the law or a wronged husband, say. Just as likely, it seems, Lee Conly Bradley erased his past so he could become someone larger than himself, much as Samuel Clemens became Mark Twain. It's the American way, after all: Hawthorne dropped the "w" from Hathorne, and Herman Melville added the final "e" to his name, as Sam Cooke would a hundred years later.

CERTAINLY BILL'S ACQUISITION of his powers have both a native and a mythic ring. Born in Lake Dick, Arkansas in 1898 and put to work early, he first made a kind of fiddle out of cornstalks and then another from wooden boxes and bits of string. His family didn't permit "sinful" music, but according to Bill, he and a little guitar-playing friend were discovered by a white farm owner who, in an eerie premonition of the troubled relation between black musicians and white managers that appears later in this century, fed them, paid them, and bought them new instruments from Sears and Roebuck, though, like "as smoothly as any courteous but vaguely menacing character in a Raymond Chandler novel," hinted that he'd rat them out to their parents if they didn't do his bidding.

Eventually, Big Bill moved to Chicago, lured in part by the writings in *The Chicago Defender*, the weekly newspaper that lured black workers north before and after World War I with questions like, "If you can freeze to death in the

< 48 >

North and be free, why freeze to death in the South and be a slave?" He soon acquired the coveted position of sleeping-car porter for the Pullman Company, a solid middle-class job for a black man in those days, but just as quickly, he turned in his porter's uniform for what seemed to be the uncertain life of a bluesman. [45] In 1925 he bought a guitar for a dollar and a half, started learning how to please a crowd at rent parties, and even cut a couple of records. More important, musicians like Georgia Tom and Tampa Red showed him how to write and sing hokum, a jokey, sexy type of blues guaranteed to make the dancers shimmy ("Uncle Bill came home 'bout half past ten / Put the key in the hole but he couldn't get in").

From there, Bill moved up. When producer and talent scout John Hammond realized he couldn't sign the late Robert Johnson for a blockbuster concert in New York City, he found another "primitive blues singer," Big Bill Broonzy. How do you get to Carnegie Hall, as the joke asks? Practice, practice, practice, which wouldn't have been a problem for a man who rehearsed before singing a lullaby to a toddler.

BUT IT'S NOT A BAD IDEA to court your audience by changing your music as well. Gutbucket blues got the mommas out on the dance floor, but progressive politics was the theme for the December 23, 1938 concert, and the adaptable Bill fit in with the other performers when he performed a new song he'd written called "Just a Dream," in which the singer dreams he visits the White House, sits in Franklin Roosevelt's chair, and shakes the hand of the president, who thanks him for coming. The lyrics aren't quite the words of Martin Luther King's famous speech, but they speak of the tumbling of racial barriers in a way that thrilled the crowd.

Within a few years, Big Bill was playing mainly to a white, left-of-center crowd. It was a good business decision: with his mix of Chicago blues and liberal politics, he was a natural for a European tour that took him to twenty-six cities in France, Germany, and Great Britain in 1951, sitting for interviews with leading jazz journalists and recording twenty-nine studio songs. The journey covered thirty-five hundred miles and included an accident in which the car in

< 49 >

which the musicians were riding rolled over. Two passengers were treated for minor injuries, but once Bill determined that his guitar was intact, he retrieved his hat and waited patiently by the roadside for a ride to that evening's concert.

A strange but telling interlude in Big Bill's life preceded the European trip, however. In 1950, he wrote Len Feinberg, a professor at what was then called Iowa State College, whom he'd had dinner with in Ames during a Midwestern tour earlier than year, and asked if Feinberg could get him a farm job; a doctor had told Bill that he would die unless he got away from the smoky clubs he performed in. The professor wrote back to say he couldn't find work on a farm for him, but if Bill didn't mind, he could be a janitor at Iowa State for $150 a month plus free housing in one of the corrugated metal Quonset huts the college had erected to provide cheap housing for the ex-soldiers who swarmed the campus to take advantage of the GI Bill.

Big Bill was making $400 a week in Chicago, so Feinberg was surprised that he accepted the offer. Later he said, "I think he was regarded in a special sense as a musician who was temporarily a janitor rather than as a janitor who played music." There weren't a whole lot of Big Bills in largely white Ames, so everyone knew who he was as he walked to work in the morning, and they liked to have him play at parties and, as he always did, perform for the children.

The feeling must have been mutual: when the offer for the European tour came, Bill held out as the promoter threw more money at him; it turned out that he would only go if the college guaranteed he could return to his janitor's job on his return (it did). Mopping floors wouldn't be the first vacation choice for most successful entertainers, but the nearly year-long stay in Ames was Big Bill's version of what academics have always had recourse to when they need to revive their energy: a sabbatical.

So why didn't Big Bill Broonzy find a world audience the way a Muddy Waters or a Howlin' Wolf did? Certainly he projected a vibe much different from theirs. The song that Bob Riesman chose for the title of his biography, "I Feel So Good," showcases the cheerful, optimistic voice of a singer who's about to go down to the station and meet his baby for what he hopes is some good

< 50 >

loving. There's none of the typical boasting and bragging, though, no claims to be a sixty-minute man or threats to annihilate rivals. The singer feels comfortable with his prospects, and while there's no guarantee, he sounds confident that things will turn out his way.

Politically, though, Big Bill Broonzy couldn't or wouldn't project the same confidence in humanity that he saw in himself. That's a problem with white audiences: liberals like to hear that things are getting better.

The original phrase is probably not his, but one of Bill's better-known songs, "Get Back (Black, Brown and White)," promotes the old saw that if you're white, you're all right, and if you're brown, stick around, but if you're black, get back. This indictment applies to everybody; liberals also like to hear that they're part of the solution, not the problem, but Bill never gives them that easy out. And in the end, he simply may have been too apolitical for his sponsors: after a dinner with Richard Wright, who had been a Communist Party member in the thirties and forties and continued to write and speak on controversial topics after breaking with the party, some friends asked Big Bill what he thought of the famous writer, and he replied tersely, "Too many -isms."

Now it's not as though your average iconic bluesman was unwilling or unable to pitch his music at any audience who wanted to hear him. I was researching a piece on Blind Willie McTell when I had one of those lucky meetings that happen when you're out and about in the world; I mentioned Blind Willie to someone I'd met in Macon, Georgia, and she said, "Oh, my uncle knew him!" Two days later, I found myself talking to the late Smith Banks, who told me he knew Blind Willie McTell back in Statesboro.

Mr. Banks described an unforgettable memory that occurred one auction day, when tobacco that had been cured in barns, graded according to the quality of the leaf, and wrapped in burlap to make 100-pound "sheets" was brought to town for sale. People came from the Carolinas and all over "in every kind of vehicle imaginable," according to Mr. Banks, with sheets of tobacco tied to their rooftops or hanging out of their trucks. Ordinarily Statesboro was sleepy, but on auction day, it was "crowded like a New York sidewalk." The best part is that Smith remembers Willie moving through the crowd strumming and "telling how to move by the way the sound bounced off people." He was on his way to

< 51 >

the Jekylly Hotel where the buyers stayed who would tip Blind Willie well when he played for them.

And here's the thing: he'd play whatever they wanted to hear. Not everybody was a fan of the blues, so if they requested (or more likely, demanded) a song, Blind Willie would play it if he knew it, and if he didn't know it that day, you can bet he'd know it the next. There's an annual Blind Willie McTell Blues Festival in Thomson, Georgia (his birthplace) which features acts of all kinds. Festival organizer Don Powers estimates a recent crowd to be around 2,000, up from roughly 800 in past years, thanks to a broadening of the lineup. While blues will always be center stage, jazz, rock, folk, and country stepped out of the wings as well. After all, says Powers, "Blind Willie played all kinds of music, especially when performing on the street, because that's what it took to make a living."

So, sure, Big Bill could have written and sung political songs or done what singers as diverse as Van Morrison (in "Tupelo Honey") and Sam Cooke ("A Change is Gonna Come") and mix the political with the personal. But he didn't, and in that way he reduced his immediate audience to a fraction of what it might have been.

By sticking to what he did best, though, he may have just created a smaller, more enduring and permanent if less visible audience, for where Big Bill Broonzy continues to live is in the effect he had on others. In his lifetime, he was renowned for his mentoring of younger bluesmen: Memphis Slim said, "Big Bill was the greatest I have ever known. There may have been some better, but I didn't know them. He was a wonderful person and a lovely artist." And Muddy Waters said simply, "Big Bill, that's the nicest guy I ever met in my life."

His influence on rock 'n' roll is indelible. About the time of his visits to the United Kingdom, "skiffle bands" began to appear, four to six musicians playing American folk and blues tunes on acoustic instruments; these groups set the still-dominant template for the rock combo. Alexis Korner promoted Bill's type of music in England, and seminal rockers acknowledge his influence. Pete Townsend of the Who says, "When I first heard Big Bill, I knew I was listening

< 52 >

to the music behind the music." Ray Davies of the Kinks notes that he "loved the rough edges and the mistakes, and it made me realize that you don't need to be a virtuoso to make good music." And when Eric Clapton saw a film clip of Big Bill playing an instrumental called "Hey Hey," he recalled that "I felt like I was looking into heaven."

Like the other songs mentioned here, "Hey Hey" is available on YouTube. The clip is very brief, but if you love music, it may be one of the most instructive minute and twenty-seven seconds you ever spend on the internet. When I showed it to a musician friend of mine, she said, "My god—I can't move my hands that fast and do nothing, much less make music." I played just the audio for another musician and asked him who it was, and he said, "Um, Clapton? Sounds better than Clapton, though?"

Big Bill Broonzy was one of the many black musicians who grew up with nothing, changed the lives of everyone he came in contact with, and disappeared too soon; he got out of the clubs too late, because he died of lung cancer at the age of sixty. Yet he'll live forever as a ghost, the invisible, unacknowledged, yet essential member of the countless rock acts that followed. Let's hope that at least some of today's musical millionaires and their fans remember the debt they owe to a cheerful, hardworking, ultimately unknowable man whose first instrument was made of corn stalks.

< 53 >

Sam Cooke, You Send Me, Honest You Do

An interviewer once broke the ice with Rod Stewart by asking how he was doing, and Stewart said, Not so great—Sam Cooke was still dead. Since this exchange took place roughly two decades after Cooke had been shot to death in the front office of a seedy L.A. motel, it suggests how hard Rod Stewart took his idol's demise.

But then Sam Cooke was not ordinary either as a singer or a person. Some achieve gold status and some have it thrust upon them; when you listen to Sam Cooke sing, though, you're convinced that probably he shone in the womb. Certainly he was a golden child to everyone who knew him, and not just because of his incandescent smile and inherent sweetness. From his earliest days, Cooke not only seemed to know that he was destined for greatness but also planned for it. Sam's brother L. C. recalls in Peter Guralnick's *Dream Boogie: The Triumph of Sam Cooke* that "when we was very little boys, we were playing, and he had these popsicle sticks—you know them little wooden sticks? He had about twenty of them, and he lined them sticks up, stuck 'em in the ground, and said, 'This is my audience, see? I'm going to sing to these sticks.' He said, 'This prepare me for my future.'"

Even if the prepare-me-for-my-future line sounds a little too prescient for a kid playing in the dirt with popsicle sticks, there is no doubt that, from his earliest days, Cooke consciously took his part within a venerable musical tradition and then worked doggedly to advance it. The young Sam Cooke fell hard for the Ink Spots and was singing their 1939 signature tune "If I Didn't Care" to a girl in the hallway of a Chicago building in 1947 when a couple of other teenagers he'd never met began to harmonize with him and then asked him on the spot to join their gospel quartet, the Highway QCs.

This wasn't his first group—along with his siblings, he'd already debuted

< 55 >

with the Singing Children, his pastor father's chorus and prime recruiting tool for salvageable souls ("Anytime you can't come, Preach," pastors at other churches would say, "just send the children to sing")—but the Highway QCs got him onto a professional track that eventually landed Cooke a spot with the Soul Stirrers, one of the biggest gospel groups in the country. Servants of the Lord though they may have been, the Soul Stirrers' one goal was to "dump house" on the groups they shared the bill with, to turn the auditorium upside down and shake it like a doll house—not bad preparation for the future, considering that, within a few years, Cooke would turn secular and become one of the greatest singer-songwriters of his day and ours.

And performers: in that day, both gospel and pop groups tended to appear as part of a multi-act revue instead of performing solo, and the idea was always to outdo the competition. In the second half of his career, Cooke was touring once with Little Richard, and every night the two vied for the final spot on the bill. One night, Little Richard apparently collapsed as he sang and played "Lucille" on the piano. Worried band members and stage hands gathered over him, but then the prostrate singer began to vibrate and shout "A-wop-bob-a-loo-bop-a-lop-bam-boo!" as he leapt to his feet and launched into "Tutti Frutti."

FROM SERENADING POPSICLE STICKS in his yard to dumping house the world over, Sam Cooke seemed to stay the same sweet kid until his final hours on earth. Clarence Fountain of the Blind Boys of Alabama recalled that, when Cooke was still a Soul Stirrer, he "didn't mind taking you to the bathroom, doing things with blind people that a lot of people don't like to do" and would also read westerns to the boys on the tour bus, noting "he could almost put you there, right back in the same time when the book was wrote."

Meanwhile, he was working on his own sound, the hallmark of which is clarity; as a singer and then as a mentor to up-and-comers, he emphasized that a crooner could get to the audience in a way that a screamer couldn't. Provided he had something to say, the singer whose every word can be heard appears to be singing to each audience member separately, a point made about Cooke again and again over the years.

< 56 >

"He just made you feel like it was all about you," observed Aretha Franklin. Mabel John, sister of R & B great Little Willie John, said, "You would feel that he was talking to no one else in the room but you," and added that Cooke seemed to be taking the advice of the mother of Motown titan Berry Gordy, a success in her own right in the insurance business because Mrs. Gordy believed that "if you want to be good at anything and you want a following, don't try to sell your product first, sell yourself. Because once they trust you, people will buy [whatever you're selling]."

Early in his career, Cooke came across a book called *How to Write a Hit Song and Sell It,* and its lessons about the value of a simple, danceable tune were ones he never forgot: when producer Bumps Blackwell first heard Cooke sing "You Send Me," with its seemingly endless repetition of the three words of the title, he thought for a moment that the singer had forgotten the lyrics and asked, "When is the song gonna start?" But "You Send Me" became Cooke's signature tune.

What the golden child was selling, though, was not something that glittered. There is a quality that Peter Guralnick calls "lostness" in Cooke's voice, an ache that comes through even in his happy tunes. He may have appeared to sing to everyone individually, but nobody seemed to know what Sam Cooke was thinking, maybe even himself. He "maintained an inscrutably cheerful and impenetrable calm," Guralnick writes, which "might merely have masked the simple fact that it was all as much a mystery to him as it was to them."

In a 1958 interview, Cooke utters what amounts to a found poem whose ending seems to express a wistful desire for self-knowledge: "I like the Ivy League look in clothes.... I am fashion conscious.... I'm impressed with New Yorkers. They seem so well polished, well versed and they keep you thinking. I would like to know more about psychology."

OCCASIONALLY THE FACADE CRACKED: once, when a loudmouth in a café badgered Cooke to stand up and sing, the singer threw the heckler over a chair and threatened to break his neck. But as soon as that happened, Guralnick says, the fracas was over, and Sam had gone back to his inscrutable calm. Eerily, that

< 57 >

calm could manifest itself smack in the middle of the churning cauldron that was a stage show: the band would be dumping house, yet "if you had studied Sam closely, you might have wondered at the vague look of dissatisfaction in his eye, at the oddly dispassionate manner in which he took in everything going on around him without ever fully taking part. . . . Sometimes it seemed like Sam was looking past his immediate surroundings to a place that existed only for him, or one to which, for whatever reason, he was not able to go." Well into his singing and recording career, he who had been born "Sam Cook" added an "e" to his name, just as two other American discontents, Herman Melvill and Nathaniel Hathorne, had added letters to theirs. Perhaps that way he became the person he strove to be, the one he couldn't become.

Another way to put it is that Sam Cooke was always in the moment—he wrote "Chain Gang" while he was looking at a chain gang he came across during a Southern tour, and after a child shouted, "Everybody, cha, cha, cha!" at a Christmas party, he wrote "Everybody Loves to Cha Cha Cha."—yet he was always looking ahead. For one thing, he was a nut on self-improvement: producer Lou Adler recalled that Cooke "was conscious of anything that was new to him—a film, a book, clothes—and he didn't hesitate to ask, 'Where'd you get that, where does that kind of thing come from?'" And later he told protégé Bobby Womack, "Bobby, if you read, your vocabulary, the way you view things in a song—it'll be like an abstract painting, every time you look back, you'll see something you didn't see before."

One thing Cooke would have seen if he had spent too much looking in the rearview mirror was the string of children he fathered besides the three he had with his wife Barbara, who might be described as long-suffering had she not been so involved in a fair amount of feline behavior on her own. Not to mention the kids' moms: Marine Somerville, Evelyn Hicks, Connie Bolling, and "some poor schoolgirl from New Orleans" are among the women we know of, and one has to assume there were others. (Before he married Barbara, he was wed briefly to Dolores Mohawk, who already had an illegitimate son—apparently somebody had got to her before Cooke did.)

Like other charismatics, he was chronically late, simultaneously generous with money yet always out of cash, and, if busy in bed, indifferent as a lover,

< 58 >

though, as a dressing-room fixture with the one-of-a-kind name Lithofayne Pridgeon said, "He wasn't the most dynamic bed partner, but he was so cool it took up the slack. He was a gentleman, which was all the way the other way from what I was accustomed to."

One of the pleasures of delving into any historical figure's life is that of mapping out the world in which they lived, which is usually a lot funkier than we expect. Sam Cooke's was the world of the Platters, the Drifters, and the Coasters, but also the Turks, the Pharoahs, the Flairs, and the Penguins. Along with Cooke, there was Fats Domino, Little Richard, and Chuck Berry, but also Jesse Belvin, Thurston Harris, and Ed Townsend. There were big-name DJs like Casey Kasem, Alan Freed, and Murray "The K" Kaufman, but also such small-timers as Bugs Scruggs, Okey-Dokey, and Georgie Woods, "The Guy With the Goods," all of whom played their part on a stage that shook with sound and fury.

Meanwhile, the skies themselves were filled with signs and portents: at the end of a 1957 Australian tour, Little Richard announced he was quitting show business after he saw the Sputnik satellite pass over the Sydney stadium like a fireball and took it to mean the Day of Judgment was coming (he went back to gospel music briefly, but the same thing happened again five years later, when he decided that the Cuban missile crisis was largely due to his return to secular music). And when Cooke was involved in a terrible car wreck (he suffered only minor injuries, but one of the other passengers died), more than one observer said that had to be expected once a man turns his back on God.

Given some of the venues Cooke played in and the fact that he often toured in the segregated South, it was also a world of personal violence; in Peter Guralnick's account of Cooke's action-packed life, a line like "he was just getting over a bullet wound that he had sustained in a fight over a woman after a party in the old neighborhood" is a throwaway. (The "he" here is Cooke's brother Charles, who had a gift for this sort of thing; on another occasion, he is quoted as saying, "So me and him got into it, and somebody stepped between us and pulled a knife, which I didn't see, and I knocked him down, but then I felt this blood just oozing out. They had to operate on me for about twelve hours, give me a fifty-fifty chance. But I know damn well I got a fifty-one-forty-nine.")

< 59 >

THE LAST NIGHT OF HIS LIFE, Cooke checked into a Los Angeles motel with a hustler named Elisa Boyer and went into a room where, Boyer would later testify, Cooke began to rip her clothes off. She escaped, taking most of his clothes with her; a police report would verify that she made a practice of insisting that her marks bathe before sex and then fleeing with their clothes when they went into the bathroom. Cooke, clad only in a sport coat and shoes, chased her and began pounding at the motel manager's door, demanding to know where Boyer was and eventually breaking in on the 55-year-old manager, Bertha Franklin. She shot at him three times with a .22 revolver, and when he kept coming at her, took up a heavy walking stick and began clubbing him. He was dead when the police arrived.

The quintessence of Sam Cooke's art and life can be found in "A Change Is Gonna Come," ostensibly a protest song Cooke wrote the civil rights turbulence of the early sixties. Like all of his songs, though, the simple, three-chord arrangement and elemental lyrics—"I was born by the river in a little tent"— reveal more than they seem to at first, especially the verse where he sings, "I go to the movies / And I go downtown / Somebody keep telling me / Don't hang around." Who tells him, though? A girl? A cop? Himself? As Cooke said to Bobby Womack, a good song is like a painting in which you see new meanings every time you look. "I never met a man like him in my life," said Lou Adler; "he was a shining light."

Rod Stewart is right to be sad: that light's out now. But when you listen to the music, it's as though it's brighter than ever. So much about his life is premonitory, and the story of the little Sam Cooke playing with popsicle sticks makes you think that even he knew he was a magician of sorts. Always in the moment, he was always able to make you feel the song he was singing was "all about you," in Aretha Franklin's words. Sam Cooke built out of his own solitude an audience of millions of fans, each sure that he sang to them alone.

< 60 >

Our Other National Anthem: "Tutti Frutti" and the Integration of America

IT'S LATE, WE'VE HAD TOO MUCH TO DRINK, and just then "Shake a Tail Feather" by the Five Du-Tones pops up on the mix tape, and Mark says, "Why isn't *this* our national anthem?" and Paige and Tara laugh, and the party just keeps rolling. The next day, though, I'm thinking, why not? Why not that song or some other song that incorporates all of America, all the optimism and hope but everything that's bizarre and outlandish and wacky, too? The America of Washington and Jefferson is a beautiful one, but it shows only one side of the coin; it took a generation for Melville and Poe and Harriet Beecher Stowe to come along and show the other. Why can't our national song show both sides?

And then I thought, why can't our national song be "Tutti Frutti"?

The story behind Little Richard's biggest hit is well known. Originally a staple of gay bars, it's a paean to backdoor sex ("Tutti frutti, good booty"), but it's also a song with no real start and finish and therefore one that can include anything—like "Song of Myself," say, another grab bag of a work by a gay artist. In researching my book on Little Richard, I was told by the old timers that, as one said, "If a man with a blue suit walked into the bar, bam! He was in that song."

Not that "Tutti Frutti" was on the demo tape that Richard sent to Specialty Records owner Art Rupe in February 1955. But there was something in his sound that convinced Rupe he might have a hitmaker on his hands, so he arranged for the singer to travel to New Orleans and record in Cosimo Matassa's tiny J & M Studios in September of that year.

The first few attempts at getting something marketable on tape were dismal, but when producer Bumps Blackwell heard Little Richard sing "Tutti Frutti," he knew he had a hit on his hands. Not with those lyrics, though. The

< 61 >

"wop-bop-a-loo-mop" part was catchy, sure. According to the singer, the nonsense syllables are what he used to shout instead of cuss words when he washed dishes at the Macon bus station and his overbearing boss harassed him; later, Keith Richards of the Rolling Stones would say that when Little Richard kicks off his song with that Tarzan whoop, it was as though someone flipped a switch, and in an instant the world went from monochrome to technicolor.

But the good-booty bits were a little too sulphurous for America's living rooms. So Blackwell called in a local songwriter named Dorothy La Bostrie, who quickly came up with lyrics that sounded as though the vocalist was singing about, um, ice cream. But that's how song writing works: "The Star Spangled Banner" sets Francis Scott Key's words to the tune of a popular British drinking song, "To Anacreon in Heaven." Vice lies behind every virtue in our culture, or at least that's what the music says.

A COUPLE OF MONTHS after the "Shake a Tail Feather" party, I ask my wife to give me for Christmas *Song of America*, a three-disc boxed set that chronicles the history of the United States in music. The project has an interesting backdrop: in 1998, former U. S. Attorney General Janet Reno listened as her niece's husband, a musician named Ed Pettersen, played two of his compositions, folk ballads about Mexico and the Old West, on his guitar, and she found their density of historical detail so compelling that she urged him to put together an entire album of songs focusing on key events in American history.

Politically charged, the songs include everything from "Go Down Moses" to "John Brown's Body" and "Johnny I Hardly Knew Ye," all the way to "Little Boxes," " The Times They Are A Changin'," "Get Together," and "Ohio," winding up with "This Land Is Your Land." I made my way through the whole set once, listened to a few selections a second time, and now the discs are floating around the floorboard of my car, maybe, or gathering dust in a box uder the bed. It's good music, but it's official music: these are all protest songs that our teachers and PBS and the former attorney general and NPR and the preachers (or at least the lefty preachers) would all approve of.

"Tutti Frutti," on the other hand, still sounds sulphurous to me. It sounds

< 62 >

dangerous. It sounds as though it'd be bad for me if I listened to it too many times. And that's because it comes right out of our cultural heartland, by which I mean, not Kansas and Missouri, but the America that sports a slouch hat and a toothpick and has a Case knife in one pocket and a rigged land contract in the other. It's a country Greil Marcus calls the Old, Weird America, a land of itinerants and con men and riverboat gamblers, a place described in the poems of Whitman and the songs of Bob Dylan, an America that once was and still is, if you know where to look. The Old, Weird America is "a kind of public secret," says Marcus, "a declaration of what sort of wishes and fears lie behind any public act."

In his book-length description of this invisible empire, Marcus offers no better introduction to the Old, Weird America than the *Anthology of American Folk Music*, a 1952 Folkways Records issue that is now available as a set of six CDs. Originally recorded between 1927 and 1935 and consisting of everything from country blues to Cajun social music to Appalachian murder ballads, these are the songs that set Dylan and a thousand others like him on a road of discovery; in Marcus's words, it was Dylan's "first true map of a republic that was still a hunch to him." And as Little Richard was born in 1933 in Macon, a town as handmade today as it was then, these songs map out the world he came from as well.

Not the world he created, of course: there are some up-tempo songs here, but nothing anyone would call rock 'n' roll. Yet Marcus sounds as though he's talking about "Tutti Frutti" when he says a typical song here "may be a sermon delivered by the singer's subconscious, his or her second mind. It may be a heretic's way of saying what could never be said out loud, a mask over a boiling face."

Go to track one of disc five of the *Anthology of American Folk Music*, for example, and take a listen to " The Coo Coo Bird," where the banjo begins manically and then actually gets faster. The chorus is repeated, but one of the verses is repeated before that happens, throwing into doubt what's chorus and what's not. Vocalist Clarence Ashley breaks into manic humming a couple of times, but he sounds less like a carefree musician than a man who needs more fiber in his diet. The whole thing is sloppy and amateurish, and you can't get it

< 63 >

out of your head. Listen to it in the morning before you go to work, and you'll be singing it under your breath on the elevator as your colleagues edge away from you.

To hear the coo-coo song is to be an extra in the HBO series *Deadwood*. Nobody you know will have all his eyes or fingers, and you yourself will have mud on your shoes and murder in your heart.

Speaking of killers, some of the songs in the *Anthology* are about good guys—John Henry, Casey Jones—but more are about stick-up boys and psychopaths. Not that the mayhem gets in the way of a little wordplay: in "Cole Younger," the singer talks about pulling a bank job in the godforsaken country of "Minneso-tio," and one robber cautions another to consider whether or not he should "under-to-take" the theft. The protagonists are Tom Sawyers to a man: if they have to shed a little blood from time to time, by God, they're going to have fun while they're doing it.

A tribute to presidential assassin Charles Guiteau (though it's spelled "Giteau" on the album, just as the song about the heroic train engineer is "Kassie Jones") includes a dressing-down from the killer's sister, who tells him he's going to the "scay-fold" for "the murder of James A. Garfield," right down to the middle initial. Middle initials, like other details of portraiture, are essential to these songs: "Stackalee" does in Billy Lyons because Billy stole the bad man's "John B. Stetson" hat, also referred to simply as Stackalee's "John B." throughout the course of the song.

Guiteau could have been the poster boy for the Old, Weird America: he was nicknamed "Charlie Gitout" and rejected from the free-love Oneida Community in New York, became a Chicago lawyer, plagiarized a theology book, and tried his hand at political speech writing before settling into his true calling of homicide. But then so could Little Richard, at least before Hollywood got hold of him and put him in the movies. His most famous song is a cleaned-up version of a paean in praise of anal intercourse. Does that not sound, in the words of Greil Marcus, like "a heretic's way of saying what could never be said out loud"?

With "Tutti Frutti," as with the songs in the *Anthology of American Folk Music*, it's as though you're looking at a painting of official America, of a town

< 64 >

square, say, with a church and a bank and a courthouse past which men stroll in shirts and ties and women push baby carriages. Then, pow! There's a tearing sound, and Little Richard's pomaded head bursts through the canvas, his mouth wide in song.

There's nothing more delicious than a cultural shift caused by the unexpected, the quirky, the totally improbable. And among the best of these unlikely upheavals is the fact that a gay black cripple from a town nobody ever heard of gave the world rock 'n' roll, and in so doing, gave the world—the whole world—the gift of itself. "Suddenly now you could be black, purple, moronic, delinquent, diseased, or almost anything on earth," writes Nik Cohn, and you were as good as those churchy folk sitting down to their Jell-O salads at the country club.

"For the first time," writes Marcus, "people from isolated, scorned, forgotten, disdained communities and cultures had the chance to speak to each other and to the nation at large. A great uproar of voices that were at once old and new was heard, as happens only occasionally in democratic cultures," though when it does happen, it's always "with a sense of explosion, of energies contained for generations bursting out all at once," like the nonsense syllables Little Richard roars at the start of his iconic song.

THE OLD, WEIRD AMERICA is not a world of monumental figures posing like statues in a park or at least not only that kind of world. It's a handmade world, one that's full of improvisors and wannabes, the has-been and the never-was. The Old, Weird America is everywhere, and it's always been invisible. It's not as though mountebanks and cardsharps and banjo players strolled down the thoroughfare in broad daylight; the sheriff would just catch up with them that much sooner, and besides, their clientele preferred the shadows. And just as the burghers of Boston and Philadelphia never saw the Old, Weird America a hundred and fifty years ago as they made their way from banks and law offices to their townhouses and back again, we don't see it now if we choose not to.

I live in a college town where people take yoga classes and shop organically, but I volunteer once a week at a soup kitchen; a woman there is convinced she

< 65 >

had a baby by me named Barack Obama, and not long ago I stopped a hungry man from pulling a knife on a guy who had cut ahead of him in line. My 85 year-old mother-in-law has finally learned how to work the internet, but she uses it to track down the fire-and-brimstone preachers she remembers from her girlhood in western Kentucky. My wife and I live in a many-roomed mansion conveniently located between a major research university and two thriving strip malls, but a couple of times a month, we have yard work done by two and sometimes three people who live in their car with a bulldog named Lucille; the third worker can't always be relied on account of him being a frequent guest at what he calls the Razor Wire Motel out on the truck route. I'm a pinot-noir sipping PhD who drives a Prius, but at times I feel like Ol' Massa.

And that's another thing about the Old, Weird America: it's not all fun. I don't let my students get nostalgic over the sixties that they never knew. There was sex and acid and the Jefferson Airplane, yeah, but also sit-ins and lynchings and head-whippings, not to mention the little matter of that war we lost in southeast Asia. So taking a swig from my own bottle of patent medicine, I don't let myself get sentimental about Walt Whitman's America. We laugh at the King and the Duke in *The Adventures of Huckleberry Finn*, but Pap is a drunk who beats the son who eventually stumbles across his father's drowned and bloated body.

Slavery is real in that work of fiction, just as it was in America for 300 years. Funny thing is, it's real today: a woman I know who directs a refuge for battered women says that every time we pass through a crowded Wal-Mart, we walk by people who work for no money, who've been smuggled into this country and are too traumatized and afraid of their handlers or the law or us to pull on our sleeves and ask for help.

Even when we're looking the truth right square in the face, we don't always see it. We can see the present-day Little Richard in concert or catch his fifty year-old shows on YouTube. But how different his career is when we reflect that he recorded his biggest hit just weeks after Emmett Till was murdered, and by 1964, when James Chaney, Andrew Goodman, Michael Schwerner were killed in Neshoba County, Mississippi, Richard had long since called a halt to a career that would revive only fitfully. His are some of the greatest songs in the rock

< 66 >

canon, yet their birth is bracketed by the ugliest murders of the Civil Rights era.

And those murders might not beat in your blood, but they're real to plenty still. So much of what we do as human beings results in outcomes that are at least different and often the opposite of what we want, yet lynching has exactly the effect its perpetrators intend. *New York Times* columnist Bob Herbert quotes a Willie Banks who remembers seeing photos of Emmett Till's disfigured face, with one eye shot out and a bullet through the skull (Till's mother insisted that the world see what the killers had done to her son). "Those pictures really stuck in my mind," he says. "And the message I got was that if I stepped out of my place, that could happen to me. You shouldn't have to think that way, but that's the way I thought." Willie Banks was twelve years old when he saw the photos he still sees today at the age of sixty-six

Out of all this pain comes music that tells us that we, too, are alone, though the music takes it one step further and says that we're not helpless, either. Life hurts like a motherfucker; music heals at something approaching the same rate of speed.

How do unforgettable songs get written, anyway? Jerome Kern said, "Stay uncommercial. There's a lot of money in it." Kern did okay by himself when he added "Ol' Man River," "The Way You Look Tonight," and several hundred others to the American songbook.

And when Jerome Kern said that song writers should be uncommercial, he meant that most music is formulaic, so a savvy artist will startle his audience by throwing out the rules and coming up with something new, astonishing, and, once the public gets over its initial shock, addictively good.

Something like "Tutti Frutti," in other words.

Other than that, we don't know that much about how great art is produced. Jimi Hendrix is reported to have said, "Learn everything, forget everything, and play," but that doesn't explain how young men and women barely out of their teens write songs of deep yearning and profound understanding of the human condition.

The problem is that there is a hidden curriculum of songwriting that works

< 67 >

something like this: yes, there are rules, but nobody knows what they are, and nobody can explain how you learn them—not even Specialty Records owner Art Rupe, with his stopwatch and metronome, analyzing "race records" like an alchemist in search of the Universal Solvent. Then again, that's how art gets made. *Moby-Dick* was written by a solitary, hemorrhoidal genius, not some MFA who'd studied composition at an Ivy ("A whale ship was my Yale College and my Harvard," said Melville). And can you imagine Shakespeare workshopping *Macbeth*? Somebody would say nix the witches because they'll scare the kids, someone else would say to take out the swordplay because there's too much violence, and the next thing you know, you're looking at a twelve-page essay on early Scottish politics.

Art results when the deliberate is transformed by the accidental, but at times, it seems as though the accident is more important than what's planned. The studio where Little Richard recorded "Tutti Frutti" was the back room of an appliance store. When the drums got too loud, the drum kit was moved out into the hall, and when someone needed to blow a solo, someone else moved the mike from where the vocalist was to where the saxophone player stood. And then there's the whole business of the lyrics: what if Little Richard hadn't decided to clown around and play his naughty song during a lunch break, and what if Dorothy La Bostrie hadn't been nearby to sanitize it?

The sheer fun of "Tutti Frutti" is captured in the stops, starts, throat-clearings, curses, and sheer what-the-hell's-happening moments on the three-disc Specialty Records set that capture all of the clownishness, the screw-ups, and the incandescent genius of Little Richard's 1955 sessions in J & M studios. Nobody ever said that the creative process has to be fun, but when it is, invariably that joy carries over into the product itself.

Mainly, though, the songs I'm writing about here are well crafted, as are dozens of others written for other artists in the same era: "On Broadway," "Stand By Me," "Save the Last Dance for Me," "Walk On By," "Breaking Up Is Hard to Do," "Will You Love Me Tomorrow," "Do Wah Diddy Diddy," "You've Lost That Lovin' Feelin'," "(You Make Me Feel Like a) Natural Woman."

Like Little Richard's best work, these songs are still around nearly 50 years later, thanks to oldies stations, movie soundtracks, commercials, a seemingly

< 68 >

endless parade of jukebox musicals on Broadway and in London's West End, and covers by contemporary artists as diverse as Elvis Costello and the White Stripes. And so are 'This Magic Moment," "The Look of Love," "Calendar Girl," "Loco-Motion," and "We Gotta Get Out of This Place."

The songs that I've listed here all came from songwriting teams who worked out of New York's Brill Building in the late '50s and early '60s: Carole King and Gerry Goffin, Doc Pomus and Mort Shuman, Burt Bacharach and Hal David, Neil Sedaka and Howard Greenfield, Jeff Barry and Ellie Greenwich, Barry Mann and Cynthia Weil. As with Penniman and La Bostrie, not to mention McCartney and Lennon as well as Jagger and Richards, teamwork often strikes sparks where solo effort doesn't—in the midst of the necessary deliberateness, teamwork inevitably results in the fruitful accident.

Little Richard's best songs all came in a flash in the first year of his career as a serious recoding artist—in a "purple patch," to use the phrase Elton John employed to describe to journalist David Wild the "specific time periods when great artists fall into an extended groove and release much of their finest work in a concentrated blast of pure artistic excellence." (Wild lists Sinatra's early years with Reprise, Ray Charles's entire tenure on Atlantic Records, and the Beatles during *Rubber Soul* and *Revolver* as examples.)

Learn everything, forget everything, and play. To Hendrix's lesson, we should add a fourth rule, something like this: as you play, keep listening until you hear what you need to hear. Look at the parts that make up "Tutti Frutti": there are the bus station nonsense syllables, the randy club song lyrics, Dorothy La Bostrie's ice cream fantasy, Little Richard's too-fast piano playing, the backbeat drumming of Earl Palmer in response, the crafty hunch of Art Rupe, the patient engineering of Cosimo Matassa, the golden-eared production values of Bumps Blackwell.

"Tutti Frutti" is a handmade song, and many hands made it. True, some are more important than others: if any other singer could deliver the way Little Richard does, then we'd be listening to Pat Boone's Sunday-school cover today rather than the fiery original. But everybody who was in that cramped studio on the corner of Rampart and Dumaine on September 14, 1955 needed to be there.

< 69 >

When I think how art is made, I recall the words of one of the Oldest, Weirdest Americans, the Huey Long who was a liberator to some and a tyrant to others and who was shot dead by a deranged dentist in the capitol at Baton Rouge: "Every man a king," said Long, "and nobody wears a crown."

So WHY IS THERE ONLY ONE "Tutti Frutti"? For one thing, the song is the result of a lengthy and error-prone process. It couldn't be copied. Pat Boone couldn't do it. Neither, for that matter, could Little Richard himself.

Too, as black tastes in pop music evolved in the sixties and seventies, Little Richard was either involved in the church (he has continued to "repent" and return to gospel throughout his career) or capitalizing on the fifties sound. As a result, his appeal became not only static but white in hue as the audience for his music defined itself largely as the nostalgia crowd. "I was always supported by white people," he tells Charles White. "James Brown was different from me. He was big to the black market. When he came to town, you could get ten thousand blacks. When I came to town, you could get ten thousand whites, and about ten blacks. When I would go to Madison Square Garden, I'd have about thirty-five thousand whites and about fifty blacks in the audience. In the whole place."

Ever one to find a conspiracy behind his misery, Richard continues: "See, in the South the R & B stations wouldn't play my stuff because of pressure from the preachers who hated show business and couldn't forgive me for giving up the ministry." And "on the West Coast, especially in LA after the Watts riots, the colored DJs wouldn't play my stuff because I've always been an artist for all the people and not just the blacks." Yeah, but if your white audience is gray-haired and thick-waisted and has no interest in your new stuff, then essentially you have no audience at all.

For recorded music, that is: the live work is another matter altogether. "I couldn't get on no TV shows," laments Richard after his honeymoon with that medium was over. "I had to do it the hard way. I had to work and try to *create* the demand." Which he's still doing today. Which is why he is the most exciting

< 70 >

live performer still in the business, regardless of whether you're white, black, young, old, or anything in between.

Meanwhile, his greatest song endures because the music still has the ribald energy of the Old, Weird America while Dorothy La Bostrie's lyrics capture the child-in-us-all hopefulness that is timeless. It's shorter than "The Star-Spangled Banner," meaning you can get to the main event (game, town hall meeting, commencement ceremony) that much faster. And "Tutti Frutti" is more sing-able, since it's contained within a single octave. Besides, who doesn't like to shout, "A-wop-bop-a-loo-mop, a-lop-bam-boom"? In 2008, we elected a new kind of president. Why not a new kind of song to go with regime change?

Then again, if "Tutti Frutti" were to become our national anthem, before long it'd become as boring as the official protest songs in the *Song of America* compilation. Let it be what it is already: the song that tells the other half of the story, the one that stands for, not the America of the Declaration and the Constitution, but the Old, Weird America. Let it be our country's other national anthem.

< 71 >

The Joe Blow Version:
Otis Redding as Torch Singer

I'M HAVING A BEER, or more than one, with Newt Collier in the Hummingbird Soundstage and Tap Room on Cherry Street in Macon when a big man comes in. A really big man, as a matter of fact, maybe six feet six, 280 pounds, and Newt, whose first gig was with the Pinetoppers, which was Otis Redding's original backing band, says, "That's what Otis looked like when he walked into a room." Which makes sense, because, when his father contracted TB, Otis dropped out of high school and took up well-digging, which, in the day, probably involved a lot more picks and shovels than power tools.

Earlier that evening, Newt and I had been at a club called 550 Blues, and a decent band was working hard on stage, though the audience was holding back. So the girl in front of the stage hooks her thumbs in the top of her dress and pulls it down to show the boys in the band her sugar dumplings, and Newt says, "That's a gimmick," and I say, "Hmm?"

Newt tells me that Sam and Dave had a gimmick called "getting the Holy Spirit," which means they'd be working up a sweat and "rocking back and forth the way church people do" when suddenly Dave would fall out and the roadies would rush over to revive him, and just when it looks as though the show will have to be called off and everybody given their money back, Dave leaps to his feet and rushes back to his mike—I'm a soul man, bah-bah-bah-bah-bah-bah-bah-bah-bah!

In a day when big-budget advertising was still on the horizon, could word-of-mouth audience reaction be more valuable?

And now Newt's saying the girl's plum cakes are a gimmick, too, that she's with the band, which turns out to be the case, because after the show I see her chatting with them in an amiable rather than a sexed-up or groupie-ish manner and then scooting behind the merch table to hawk their tee shirts, CDs, and

< 73 >

posters, all the while perching on a folding chair and making change out of a cigar box like an enterprising small businesswoman.

But a gimmick doesn't necessitate disrobing or elaborate choreography. Some of the most primitive still work: Newt told me that sometimes when they had a soul revue at the historic Douglass Theatre, where all the great Macon musicians got their start, a guy would run up to the MC and whisper and point to the balcony, and the MC would shade his eyes with his hand and look up there, and a big grin would break out on his face, and he'd take the microphone and say, "Ladies and gentlemen, we have a very special guest this evening: Mister . . . James . . . Brown!" And the house would go dark, and there'd be a drum roll, and a pencil spot would shine down, and a guy crouching just under the balcony ledge would slowly raise a tongue depressor that had a picture of James Brown stapled to it. As P. T. Barnum knew, people don't mind getting tricked if the trick is good enough.

"It was a gimmick," Newt says, "but a good one, because it worked."

Newt says Otis told manager Phil Walden he *never* wanted to be on the bill with Sam and Dave again, because Otis couldn't dance, and he couldn't stand it when Sam and Dave would "pull out that goddamned Holy Spirit gimmick every goddamned show!"

Even though it was a good gimmick, getting the Holy Spirit was a gimmick nonetheless, and after a while, gimmicks become tiresome. Otis was only 26 when he died, but already critics were getting on him for that gotta-gotta-gotta stutter he used more and more frequently in every show.

I'M IN MACON FOR RESEARCH on a book I'm writing on Little Richard and especially "Tutti Frutti," the song that, as Keith Richards says, turned the world from one color to many. Earlier that day, I'd had lunch at the Market City Café with Karla Redding-Andrews, who was only four years old when her father died. She had a salad, I had the meatloaf sandwich, and then we decided to split a serving of the Market City's deservedly famous banana pudding, which comes in a cinnamon-dusted pastry shell.

It is, hands down, the best dessert in the world. I've been back to the Mar-

< 74 >

ket City Café many times, and I always get the banana pudding. Now banana pudding is one of those things that turns folks prideful, and every time I tell somebody in Macon that I know where to find the world's best banana pudding, it's a little like claiming that the baby you just saw is more beautiful than all the other babies in town. "I'll put my banana putting up against theirs any time," they'll say, or "No, baby, you got to try my mama's before you can say you had real banana putting."

But no matter how good it is, when you're splitting a banana pudding with Karla Redding-Andrews, you've got to be a better man than I am not to salt your creamy dessert with your own tears. Karla is the spitting image of her dad. So I'm okay as long as I'm asking her what makes a song a standard as opposed to a piece of pop fluff that's here today and gone tomorrow. "I don't mean to be rude," Karla says, "but do you think that, in ten years, anybody is going to be singing a song by _____," and here she says the name of a popular r 'n' b artist whom I'd better not identify, either for fear that I'll want to write about him one day and he'll snub me or, worse, beat my ass. But if I let myself think "I'm having lunch with Otis Redding's daughter!" I hear "Security" and "Mr. Pitiful" and "Dock of the Bay" and begin to tear up.

Yet I hang in there, and after I finish my lunch with Karla, who likes the banana pudding so much that she gets a to-go order for Zelma, her mother, I hit the streets, looking for places to go and people to talk to When I realize that I kept my camera in my pocket the whole time we were having lunch and forgot to get a picture, I track Karla down at the Macon City Auditorium where she's meeting Zelma to plan the tribute concert they're having to commemorate the fortieth anniversary of Otis's death. There I meet Zelma and get pictures of Karla and Zelma, Karla and me, Zelma and me, Karla and Zelma and me.

Otis was only 26 years old when his plane went down, and Zelma was barely out of her girlhood. At the funeral, she broke down as Joe Simon sang "Jesus Keep Me Near the Cross," and there are people in Macon today who still recall with horror her screams.

Sometimes interviewers want to know what dead people I'd like to have dinner with, but my answer to that is nobody. I mean, I wouldn't mind following Dante around and seeing who he talks to and where he shops and what his

< 75 >

writing schedule is, but can you imagine trying to have a conversation with Dante? Yeah, he wrote the greatest poem ever, but his world view would be totally different from mine, plus his temper was supposed to have been terrible.

Shakespeare wouldn't say anything, probably; he'd be storing up bits for his next play. Whitman would probably talk your head off, and then you'd be bored and not like his work as much as you used to. No, I don't want to have dinner with anybody.

But if I could time-travel, I'd like to go to Jamaica in 1967 and be sitting at a table and drinking a Red Stripe in the after-hours club where Bob Marley is playing, and Otis Redding, who is touring the island, comes in "like a god," according to eyewitness accounts, and Bob Marley looks up and begins to sing "These Arms of Mine."

Wow. I wouldn't be myself. I'd be Troilus or Tristan or Lancelot, crying my eyes out for Cressida or Isolde or Guinevere. She'd be on the battlements of a castle in Troy or Wales or England, all beautiful and sad-eyed, and I'd be clank-ing up a storm as I drop my lance and brush
back my visor and pound the table with my mailed fist while all the rastas look at me and say "I and I a-go cool out wit' a spliff, mon!"

But my arms are burning, burning from wanting you and wanting, want-ing to hold you because I need me somebody, somebody to treat me right, oh, I need your woman's loving arms to hold me tight. And I . . . I . . . I need . . . I need your . . . I need your tender lips, and if you would let these arms, if you would let these arms of mine, oh, if you would just let them hold you, oh, how grateful I would be.

BACK IN THE HUMMINGBIRD, Newt is telling me Otis's secret. "He's a torch sing-er," Newt says. "Everybody puts him in with Little Richard and James Brown, but that's rhythm 'n' blues and funk." I agree vaguely, not knowing what a torch singer, exactly, but when I get back to my hotel, I look it up on Wikipedia, which defines "torch song" as "a sentimental love song, typically one in which the singer laments an unrequited or lost love, where one party is either obliv-

< 76 >

ious to the existence of the other, or where one party has moved on." (The phrase comes from "'to carry a torch for someone', or to keep aflame the light of an unrequited love.") Of the 66 notable torch singers listed in the Wikipedia article, only one, Frank Sinatra, is a man.

Add Otis Redding to the list. Wait, I just did—I logged into Wikipedia and entered Otis's name those of between Ma Rainey and Della Reese.

And of all his songs, none is torchier than "I've Got Dreams to Remember," or at least one version of that hymn to heartbreak is.

Back at the Hummingbird, Big Man is sitting at the bar looking sad, and when a man that size is sad, he's *really* sad, so sad that you have to work hard at not being sad yourself. Too, Big Man's throwing them back like nobody's business, like he's cruising to get a DWI for not having enough blood in his alcohol stream. If he keeps it up at this pace, Big Man's going to be toxic. If rattlesnakes bite Big Man, they'll die.

And I wonder if he isn't thinking about a girl, which is when I think of "I've Got Dreams to Remember." That's Otis's saddest song. And that's saying a lot, because he had a lot of them —even his happy songs are sad—though the saddest of them all is "I've Got Dreams to Remember," the standard version of which tells of a man who sees his baby in another man's arms, and the woman says that other man was just a friend, and the singer says yeah, but I saw you kiss him again and again and again, and every time he says "again," it's like a door slamming on your hand, a pipe coming down on your head, a nail going into your heart again and again and again. You can find that one on *The Very Best of Otis Redding*, which is the CD most people are likely to have; it's also the only version you'll hear on oldies stations.

But there's a much more tortured version of "Dreams" on the Stax Profiles CD that Steve Cropper compiled and that's called simply *Otis Redding*. Cropper played guitar on and helped produce all of Otis's studio sessions at Stax between 1962 and the singer's death in 1967, and in his liner notes, Cropper says that "Otis had the gift of getting musicians to play things they normally wouldn't play." On this song, the singer gets something out of himself that appears nowhere else in his music, something so painful that it seems to come

< 77 >

from the underworld, a razor-wire tentacle pulling you down into the fire as you claw at the ground and grab at the roots of trees and try to hang on to the last happiness you'll ever know.

You'll have to hear it to experience it. Here, though, suffice it to say that, in the version I'm talking about, the singer says he dreamed they were walking down the street together, him and his girl, and Joe Blow comes up and grabs her, and she just turns and walks away with him.

And you think, Joe Blow? Not Sam Cooke or Elvis or Muhammad Ali, but Joe Blow, i.e., anybody, any mullygrubbing, chicken-and-biscuit eating dipstick, only now he's got your baby and you're, like, dead, I mean, you can see what's going on around you and hear people talking and laughing and having fun, only you're not having any of it, and you feel the way Muslims feel when they undergo the "torments of the grave," which is when you die and are grilled by the angels Munkar and Nakir, and if you give the right answers, a window to paradise opens and you go back to sleep and wait to travel to the wonderful place you've just had a glimpse of, whereas if you answer wrong, demons are unleashed on you front and back, the grave closes in, and your ribs break. Where's my baby? Where are my friends? Fuck! Lemme out of here!

WHAT DO DREAMS MEAN, if anything? In *The Interpretation of Dreams*, Freud says every dream is a wish fulfillment, which is not especially comforting if you've just dreamed that you hacked your mother to death with a butcher knife (unless, of course, that's something you're looking forward to). Freud being Freud, he'd say the problem there is not examining the dream fully, looking at its every feature, even the minor ones— especially the minor ones.

The classic example in *The Interpretation* of a dream that is morbid on the surface but nonetheless expresses a healthy wish is the one in which a troubled young woman comes to see Freud because she has a recurrent dream in which she is at the funeral of a nephew she loves. Does this mean she wants the little boy to die? By going over the dream with his patient repeatedly and getting her to describe the funeral in detail, Freud finally elicits her memory of a shadowy

< 78 >

figure, a young professor she has a crush on and whom she saw once at another funeral, this one also of a child.

That's the wish, then: not for the boy to die, but for the dreamer to be near the man she loves, yet in a situation that calls for the utmost decorum, that is, one where there is absolutely no chance of her betraying her feelings.

Freud was to change his mind about the nature of dreams in *Beyond the Pleasure Principle*. After treating shell-shocked World War I veterans who repeatedly dreamed of their woundings, he conjectured that not all dreams were wish fulfillments, after all.

Most recently, it's been suggested that the main function of dreaming is merely physiological in nature rather than psychological. Benedict Carey suggests in *The New York Times*, that, according to Harvard sleep researchers, the dreaming brain is simply "warming its circuits, anticipating the sights and sounds and emotions of waking."

Yet Freud's wish fulfillment idea remains the most satisfying way to think about our dreams, *even if it's wrong*. Why? Because it compels us to do the two things that the distressed young woman did, which was, first, to look at all the evidence (including the adorable professor), not just the dominant bits (the dead nephew) and, second, to interpret. We look at poems that way, and a dream is a unedited poem of sorts, which is why, though Freud may be dead to cognitive behavior therapists, he will always be important to readers of poetry.

So what is the singer in the Joe Blow Version of "I've Got Dreams to Remember" saying? One of Freud's central tenets is that we have mixed emotions even about those we love, a revolutionary idea in his lifetime. For millennia before Freud, civilization had been in denial, even though Sophocles and Shakespeare told us otherwise. Now we talk it for granted that, simultaneously, we can feel desire and repulsion and a dozen other urges.

So maybe the singer's trying to get the girl to rush to him, to say there is no Joe Blow, to declare her love. Or maybe he's trying to drive her off! Maybe he doesn't love her any more, and maybe he's not ready to admit that, and this is the worse of two thoughts for many of us. Sometimes it's easier for us to have our hearts broken than to break another's.

< 79 >

Or maybe the singer is just having a good time feeling bad. Sometimes you want to induce what Keats calls a "waking dream," and that can mean an intense dream rather than a pleasant one.

AFTER AN EVENING OF WATCHING Big Man try to drown his miseries and, perhaps in half-conscious empathy, ordering at least one drink to every two of his, the next morning I am on my way to Nu-Way Weiners on Cotton Avenue for their hangover cure, even though they don't call it that. I'm talking about the Scrambled Dog Platter, an open-faced hot dog smothered in chili and—and I suggest you not laugh at this, reader, because by doing so you would be exhibiting a churlish disregard for one of the great dishes in the roadside diner repertory—oyster crackers, crunchy hexagons that contrast nicely with the rich stew of beans and bread and meat.

On my way to the Nu-Way, whom do I run into on the sidewalk but Zelma, who is coming out of the Nu-Way and heading to the Macon City Auditorium again with two chili dogs, one for Karla and one for herself. We chat for a minute, and then I wash my Scrambled Dog Platter down with a pot of black coffee and head over to the Georgia Music Hall of Fame to talk with then-curator Joseph Johnson.

When I tell him about my obsession with this one song, Joseph shows me a piece of paper with the chorus of "I've Got Dreams to Remember" in pencil in Zelma's schoolgirl hand. Again, I tear up. Zelma was in her early twenties and close still to the blush of first love when she wrote these words. Otis was away on tour, and according to an e-mail from Jared Wright, current curator of the GMHF, Zelma meant to say she "had all her memories of Otis to keep her company while he was gone."

So you're thinking how handsome your sweetheart is, how much you love him, how you'll part one day, sure, but that won't be for years. And then you find out it's one year, the plane falling out of the Wisconsin night, trumpeter Ben Cauley alone surviving by unbuckling himself and grabbing the seat cushion that keeps him afloat and listening to the others as they thrash and scream in the icy water. When I even think about those lyrics in Zelma's handwriting,

< 80 >

I suffer the tortures inflicted on the unworthy dead by the angels Munkar and Nakir. When you're fighting against death, though, sometimes that's when you feel the most alive.

When they found Otis Redding's body in that lake the next day, he was still wearing his seat belt. Observers say he looked as though he were taking a nap.

JARED WRIGHT CONTINUES THE STORY of the song's composition in an e-mail to me: "When Otis returned from the road, she gave those handwritten lyrics to him, saying that she had written out an idea for a song. Otis took the paper and later added the verses, which significantly changed the meaning of the song. . . . The handwritten copy that you're thinking of is the one she gave to Otis which contained the eventual 'dreams to remember' hook plus some other lines that were left out of the version that was recorded."

So there are at least three versions of "I've Got Dreams to Remember": the canonical one on *The Very Best of Otis Redding* that everyone knows; the virtually private "Dreams" on the *Otis Redding* album; and the original manuscript that contained the song's most important words as well as the ones Otis ignored during his rewrite but without which there would be no song at all. (Credit is given to both Otis and Zelma on both albums, as "Redding/Redding" on the first and "O. Redding-Z. Redding" on the second.)

And we can only speculate about the lost versions that were sung in live performance but never recorded; I have a feeling that the Joe Blow Version is a variant on one of these. After all, in shows, so many songs become anthems, liable to change at any moment and seemingly without end. Cosimo Matassa, who produced the "Tutti Frutti" that changed music forever, told me that song would go on for 20 minutes or more, and whatever the singer saw or thought or felt at the moment would go in, never to be used again.

Some of the songs that get under our skin the most aren't written so much as assembled. I've already written about "The House of the Rising Sun," which, like "I've Got Dreams to Remember," exists in different versions. There, too, the singer knows what to do, but will he do it? He could be free—why's he going back to New Orleans, to the thing that will kill him? Because it's the thing he

< 81 >

can't resist, just as the singer in "I've Got Dreams to Remember" knows he can't stay away from the woman who will destroy him. In both cases, it's like being offered the Hope Diamond: it's going to take your life, but you can't say no.

Most of us will never face such a dilemma. Yet each of us is to some degree a slave to the poison in our own veins, to the darkness that we fear and despise and that makes us human.

WHEN I WRITE MY COLLEAGUE Anne Coldiron, a textual scholar, about my interest in the instability of the lyrics to "I've Got Dreams to Remember," she says this: "Your Otis example stands in a venerable line. Some of us more recent textual scholars say that variablity *is* the norm, and that the older ways of handling texts, ways of attempting to stabilize, to create and/or to declare 'definitive' editions, to establish copy text (a loaded term in this field), and so on, are not just out of date but do not reflect the truth of things."

Coldiron describes the canon making that shaped the literature curriculum for decades and that broke only under the call for new texts that began in the sixties and continues today: "The nineteenth century in particular was an age of canon founding," she writes, "and thus of efforts to establish copy text, fix authorship, lay out national literary histories, and set up curriculum."

Of course, canon making extends well beyond the confines of the university English department, just as it goes back much farther in time. The Bible that is the basis for every form of Christianity was assembled in the fourth century by a papal synod that included the books we have today and excluded others, notably the Gnostic books. And Shakespeare's plays exist in different versions. Shakespearean scholar Christie Carson writes in "The Quarto of *King Lear*" (available on line) that "some would argue that the differences between the Quarto and the Folio reflect changes made to the play as it was performed in Shakespeare's theatre—changes in which the playwright may or may not have had a hand."

Today textual scholars work less to create literary canons and more to show how variants not only exist but challenge, enrich, and, as I say of the the Joe Blow Version of "I've Got Dreams to Remember," exceed the accomplishments

< 82 >

of the better-known variant. W. H. Auden notoriously revised his poems, and his literary executor, Edward Mendelson, writes this in his introduction to the *Selected Poems*:

> By revising his poems, Auden opened his workshop to the public, and the spectacle proved unsettling, especially when his revisions, unlike Yeats's, moved against the current of literary fashion. In the essays he wrote in the later part of his career, Auden increasingly called attention to the technical aspects of poetry, the details of metrical and stanzaic construction—much as Brecht had brought his stagehands into the full view of the audience. The goal in each case was to remove the mystery that surrounds works of art, to explode the myth of poetic inspiration, and to deny any special privileges to poetry in the realm of language or to artists in the realm of ethics.

Revision also both challenges audiences familiar with the work and appeals to new ones. Does a musical "textual scholar" like the Steve Cropper who preserved the Joe Blow Version of "I've Got Dreams to Remember" remove the mystery and, in so doing, heighten the pleasure? In Cropper's version of Otis's song, the first sound you hear is a producer saying "Three, four" and Otis starting to sing and then saying "Al, don't say four, because then I'm on you" as the producer counts "One, two, three," and the song starts over.

You songwriters and poets and playwrights, keep revising—keep changing up your pitches. And you Steve Croppers, Anne Coldirons, Edward Mendelsons, and Christie Carsons, keep doing what I have done here, which is to argue for one version over another, sure, but, mainly, show all the versions in their variety.

For what works in art is that which startles and surprises, and what doesn't work is the rote, the familiar—the tired "gimmick," as Newt Collier calls a hack piece of showbiz trickeration. In *Gravity and Grace*, Simone Weil writes of the

< 83 >

"monotony of evil: never anything new. . . . That is hell itself."

Besides, your audience is going to take what you spent years (or maybe minutes) writing and do what they want with it. Journalist and musician Bob Stanley quotes Michael Stipe of REM as saying, "I doubt very few people in the world can tell you all the words to, say, 'Tumbling Dice' by the Stones. It probably holds a lot more meaning to be able to make up your own words and to make up your own meanings about what the words are saying."

We should ask of art no less than we ask of life, which, as they say, is full of surprises. When I run into Zelma Redding the day after I had lunch with her daughter Karla, we chat awhile, and I wish her luck with the tribute concert, and I start to walk away, and then I turn and say, "Oh! Zelma! Wasn't that banana pudding good?"

And Zelma says, "What banana pudding?"

< 84 >

The Devil and Jerry Lee Lewis

IT's NOT EXACTLY NEWS that musicians attract a certain kind of woman, and, given the kind of venues that Jerry Lee Lewis loved best, it will come as no surprise to learn that the women who flocked to him were often associated with men who didn't take kindly to the performer's amorous ways. In practice, this sometimes meant that he found a .45 bullet resting on the lid of his piano, a big-caliber IOU that just might be cashed if he started (or didn't stop) messing with the wrong gal. Jerry Lee always knew what the bullet meant, always had an idea of what he had done, although, given the times he was tempted and the occasions on which he succumbed, which seem to be identical in number, he didn't always know with whom. "But I knew," he said.

Bullets play an important role in Rick Bragg's biography of the entertainer, starting from the very beginning. "I approached him with great anticipation," says Bragg, "and one reservation, as to getting shot. People told me he was mercurial; some said he was crazy. He shot his bass player, they said. Why not shoot a book writer?" Okay, maybe he did shoot Butch Owens while entertaining folks at a birthday party, but everybody had been drinking a lot, and besides, Jerry Lee says he didn't know that gun was loaded and even that it was flying glass that wounded the bass player, not a bullet. ("I believe it was a piece of the Coke bottle that went into Butch. . . . He stuttered a lot when it happened, whatever it was.")

As it turns out, Jerry Lee was "mostly" gracious during the days Bragg spent with him, even though the shooting, or at least the opportunity for it, never seemed to abate: there was a "small arsenal" of weaponry in the bedroom where Bragg conducted many of his interviews, and the walls and furniture bear the unmistakable signs of indoor target practice. Once he realizes that the armoire is in more danger than he is, Bragg says to Jerry Lee, "You know, you

< 85 >

can load that .357 with .38 shells, and you won't blow such deep holes in . . . things."

The singer thinks for a bit. "Naw," he finally says. "I don't think I'll do that."

Bragg won the 1996 Pulitzer prize for his journalism; his best-known book, *All Over but the Shoutin'*, is a memoir that describes a hard-scrabble early life similar in many ways to Jerry Lee's. Like a lot of people who fought their way out of a world without indoor plumbing and paved driveways, his subject here is a born phrase-maker, but when Jerry Lee isn't spinning the homegrown metaphors, Bragg does a grand job of it himself.

Speaking of Jerry Lee's aversion to introspection, he writes, "remembering, if you are him, is like playing catch with broken glass." Later, Bragg says that "tragedy in [Jerry Lee's] private life seemed to rattle and clank behind it all, the way tin cans do when tied to the bumper of a car," a fair assessment when you count up the damage and reckon that he buried two sons, saw six marriages go down in flames (he married a seventh time recently), and got in more bar fights and car wrecks than any man has a right to survive. By his own account, he did everything he could to keep the Corvettes rolling off the assembly lines ("wrecked a dozen of 'em," he says).

Jerry Lee came out of what cultural historian Greil Marcus called the Old, Weird America, a time when people did what they wanted in part because they knew nobody would find them. When Melville was an ordinary seaman in the South Pacific, sailors who were tired of being beaten and starved regularly jumped ship whenever they reached a warm tropical island, and they seldom paid the price for desertion.

Technologically, the Ferriday, Louisiana where Jerry Lee grew up was closer to Melville's time than ours. There were no security cameras, no television, only a few radios, and most people who wanted to make a call had to walk to a neighbor's house to find a phone that worked, which meant that a young scamp could spend a lot of time getting in and out of trouble without the grown folks knowing.

And there was plenty of trouble to get into: Ferriday was incorporated in 1906 when two railroads decided they needed a terminal in Concordia Parish

< 86 >

for trains hauling wood and cotton, and like other places founded overnight and that brought in thousands of roughnecks with money to spend and time on their hands, it became one of the wickeder towns in a part of the country not entirely unacquainted with sin, a town where brothels, gambling houses, and saloons opened early and, well, never really closed.

Jerry Lee was lucky in having a mother who adored him and a father who did a couple of stretches in prison but recognized his son's musical precosity. The boy was playing in the yard one day when he saw his father's old truck come up the road with an upright piano in the back; he found out later that Lewis senior had mortgaged the farm to pay for the instrument. At the age of thirteen, Jerry Lee was playing before at the Blue Cat Club in Natchez. Largely self-taught, he didn't merely keep time with his left hand, like most piano players, but used it as deftly as his right, so that it almost seemed as though he was playing two melodies at once.

Still, he needed more. He'd been steeped in gospel and country music within the family circle. Those are sturdy tools, but he knew there were depths to be plumbed, so he looked for a way to dig deeper into the human heart and soul. He found what he wanted at Will Haney's Big House, a temple to the blues where men routinely carried pistols and women slapped the wigs off each other. In segregated Ferriday, that meant Jerry Lee couldn't walk through the front door, though he could and did sneak in. Everybody knew everybody in the little town, which meant Will Haney had to pull him out from whatever table he was hiding under and tell him to crawl back through his bedroom window before his parents raised a fuss. He underestimated the Lewis stubbornness, though, and it became a common occurrence for Haney's customers to call him over and say, "They's a white boy under my table."

Like a lot of American originals, Jerry Lee Lewis describes himself as his own man, one not beholding to others; if I had a vinyl LP for every time he says "I done what I wanted" or something close, I'd have to add a wing to store them all. But a lot of tributaries flow into his mighty river of sound: the gospel songs of the Assembly of God church in Ferriday, the rhythm 'n' blues he soaked up while crouching under Will Haney's tables, the country songs of the man many

< 87 >

refer to as "Hank" but who is, to this day, "Mr. Williams" to Jerry Lee. He toured and swapped musical riffs with the early rock and rockabilly pioneers: Little Richard, Elvis, Carl Perkins, Johnny Cash, Roy Orbison.

HE WAS NOT YET OUT OF HIS TEENS by the time he had targeted his core audience, one he identified with: folks with missing fingers thanks to the kinds of jobs they had, men for whom a barroom ruckus was not only an acceptable form of entertainment but a welcome one, woman who were devoted to their husbands right up to the moment when they first laid eyes on that skinny boy with the slicked-back hair who played the ivories with his rear end and kicked the piano stool clean off the stage.

Rock 'n' roll is the most audience-driven music in the world if you measure it by its geographic and generational scope and consider all the forms that have flowed out from it, from punk to hip-hop to house and techno and beyond, and with his country-boy savvy, Jerry Lee Lewis picked up on rock's appeal early and worked it to the max. When he was thirteen and had already left home to play at a club in Natchez, Mississippi, he learned how to play every kind of music, that "a request," as Rick Bragg says, "was not always a suggestion, not from a man who cut pulpwood for a living and drank his whiskey by the shot."

Rock 'n' roll hadn't really been invented or at least named yet, but Jerry Lee knew how to please a crowd. We'd take an old country song, he'd say, "and we'd watch the crowd, and if you hit some jagged notes they liked and they stomped the floor, you knew to just keep goin'. We didn't know that was rock 'n' roll."

By the time the new music had a name, it was already spreading like fire leaping from tree to tree in a pine forest, and that was because the early rockers knew how to sell it. Bragg says of "Whole Lotta Shakin' Goin' On," Jerry Lee's first big hit, that black music had sounded that way for years, but "it took a little touch of hillbilly to make it slide down easy for most white audiences, like a chunk of busted-up peppermint in a glass of home brew."

Even Jerry Lee's signature piano stool kick started as an accident before it became a surefire audience pleaser. Somewhere on the road, he got tired of being the one band member who sat down all night while the others got to pace

< 88 >

and shake what their mommas gave 'em, so he stood up one night and then decided to make a little room by pushing the piano bench back. "But my boot got caught and I gave the bench a flip across the stage, and man, it tore that audience up." Well, what if he kicked it all the way across the stage at the next show? So he did, and the audience howled and the women screamed, so he did it again every time after that.

"Whole Lotta Shakin' Goin' On" was followed by "Great Balls of Fire" and then hit after hit, tour after tour, blackout-level drinking bouts, plenty of amphetamines to fuel the frenzy, and women, women, women: wives and girlfriends, one-night stands and dressing-room grapples of considerably shorter duration.

Along the way, there was Elvis. Theirs was a rivalrous relationship, though it was always friendly. Once Elvis abandoned gutbucket rock 'n' roll to sing pop songs and make silly movies, Jerry Lee appointed himself the true embodiment of rock, a coronation that even Elvis agreed with, or so Jerry Lee says.

In the late fifties, the two entertainers saw the first great age of rock 'n' roll come to a sorry end as Little Richard quit show biz and returned to the church, Chuck Berry was given a prison sentence for transporting a fourteen year-old girl across state lines, and Buddy Holly died in a plane crash along with Richie Valens and J. P. "The Big Bopper" Richardson. Elvis himself felt he had to answer his country's call and entered the army in 1958; Jerry Lee got a draft notice as well, but he threw his in the river.

And then he married his cousin Myra, who was only thirteen. Actually, she was his third cousin, and she was almost fourteen at the time of the marriage. Besides, marrying kin and marrying young were not all that unusual in the part of the world where the two lovebirds grew up. But rock 'n' rollers were being scrutinized carefully at the time (a factor that no doubt contributed to Elvis's decision not to contest his call to duty), and when the press found out that Jerry Lee's bride was just a few months away from jumping rope in a swept-dirt schoolyard, the frenzy of condemnation exploded like an H-bomb.

It didn't help that the story broke in England, where the opportunity to lash an American hillbilly was too good for the press to ignore. And Jerry Lee didn't do himself any favors by telling the press that his bride was fifteen, as though

< 89 >

two extra years would give her the status of a matron. When the gentlemen of the fourth estate found out he had lied, the headlines became hysterical: "Baby Snatcher!" said one. Even his fans turned on him: during one London show, the papers reported, audience members shouted, "We hate Jerry!" and "Cradle robber!"

While the scandal would have been a career-ender for anyone else, all it did in this case was change that career's trajectory. Jerry Lee loved playing live too much to quit, and if that meant smaller clubs in more out-of-the-way places, so be it, and if it meant that men bigger than him called out of the crowd every night and threatened to whip his ass, so be that as well.

His core audience stayed the same over the years; it was made up of "people who worked in the pipe shops and steel plants and cotton mills, who sold insurance and slung wrenches and drove taxis and trucks and wiped the tables at Waffle House." He had known them since his first outings as a thirteen year-old in that Natchez club, so he could truly say, "I can read my audience like *that*. I can tell what they want and what they don't what. . . . I can deliver it to them." He led his band as sure as a conductor led his orchestra: "I train my boys to follow me," he says. "I build up a show. . . . And I pick up my tempo at certain times, like I want it," demonstrating with a jerk of his thumb. "When I do that, it means pick up, *or else*. It means pick it up, or *get off the stage*." When the band follows his or-else lead, "it brings the crowd up," and everybody's happy, not least the man pounding the piano.

"You give 'em what they deserve," he says, "always." And that meant not varying the show that much except to take note of what the audience wanted and then giving them more. He beat his pianos up so badly that one night in Florida, after trying to get his signature sound out of some old wreck of an instrument that a promoter had palmed off on him, he pushed the piece off the stage, onto a ramp, and out the stage door.

A crowd followed him down the sidewalk, shouting, "What're you doin', Jerry Lee?" He shouted back, "I'm takin' it swimmin'." Later he said, "It was harder to do than you'd think," but just as a pro athlete will give his body to the game, a true entertainer will do what he has to to give his audience its money's worth. There as a great splash, and the people cheered their fool heads off. No

< 90 >

wonder a journalist would write, "What Jerry does on stage is so beyond the realms of human imagination that no one can fully anticipate" it.

That doesn't always mean a piano drowning. But it does mean a show that usually defies expectations. In *Jerry Lee Lewis: Lost and Found*, Joe Bonomo writes that "there's a lot of treasure and a lot of garbage" in Jerry Lee's career, though you can take a sly pleasure in the garbage the way you can when you're watching some jackass make a fool of himself and not minding because you knows he's going to knock his audience's socks off any minute now.

Certainly that was the case when I saw Jerry Lee and his band play in Jacksonville a few years back. Even then, he looked like the undead, only cooler— not even the undead just sit there staring and suddenly churn barrelhouse piano as though the devil himself has his forked tail up their butt end. He dashed through "Big Legged Woman" and "Breathless" and "Wild One," pausing only to say, "I think Satan done it!" when an amp went out, all the while cheerfully interpolating his name into virtually every song: "Other arms reach out for ol' Jerry Lee, / other eyes smile tenderleeee!," thus celebrating himself and singing himself much as Whitman did.

The 1500 or so audience members looked as though they came mainly from Jacksonville shipyards and the ranches that begin around just outside of town and go clear down through central Florida. There were lots of sunburned, bowlegged guys with Popeye forearms, and they might have belonged to the last generation to take men's hair seriously enough to make a wavy sea of ducktails and pompadours anchored by what appeared to be gallons of melted yak butter. Most of them were accompanied by faded beauties, good-natured women who were a little hard around the edges but smiling and tolerant when they needed to be, which was most of the time..

A week before the concert, Johnny Cash died, and Jerry Lee begins his concert by saying, "Before we start rockin' and gettin' it and throwin' stuff and goin' to jail, I wanna sing a song for Johhny Cash," the song being "I'm Going to Take My Vacation in Heaven," which brings tears to the eyes of men you wouldn't associate with a whole lot of crying. Sun Records founder Sam Phillips was long

< 91 >

dead, as were the other members of the Million Dollar Quartet: Elvis Presley, Carl Perkins, and now Johnny Cash. Yet there is Jerry Lee Lewis, still smokin', drinkin', and rockin'.'

A few years earlier, I was living in Paris and found myself walking past the Hôtel-Dieu on Christmas Eve. The Hôtel-Dieu is the oldest hospital in the city, dating back to the seventh century, if you can imagine that, but still a working hospital. Anyway, as I walk past, just about frozen to death, I hear "Great Balls of Fire" coming out of an open second-story window,   and when I look up, I see doctors and nurses in surgical scrubs, just dancing their hearts out. They're swing-dancing, complete with flash moves, and dripping with sweat and laughing and boogie-ing away all their stress and tension and unhappiness over their inability to make people live longer, just better, and that only for a while. The music was saving them. The music was healing the healers.

Back on stage in Jacksonville, Jerry Lee works his way through "Once More With Feeling," "Workin' Man Blues," and "Waiting for a Train." Out of nowhere, he says, "If God made somethin' better than a lady—umm!— he musta kept it for himself!" And at that point, one can't help reflecting on the fact that he was married six times and that every one of those unions followed the arc suggested by the titles of such songs that night as "Let's Talk About Us" but then "We Live in Two Different Worlds" and, finally, "She Even Woke Me Up to Say Goodbye."

According to the program notes, "he has never claimed to be a role model." He's not? Well, that's news to the 1500 audience members who love everything he does even though fear or a godly upbringing keeps them from copying his example. For tonight, as in his whole life, he does exactly what he wants, and it works, and when it doesn't work, he blames the devil.

There is one long period where he does nothing except play a note or two and then pause to clown around with the members of his band the way he might do if they were in a studio waiting for an engineer who is running late. At one point, he knocks over a can of Sprite and begins to laugh helplessly and then wipes it up and holds the towel over his face bandanna-style and say, "This is a stickup!" and mug for the band. Finally, a heckler shouts "Play something!," and he swivels on his piano stool and look outs as though seeing the audience for the first time.

< 92 >

And then he goes back to doing exactly what he wants to do, and you can't help but think, Jerry Lee Lewis, Jerry Lee Lewis, may you have as much fun in hell as you did getting there.

NOWHERE IS IT WRITTEN that a life in show business must exact a certain price, but many entertainers do seem to give up a certain amount of ordinary happiness to reach the peak. And when you look back over the life of Jerry Lee Lewis, you do have to wonder if the old story about signing your soul over to the devil just might be true. Jerry Lee himself recognizes what he gave up to get where he did, or almost. Again and again he says in Bragg's book, "if I wanted to do something, I just did it" or "I done what I wanted to do"; if you got a dollar every time he said some variation on "it didn't bother me none" or "I didn't think that much about it" in his actual life, you'd eat dinner for free the rest of your life.

Jerry Lee Lewis might not be the most introspective guy in the world, and for good reason. As Rick Bragg says in his own memoir, "dreaming backwards can carry a man through some dark rooms where the walls seem lined with razor blades." But he recognizes that his audience lives through him when he notes that "other people just wished they could have done what I done," and occasionally he seems to be aware that a price must be paid, though the way he sees it, his way of living is harder on others than on him. "You have to give up a lot," he reflects in a moment of candor. "It's hard on a family, on your women, on the people that loves you." Still, he says, "I picked the dream."

That he did. And it's Jerry Lee Lewis's unrepentant outrageousness that makes his life story irresistible. If you've ever wanted to poke your boss in the eye or throw a brick through your neighbor's window or just walk out the door one day and keep walking, at least you get to spend a few hours with someone who wouldn't think twice about doing that and more.

There were two stories I'd always heard about him that I expected to pop up sooner or later in Bragg's account of his life. One has Jerry Lee jerking his thumb at the back of the auditorium when an audience member complains about the quality of the show and saying, "Them doors swing both ways." In the

< 93 >

other story, Jerry Lee opens for the Doors at the L.A. Forum in December 1968, and, after being roundly booed by fans who shouted "Jim, Jim" and "Doors, Doors," he says, "For those of you who liked me, God love ya. For the rest of you, I hope you have a heart attack."

Did those things happen? Sure, or if not, something similar (or worse) did. At one point, says Bragg, he asks the singer, "Didn't I hear once that you . . . ," but he is cut off before he can finish his query. "Yeah," says Jerry Lee. "I probably did."

< 94 >

The Italian-American Decade
in American Music

1947 WAS A SPLENDID YEAR for Italian-Americans. For decades, Italian immigrants, especially those from the poorer southern regions, were feared, discriminated against, even lynched on occasion. Then suddenly the whole country was going nuts for a bunch of boxers whose forebears came from Italy's bootheel: Rocky Graziano, Jake LaMotta, and the only undefeated heavyweight champion ever, Rocky Marciano. Roland La Starza knocked out Jim Johnson, Joey Maxim (born Giuseppe Antonio Berardinelli) defeated Clarence Jones, and Willie Pep (Guglielmo Papaleo) successfully defended his featherweight title.

That same year marked the death of the beloved Fiorella La Guardia, New York mayor from 1934 to 1945; forty thousand mourners filed past his coffin at the Cathedral of St. John the Divine. And in September, Joe DiMaggio, a Sicilian fisherman's son, played in the first televised World Series as the Yankees faced the Brooklyn Dodgers; the Yanks won, and Joltin' Joe earned his third American League MVP award.

What was good for Italian-Americans was good for American culture, which was now richer, warmer, and just plain more fun—and I haven't even gotten to the music yet. What is sometime called the Italian decade in music is actually ten years and change: from 1947 to 1964, or roughly from the end of the big band era to the arrival of the Beatles on these shores. Mark Rotella points out that other writers have given this period other names: the years between the Korean and Vietnam wars, from the A-bomb to JFK's assassination, the Eisenhower years. These labels are all accurate, but no matter what the era is called, it's scored by a soundtrack dominated by Italian American artists, a jukebox full of hits shaped primarily by that smooth, airy delivery opera singers call bel canto.

< 95 >

The transition of Italian-Americans from pariahs to heros wasn't easy, of course. A decade earlier, stereotypes abounded that seem jaw-droppingly crude today. A grinning DiMaggio appeared on the cover of *Life* in 1939, but the magazine's writer described him this way: "Although he learned Italian first, Joe, now 24, speaks English without an accent and is otherwise adapted to most U.S. mores. Instead of olive oil or smelly bear grease he keeps his hair slick with water. He never reeks of garlic and prefers chicken chow mein to spaghetti."

It's hardly surprising that DiMaggio adapted to life in this country so quickly, seeing as how he was born and raised in California. Nor is it a wonder that, with the kind of thinking that "Life" exposes, almost all of the great Italian crooners "Americanized" their names. Pierino Como changed his first name to Perry, and Vito Farinola became Vic Damone. Ten year-old Anthony Dominick Benedetto appeared with Mayor LaGuardia in a photo marking the opening of the Triborough Bridge, but the musical tyke became Tony Bennett when he started in show biz.

Giovanna Carmela Babbo (Joni James), Dino Crocetti (Dean Martin), Francesco Paolo LoVecchio (Frankie Laine), Concetta Maria Franconero (Connie Francis), Alfredo Arnold Cocozza (Mario Lanza), Alfred Cini (Al Martino): one by one, they either took on less ethnic-sounding names or, in the case of Cocozza/Lanza, sacrificed syllables. Some of the stories behind the name changes are hilarious, the more so for not being entirely credible: Walden Robert Cassotto probably got "Bobby Darin" out of the phone book, but it's more fun to think of him walking past a Chinese restaurant, as one story has it, and noticing that the first three letters had burned out on the neon sign that advertised Mandarin-style cooking.

Of course, name changing is what artists have always done in America. David Henry Thoreau changed the order of his given names, and Samuel Clemens became Mark Twain. Why shouldn't Francesco Paolo LoVecchio do the same?

Each of these singers has a different story, but in addition to Italian ancestry, certain common factors crop up so often that it's safe to say that three key figures stood behind almost every one:: a bill-paying blue collar dad who kept the family together; a mother who insisted on music lessons for a promising little songbird; and Enrico Caruso.

< 96 >

In 1904, the young tenor from Naples recorded "Vesti la giubba" from *Pagliacci* for the Victor Talking Machine Company; by 1907, the aria had become the first record in history to sell a million copies. In interviews, the singers mention Caruso again and again. His songs were both a source of pride and a connection to the Old Country, and it seems that every family, no matter how poor, had a Victor phonograph and, if no other records, at least a few heavy shellac 78 rpm discs with Caruso's voice on them. Incidentally, by going with Victor, Caruso helped shape the course of the American recording industry. There were two competing formats at the time, and by choosing a company that used the flat disc rather than the cylinder invented by Thomas Edison, he paved the way for the vinyl era that would dominate recording well into the twentieth century.

In terms of audience, what makes the Italian-American experience so interesting is this. Not only did that huge wave of immigration toward the last half of the nineteenth century create a seed bed for great singers, it created one for great listeners as well, a never-ending loop of sound that grew as more little Giovannas and Paolos joined church choirs and their mothers and fathers and aunts and uncles called them into the parlor to sing. Soon, everyone was listening. Everyone was Italian, the way everyone is Irish on St. Patrick's Day.

THE GREATEST OF THEM ALL, of course, didn't change his name. If he had, "It Was a Very Good Year" and "My Way" would have been sung by a guy named Frankie Satin. "Are you kidding?" said Sinatra when bandleader Harry James proposed the change. "That name is all I got." Actually, a liquid voice, a delivery so intimate that it sounds as though it's coming from a guy a couple of barstools down, and the bluest eyes in show biz till Paul Newman strolled into the joint probably had something to do with Sinatra's rise as well.

Sinatra's career path looks more like a roller coaster track than a steady climb to the summit; in a sense, his story is that of Italians in America generally. Early on, Sinatra was the darling of the bobbysoxers, but after the married singer began to be photographed in public with actresses like Lana Turner, his fan base started to erode. Worse, he had rubbed shoulders with Lucky Luciano

< 97 >

and other mobsters, which brought him unwelcome attention from the government. Testifying to the Senate's Special Committee on Organized Crime in Interstate Commerce, Sinatra said, "Hell, you go into show business and you meet a lot of people. And you don't know who they are or what they do."

But it was too late: his agent dropped him, his label did as well, and MGM didn't revew his film contract. Ironically, it was a movie that revived Sinatra's singing career: after MGM reconsidered and cast him in *From Here to Eternity*, the publicity helped sell records; he won an Oscar for Best Supporting Actor in March 1954, the same month that "Young at Heart" went to number two and stayed on the charts for twenty-two weeks.

But the Mob was a real factor in the lives of these singers. As Al Martino says matter of factly, "We befriended them, we worked for them, they owned the nightclubs."

Then again, what would the music have been like if it had been born of and sustained by the virtues of whitebread American officialdom? This is another unique aspect of Italian-American music. The singers had a large and visible audience and then an unseeable yet powerful one that wielded an influence hugely disproportionate to its size, an audience that made money from the artists, aided by ruthlessness and weapons.

Edmund Burke distinguishes between two types of aesthetic pleasure, noting that whereas the beautiful is uniformly pleasing, the sublime pleases yet frighten as well, and Sinatra is definitely a denizen of the latter realm. In 1955, a writer for *Time* said "Frank Sinatra is one of the most delightful, violent, dramatic, sad and sometimes downright terrifying personalities now on public view." As in the HBO series *The Sopranos* or the Hollywood version of the Catholic Church and especially the Vatican, from time to time Italians come off as both alluring and threatening, as powerful in ways that can't quite be articulated, and therefore both seductive and dangerous.

Dion DiMucci of Dion and the Belmonts recalls in his autobiography that "there was something about the sight of four Italians decked out in city slicker clothes, snapping their fingers, acting like Negroes. We were kind of exotic, which, back then, meant foreign, and that, in turn, meant dangerous."

< 98 >

Then again, many Italian-Americans used their outsider status to bring others into the mainstream: Frank Sinatra made a short anti-discrimination film in 1945 in which he stops a bunch of kids from beating up a Jewish boy, and in 1956, Frankie Laine brought Frankie Lymon and the Teenagers, a group of African-Americans and Puerto Ricans, onto his TV show to sing "Why Do Fools Fall in Love." (Both the Sinatra movie, which led some critics to accuse him of being a Communist during the dark days of his career, and the episode from the "Frankie Laine Time" show can be seen on the internet). In Las Vegas, Sinatra boosted the career of Sammy Davis, Jr. , though much of their racial banter is cringe-making these days, and Bobby Darin helped break the notorious color code at the Copacabana by insisting that black comedians Richard Pryor, George Kirby, and Flip Wilson be allowed to perform on his bill.

The story of the Italian-American decade in American music not only adds to what we know of a bygone era but is also deeply relevant to our own lives. As we grapple today with issues of immigration and ethnicity, it doesn't hurt to be reminded that, everything else being equal, the winds of history tend to scatter prejudice and discrimination like the leaves swirling around a singer's feet as he toddles down an empty sidewalk after a long night and before a new day dawns.

< 99 >

The Dancer from the Dance:
Peggy Lee and Mary Wells

MARY WELLS WAS A SITTING DUCK. Apparently she never ran into a a man or a drug (or a highball or a cigarette) she didn't like. And when people look at pop stars, sometimes that's all they see. As an artist, though, she was a fallen angel, and if you look past the substance abuse and the hanky panky, you don't have to look that hard to see where the music came from and how it went away.

And her story is really the Motown story as well. There are dozens of books on the subject already, notably Nelson George's *Where Did Our Love Go?: The Rise and Fall of the Motown Sound*, which describes how Berry Gordy, Jr.'s enterprise changed the music we listen to forever and then, in the end, "became just another record company." But to get inside a story, there's nothing like looking at it through a key player's eyes. You want to know about the Civil War? Pick up a biography of Ulysses S. Grant. Radioactivity? Marie Curie. And to find out where Motown came from, what made it tick and then tumble, you could do a lot worse than to slip into a pair of Mary Well's pumps and follow her into the studio.

A natural singer and entertainer from an early age, Wells was also one of the most persistent of the many singer/songwriters to pound on Berry Gordy's door. Her father was a shadowy figure at best, and her mother worked as a cleaning woman to raise a daughter who suffered as a child from both spinal meningitis and tuberculosis. By the time she was a teenager, though, she was a big-eyed beauty. At age sixteen, she began to work her way into any muscial group that would have her.

When that didn't get her what she wanted, she wrote a song called "Bye Bye Baby" and cornered Gordy in the hall of a Detroit nightclub; as he walked away, she stayed in step until he turned on her and said, "Sing it right now." She did,

< 101 >

and Gordy told her to show up at the studio the next day. She was only seventeen at the time, so she brought her mother along to sign the contract.

With that, Wells stepped onto the assembly line of America's greatest hit factory. She was told what to do, and she did it, because it worked.

THE STORY OF PEGGY LEE is identical to that of Mary Wells in many ways, utterly different in others. The beginnings are about as corny as beginnings can be: she was born Norma Deloris Egstrom in Jamestown, North Dakota, the seventh of eight children; her father was a station agent for the Midland Continental Railroad. Then life got serious fast: her mother died when Lee was just four years old. Hr father drank, and when he married a woman who disliked young Norma and treated her cruelly, the future singer began to look for a way out.

By 17, she was gone. To get out of the house, she took jobs singing at radio stations in other towns; it was a DJ in Fargo, North Dakota, who suggested she change her name to Peggy Lee. She left for Los Angeles and from there sang her way America, and she also made her way through the Great American Songbook and beyond. Grounded in the pop songs of the '30s, '40s, and '50s, Miss Lee also sang jazz, swing, blues, bebop, ballads, soul, and rock, becoming a gifted songwriter as she matured.

Like all American originals, she based her art on someone else's. Her voice was often taken for that of Billie Holiday, who complained that Lee "stole every goddamned thing I sang." Then again, she would have been the first to agree that appropriation and artifice are what show biz is all about.

Photos of the mature Peggy Lee show a woman very much turned out in the style clichés of the day: skin so perfect it seems to be made of plastic, painted-on eyebrows, hair teased out and then frozen in space with a cloud of lacquer, lipstick and eyeliner applied by a makeup artist who seems to have said, "Okay, that's enough—let's put on some more."

Once, when a fan on an elevator that was taking the singer to be coiffed and made up and draped in an elegant gown asked, "Are you Peggy Lee?," she answered, "Not yet, I'm not."

< 102 >

BERRY GORDY, JR. TOOK CARE of all that personally in his shop. He groomed his artists right down to the buckles on their shoes.

Mainly, though, he wanted his songs to be hits not only on the rhythm and blues chart but the pop chart as well; to that end, he insisted that the songs tell stories and tell them in the present tense (not "my girl broke up with me" but "my girl is breaking up with me"). He began immediately to groom Mary Wells to produce what Peter Benjaminson says "came to be known as the Motown sound, essentially a black idiom stripped of the heavier parts of its soul and lightened with the air of innocence."

Thus Wells' greatest hit, "My Guy," was not the sound of black America but of young America. In early 1964, the Beatles dominated the pop chart; when "My Guy" held the number one spot for two weeks before the boys from Liverpool knocked it out with "Love Me Do," a Motown publicist issued a press release proclaiming Wells "The Girl Who Beat the Beatles."

And like the Beatles, Wells knew how to slather a bouncy pop tune with sex appeal. Peter Benjaminson relates how Wells was clowning around in the studio when she made a stuttering sound towards the end of "My Guy." The producers told her to do it again, and Wells said she was just kidding, that she was imitating Mae West trying to entice a lover upstairs. But those come-hither hiccups made it into the final take. If you've ever listened to "My Guy" (which you can do easily on YouTube) and thought, "Gee, that's kind of sexy," now you know why.

The Beatles, of course, were the masters of looking and sounding like singing teddy bears as the sex oozed under and through the lyrics. Smitten with Wells, they invited her to join them as an opening act on their fall 1964 tour and followed her around slavishly, leaving her dressing only when she announced she had to get ready.

As a British journalist quipped, Mary Wells had "the highest-paid publicists in the world."

From 1962 to 1964, Wells was Motown's premiere female vocalist; hits like "Two Lovers" and "You Beat Me to Punch" did just what Berry Gordy hoped they would. But the Motown business model also involved using the revenue

< 103 >

from successful artists to support the careers of developing ones, such as, at that time, the Supremes.

Dissatisfied, Wells announced her intention to leave Motown; incredibly, she claims Gordy offered her fifty percent of the company, which meant that, if she had stayed, she would have had a stake in the rising careers of artists like Diana Ross. It was a decision that did irreparable damage to both parties. Years later, Wells told a reporter, "I should have stayed at Motown."

The rest of the story is not happy. Wells bounced from label to label, but no one could duplicate Berry Gordy's formula, and she supported herself mainly through touring. There were a couple of suicide attempts and a bizarre invented "kidnapping" supposedly staged by a couple of overeager fans. She grew more and more ill; she'd had a two-pack-a-day habit from her teen years and later turned to crack and heroin.

PEGGY LEE NEVER GOT INTO THE HARD DRUGS, but hers was "a profession practically based on booze," writes Peter Richmond, and Lee drank her share, often in the company of the questionable men she chose; her first husband, charismatic guitarist Dave Barbour, "even fed the goldfish bourbon," Lee recalled. Later, she went for brief, intense couplings, so many that her daughter Nicki pleaded vainly at one point, "Mother, let's make this one do, so that I won't get confused."

Like Mary Wells, she always had trouble with the fellows. She never made a good marriage; when her fourth husband, bongo player Jack del Rio, carried Peggy into her own house and thanked her for giving it all to him, Lee says she thought "*Uh*-oh" to herself.

Also like Wells, Lee's one lasting relationship was with her audience, with whom she practiced a kind of sensual restraint. Having failed in an early club date to sing over a boisterous Jack Benny and his entourage, she realized on the spot that a soft voice conveyed more feeling and made her listeners want to get in close. She had a way with a song like nobody else, giving a beatnik flair to the lyrics of Little Willie John's "Fever"and stripping the instruments down to a string bass and drums played with fingertips.

< 104 >

*

EVEN THOUGH SHE PUT ON DAZZLING SHOWS for as long as she could and stayed after for hours talking to fans, Mary Wells never struck those around her as happy. Between 1990 and 1992, a journalist named Steve Bergsman recorded four hours of interviews with Wells that have never been released; later, he gave access to them to Peter Benjaminson. On Bergsman's tapes, fellow Motown artist Brenda Holloway recalls that "there was a sadness about [Wells] from the first day I met her to the last day I saw her," and another friend says Wells "had a lot of hurt bones, but no mean ones," even in her last days.

Yet accounting for anyone's sorrow is a bit of a chicken and egg conundrum. Yes, she grew up without a father, but so have a lot of people. Maybe hers is a case of life imitating art; Peter Benjaminson quotes singer and producer Ken Fowley as saying "pop music is music for lonely people made by other lonely people," and perhaps Wells took that too much to heart.

Was that Peggy Lee's problem as well? Identifying your audience doesn't always mean identifying with it; you can tell the stars who keep a thin but impenetrable, often ironic barrier between themselves and their fans from the ones who go all in. "Fever" is Peggy Lee's signature tune, not to mention, in Peter Richmond's words, "the sexiest song that Peggy Lee—or maybe anyone— ever sang."

But in light of Peggy Lee's seeming pact with the devil to have a dazzling career instead of the domestic bliss of which she often sang wistfully, one wonders if a better theme song might not have been the Jerry Leiber and Mike Stoller hit "Is That All There Is?," a song whose Kurt Weill-ish music and lyrics are so tinged with disillusionment that Marlene Dietrich wouldn't record it. Peggy Lee did, though.

When you look at the two singers together, you see that Mary Wells's story is the stuff of fine art. Operas like *La Traviata* and *La Bohème* are centered on characters like hers. Edgar Allan Poe said that the death of a beautiful woman is the most poetical topic in the world, and Henry James's most acclaimed novels are about doomed heroines.

Peggy Lee is like some aunt of yours, a brassy dame with a salty tongue and a drink in her hand before noon. But if her story is big-screen and bombastic,

< 105 >

that of Mary Wells is muted and intimate. Like Sam Cooke, she sang to huge audiences, yet she seemed to be singing to each individual as well. The more you know about Mary Wells, the more you find that, like John, Paul, George, and Ringo (and this writer, too), you are more than a little in love with her as well.

< 106 >

The Savage Young Beatles

IF YOU'VE EVER WATCHED A DOG trying to fasten its mouth around a fully-inflated basketball, you have a sense of what it's like to get a grip on Beatlemania fifty years after the fact. Here's how Bob Spitz describes the band's first appearance at Liverpool's Cavern Club.

> The audience stirred and half turned while Bob Wooler crooned into an open mike: "And now, everybody, the band you've been waiting for. Direct from Hamburg—."
>
> But before he got their name out, Paul McCartney jumped the gun and, in a raw, shrill burst as the curtain swung open, hollered: "*I'm gonna tell Aunt Mary / 'bout Uncle John / he said he had the mis'ry / buthegottalotoffun. . . .*" Oh, baby! The aimless shuffle [of the crowd] stopped dead in its tracks. The reaction of the audience was so unexpected that Wooler had failed, in the first few seconds, to take note of it. Part of the reason was the shocking explosion that shook the hall. A whomp of bass drum accompanied each quarter note beat with terrific force. The first one struck after Paul screamed "*Tell*," so that the charge ricocheted wildly off the walls. There was a second on *Mary*, and then another, then a terrible volley that had the familiar *bam-bam-bam* of a Messerschmitt wreaking all hell on a local target: an assault innocent of madness. The pounding came in rhythmic waves and once it started, it did not stop. There was nowhere to take cover on the open floor. All heads snapped forward and stared wild-eyed at the deafening ambush. The music crashing around them was discernibly a species of rock 'n roll but played unlike they had ever heard before. *Oh bab-by, yeahhhhhh / now ba-by, woooooo. . . .* It was convulsive,

< 107 >

ugly, frightening, and visceral in the way it touched off frenzy in the crowd.

You could start in that grimy firetrap of a club in a declining English port city, then—or, in this country, at a 1964 Chicago concert, when someone in the balcony cocked his arm and threw a frozen t-bone steak onstage, nearly clobbering Paul McCartney.

What could the tosser have been thinking—that the boys needed a good meal? Certainly they were rail thin from all the speed they gobbled and their bed-to-studio-to-bus-to-show-to-club-to-bed lifestyle.

But chances are the steak slinger just figured, well, it was a good idea at the time. In those days, girls fell to their knees and gnawed their hands in ecstasy when the Beatles' limo went past, and boys lowered themselves from hotel roofs on bedsheets so they could dangle outside their idols' windows. In an era of celebrity saturation, it's hard to remember how life-threateningly Dionysian the scene was. The world was just as young and stupid and beautiful as it is now, though in an unimaginably different way.

THE DANGER OF EXTRAPOLATING is that sometimes it works, though more often it doesn't. By one estimation I've seen, there were thirty-seven Elvis impersonators at the time of his death in 1977. By 1993, there were 48,000. Extrapolating from this, it was estimated that by 2010, every third person would be an Elvis impersonator, which would probably make going to the supermarket a whole lot more interesting than it is now.

So the parents and preachers and principals were wrong: the pit-bull Beatlemaniacs didn't grow in number and ferocity. Instead, they became a smaller, more intense, more important audience. Still, who could blame the squares for their terror. The crowds were so crazed . . . who *knew*?

Regardless of your age, it's almost certain that you've crooned into a hairbrush as you practiced soulful looks in the mirror and wondered why you, too, weren't a Beatle (or Eminem or Dolly Parton or Jay-Z). As it happens, there's a

< 108 >

formula to becoming the star you were always meant to be, though it's going to help a lot if you're no older than fourteen.

First, be a fan. The Beatles relied heavily on records by the Everly Brothers and Buddy Holly as they sought to give their vocals personality, and their own first recordings include songs by Chuck Berry, Little Richard, and other American rock singers they adored.

Second, be persistent. The boys didn't really have a plan B. In the words of another Liverpool musician Mark Spitz interviewed, the alternative to showbiz success would have been the preordained misery of the Beatles' contemporaries: "no diploma, a dead-end job, a loveless marriage, too many kids, never enough money, and lots of beer to drown the burden."

Finally, if you want to make it big, be flexible: John, Paul, George, and Ringo went at stardom the way a team of safecrackers would go after the crown jewels, trying every combination of tempo, key, rhythm, personnel (Pete Best was only the most famous of the group to be sacked), girlfriend, wife, manager, pharmaceutical, religion, and haircut until they got exactly what they wanted.

THEN, OF COURSE, THEY WERE KILLED, not by the narcissistic idiot who shot John Lennon or the cancer that took George Harrison's life but by Beatlemania itself. Unlike a band today that begins by plugging into the system, the Beatles invented the system, which means they didn't know what they were doing until they had done it, and then they didn't know what they had. In 1962, they couldn't get a record deal; a Decca executive told them that guitar groups were on the way out. Less than two years later, they had sixteen Number One hits.

It was about this time that they crept into a darkened box at the Royal Albert Hall to hear Bob Dylan and realized that he was already more musically advanced than they were; having already changed the world of music, how could they possible keep changing themselves at an ever-increasing pace?

They couldn't, of course, and by 1968, with Paul proposing wistfully that the group go on the road again as a small band playing club dates the way they had in the beginning, the four Beatles took a look at each other and decided

< 109 >

that, in an echo of songs as old as "I'm Looking Through You" and as recent as "Nowhere Man," there was no one there anymore.

In 1967, you could have found me and my grad-school roommates and sitting cross-legged around a wobbly turntable, our granny glasses slipping down our noses as we furiously scribbled *Sergeant Pepper* lyrics and analyzed them long into the night instead of preparing for class. We didn't know it then, but the Beatles have reached their musical peak. Within a couple of years, they disbanded and headed, or so it seemed at the time, toward history's closet, to hang there with the Nehru jackets that would soon be too snug and the peace medallions that were already beginning to tarnish.

When the Beatles arrived long before that, they came as saviors. In the late '50s, rock was in its giddiest, most danceable phase, a time of twangy guitars and drumbeats that sounded like someone hitting a wet cardboard box with an ax handle.

Then things started to go bad—fast. In 1957, Little Richard got religion and vowed never to play rock and roll again. Elvis was drafted in 1958, and Jerry Lee Lewis was hounded off the air after he married his thirteen year-old third cousin.

1959 was the worst: Chuck Berry was convicted of violating the Mann Act; the payola scandal broke wide open; Buddy Holly, Ritchie Valens, and the Big Bopper all died when their plane went down in a snowy field outside of Clear Lake, Iowa.

But the saddest day for rock fans was November 22, 1963, because John F. Kennedy was no musician, but he was everything young people wanted to be—happy, cool, suave—and if he were mortal, that meant they were, too.

The term ended on a bad note that year, and when school started again, I wasn't the only one who was just going through the motions. But as I walked through a college dorm in January, 1964, I heard a song coming from someone's room, the chords hitting me in the chest like hammer blows. "What is *that*?" I asked. The guy with the radio said, "'I Want to Hold Your Hand.' It's by the Beatles." And then he added, though he didn't need to, "They're gonna be big."

< 110 >

For genius to appear, it helps to have not only brilliant individuals but also extraordinary times, periods in which every kind of border is crossed: geographic, technological, artistic. Shakespeare flourished in such a time, and so did Mark Twain. And so did the Beatles.

Consider: the Beatles appeared on the Ed Sullivan show on February 9, 1964. In that same year, it wasn't just fight fans who remembered Muhammed Ali's astonishing defeat of heavyweight champ Sonny Liston on February 25, 1964 and Ali's subsequent emergence as a global cultural icon. The March on Washington took place on August 28, 1963; the Voting Rights Act was signed into law two years later.

The messy auteur film *Easy Rider* was released on July 14, 1969, changing Hollywood forever. Meanwhile, no less than six James Bond movies appeared between 1960 and 1969, fitting reminders of the era in which pop culture and politics not only collided but reached critical mass, setting off chain reactions that shape our lives today. Other paradigm-shattering events of the period include the assassinations of Martin Luther King and Bobby Kennedy in 1968 and Neil Armstrong's moonwalk in 1969. The first birth control pills were marketed in the early 60s, and widespread use began a few years later.

Another quality of genius is that you can't see it coming; nobody predicted Shakespeare or Twain, either. Also, genius can't be copied; just as the two writers had their imitators, other bands based themselves on the boys from Liverpool (remember the Knack?), but the "next Beatles" never appeared. Bands can be cloned—Britney Spears and Christina Aguilera, the Backstreet Boys and *NSYNC—but not genius.

AS A GROUP, THE BEATLES COVERED the entire artistic gamut. There was John the mordant wit, Paul the ebullient showman, Ringo the madcap, and George the moral force. No single group or movement since has reproduced this complex chemistry. Punk didn't, and neither did grunge. Rap comes the closest, but rap has managed to thrive by keeping the formula basic: its mordancy is neatly balanced by glitzy showmanship, but while there are zany rap acts and even ethical ones, no single group offers the whole package.

< 111 >

In talking to younger people to find out what, if anything, the Beatles mean to them, I uncovered every possible response, from those who didn't quite know they were (one 20-year-old mentioned "Paul McCarthy") to others who owned every album the group recorded. One latter-day fan said the Beatles "created most of the sounds I listen to now"; another said "the greatest band of all time—basically invented what we know of pop music today." My most startling discovery was that young people know a lot more about the Beatles than the Rolling Stones, even though the former disbanded over 30 years ago and the Stones are currently embarked on yet another world tour.

One way or another, the Beatles' music endures. While it's their greatest legacy, it isn't their only one. Because even though they're gone, the Beatles also represent what's to come. It might be a hundred years from now and it might be tomorrow, but sooner or later, like a fast-moving weather system or a lone rider against the sky, the music that changes the world will arrive as though out of nowhere.

JUST AS THERE WAS A HARD-TO-ACCOUNT-FOR CLUSTER of events in the sixties that caused seismic cultural shifts, in the early years of the twenty-first century, a number of studies of those shifts appeared. In music, books on Jimi Hendrix, Janis Joplin, Sam Cooke, and the Brill Building songwriters seemed to tumble out one after another. In addtion to Mark Spitz's doorstopper of nearly a thousand pages called simply *The Beatles*, there was Steven D. Stark's aptly titled *Meet the Beatles: A Cultural History of the Band That Shook Youth, Gender, and the World* as well as Ian MacDonald's *Revolution in the Head: The Beatles' Records and the Sixties.*

The spate of such books makes sense for two reasons. First, it's a sign that the songs that once looked like throwaways have attained classic status; the sound engineers who saw lyric sheets that read "She loves you, yeah, yeah, yeah" figured the boys would bring the real song with them when they showed up at the studio, but forty years later, teenagers of all ages recognize the Beatles' gift of coining a simple phrase behind which lies the promise of limitless rapture. The second reason why so many books about boomer music are appear-

< 112 >

ing is that savvy biographers are realizing that many eyewitnesses from the day are lining up to buy tickets for the Big Concert in the Sky, If half the Beatles are dead, a good number of those who knew them when are statistically poised to join them, and dead readers don't buy books.

What makes Bob Spitz's book a standout among its many competitors is his attention to visual detail. The book begins with the description of a crowd forming at an early concert: "December 27, 1960 -- They had begun to pour into the village of Litherland as they always did, half an hour before the doors opened. Night crawlers: their bodies young and liquid, legs spidering along the sidewalks, exaggerated by the blue glare of the streetlamps." Meanwhile, the just-formed Beatles are slouching toward Litherland in an "old bottle green van that had been recruited for service only that morning. The four boys, riding in the dark, grimy cargo hold like astronauts in a cramped space capsule, braced themselves with experienced hands as the old crate rattled north along the Stanley Road, past shops splashed with a waxy fluorescence."

As you follow the path the boys tread, you, too, will change the turtleneck sweater, corduroy trousers, and duffel coat you wore in 1957 for the leather outfit of 1960 and then the psychedelic hodgepodge of velvet and paisley that would have been de rigueur in 1966.

Even if you were just a gleam in your dad's eye in those days, and even though a nasty war was starting in Asia and civil rights protesters were being knocked down by water cannons, Spitz's knowing, affectionate take on the Beatles will give you a sense of what Wordsworth meant when, describing the revolutions of his own time, he wrote: "Bliss was it in that dawn to be alive, / But to be young was very heaven."

Surprisingly, today's young don't find the Beatles to be dated. It's hard to walk across a college campus and not see a pretty girl in a Beatles t-shirt. Regularly I poll my students on their musical tastes. Painting with a broad brush, I'd say that roughly half of them are indifferent to the Beatles and half of them are as fanatic as we were in the sixties, even if they're not throwing steaks at them or lowering themselves through hotel windows. And I'm generalizing again,

< 113 >

but I think I'm probably right in saying that almost all of the students who are fans were or are presently in bands—talk about the perfect audience.

Recently I asked students in a contemporary American authors class to make a list of their favorites of the writers we studied but to include a "wild card," a work that isn't literary but that defines or lights up or energizes all the others. Among the authors they liked best were Raymond Carver, John Cheever, Flannery O'Connor, and Sylvia Plath. When it came to the wild card, my students nominated but passed ultimately on *Breakfast at Tiffany's* (the movie), Handel's *Messiah*, and Gershwin's "Rhapsody in Blue" and chose instead *The White Album* by the Beatles.

Why *The White Album*? How did it find this new and unexpected audience? The Beatles may have been English, but this album is rooted songs my students love, in the music of Buddy Holly and Little Richard. It includes the sounds of the Beach Boys, and, taken as a whole, became a kind of anthem to the murderous Manson family.

Can't get much more American than that.

< 114 >

Girl Groups and Go-Go Dancers: Rock 'n' Roll Comes of Age

AH, TO BE THERE AT THE MOMENT OF CREATION. It's 1958 , and Jerry Leiber is making tea in his Washington Square duplex, listening to Mike Stoller fooling around on the piano and then yelling "Take out the papers and the trash," to which Stoller instantly replies, "Or you don't get no spending cash!" Within 15 minutes, the legendary songwriting duo finishes "Yakety-Yak"for the Coasters, a song which becomes their fourth No. 1 single on the pop chart.

If you tell friends today that you're getting ready to play "Yakety-Yak" or "Along Came Jones" or "Poison Ivy" or any other Leiber-Stoller song that the Coasters recorded, they might look at you as though you've just announced you're going to have a hula hoop contest in their living room. Go ahead, though, and crank the volume. Your buddies will see that the songs are as catchy and funny now as they were then. "During recording sessions," said Stoller, "we'd be falling on the floor—all of us—and staggering around the room holding our bellies because we were laughing so hard." The duo had the intellectual courage to be stupid, you might say; some of their biggest hits were, in Jerry Leiber's words, "content-free—they're about nothing."

Mainly, though, the songs are well crafted, as are dozens of others written by others in the same era: "On Broadway," "Stand By Me," "Save the Last Dance for Me," "Walk On By," "Breaking Up Is Hard to Do," "Will You Love Me Tomorrow," "Do Wah Diddy Diddy," "You've Lost That Lovin' Feelin'," "(You Make Me Feel Like a) Natural Woman," all of which emerged from New York's Brill Building in the late '50s and the early '60s.

Well, not quite: actually, the music came from two addresses within a couple of blocks of each other, the Brill at 1619 Broadway and the unnamed building at 1650. Ken Emerson notes that the one-building-only myth persists be-

< 115 >

cause its name is so thoroughly identified with the songs that became the first rock and pop selections to make it onto the American jukebox.

But that's showbiz: the goal is not to be right but to sound right, a composer's truism that would have been roundly endorsed by the songwriting teams covered in this comprehensive account of a key moment in the history of popular music: Carole King and Gerry Goffin, Doc Pomus and Mort Shuman, Burt Bacharach and Hal David, Neil Sedaka and Howard Greenfield, Jeff Barry and Ellie Greenwich, Barry Mann and Cynthia Weil.

The paters familias of these duos were, of course, Leiber and Stoller, who in one way or another influenced, inspired, hired, worked with, and/or produced them all. In keeping with the opposites-make-the-best-music paradigm (think Lennon and McCartney, Jagger and Richards), Jerry Leiber was "manic, impetuous, and aggressive . . . a motormouth with curly red hair," writes Emerson, whereas Mike Stoller was "so laid-back he could scarcely be bothered to raise his eyelids, much less his voice."

Their personality types may have extended to choice of wives—Leiber's first wife was an actress, Stoller's a bookkeeper—and even the songwriters' friends seemed chosen according to artistic temperament; the Leibers liked to socialize with actors and painters, the Stollers with classical composers. Similarly, Burt Bacharach had "a very, very tense and hyper type of personality," according to Dionne Warwick, whereas Hal David was "kind of a father figure."

Leiber and Stoller succeeded because they not only adored the blues and boogie woogie that adult black musicians played but also figured out how to turn its raw yearning into commercial songs that an audience a generation younger and several shades paler would buy. In other cases, though, the identification with black culture was more primal: Doc Pomus (who was born Jerome Felder) was crippled by polio as a child and once wrote in a notebook: "To the world, a fat crippled jewish kid is a nigger—a thing—the invisible man—like Ralph Ellison says."

Citing a scholarly study of themes of recovery and redemption in polio narratives, Emerson connects the emotions swirling around the world-changing first kiss described in "This Magic Moment," written by Pomus and Mort Shuman for the Drifters, to a journal entry in which Pomus says that "I used

< 116 >

to believe in magic and flying and that one morning I would wake up and all the bad things were bad dreams. . . . And I would get out of the wheelchair and walk and not with braces and crutches."

GENERALLY, THOUGH, THE COMPOSITION of these songs was a good deal more prosaic. Carole King recalls that, one evening in 1960, she had gone out to play mah-jongg, adding "How Jewish can you get?" Her collaborator and husband Gerry Goffin had finished his shift at the chemical plant where he worked and gone bowling with friends, returning home to find a note from King saying that producer Don Kirshner wanted a song by the next day for the Shirelles, who had had a recent hit with "Tonight's the Night."

King had left a piano track on their Norelco tape recorder; Goffin got to work on the lyrics, and when King returned from her mah-jongg game, they finished "Will You Love Me Tomorrow" and went to bed at two. When the song topped the charts, Kirshner and King took a limo to the chemical plant and told Goffin his days testing polymers and epoxies were over.

Much has been made of the scenario in which white and specifically Jewish businessmen take advantage of naive black musicians, but the history is more nuanced than that. As in any story of business dealings, of course there was a certain amount of exploitation, yet the big picture is one of nice Jewish boys and girls being forced to take piano lessons by their Yiddishe mamas, rebelling as all kids do by embracing a culture totally different from that of their parents, then using their own skills to shape black music to appeal to an audience much like themselves. When no one in the studio could figure out how to kick off Mann and Weil's "Bless You," a pianist began to pick out a rhythm to which a startled Barry Mann responded, "That's 'Hava Nagila!'" Even better, the same notes appear a year later in the Crystals' "He's a Rebel," and thus a traditional Jewish dance became into an anthem of teen rebellion.

Some of the writers were experts at taking apart songs that were already hits and rewriting them "sideways," with different chords and a scarcely altered structure. Thus "Oh! Carol" by Neil Sedaka and Howard Greenfield, the writers least influenced by Leiber and Stoller, sounds like "Little Darlin'" by the Dia-

< 117 >

monds (a white Canadian quartet covering an original by the Gladiolas, a black doo-wop group); Sedaka also appropriates the spoken interlude from Maurice Williams' version of "Little Darlin'" and, recalling those childhood piano lessons, throws in a flourish from Heitor Villa-Lobos's "A Prole do Bebê" for good measure. (Ken Emerson notes that because Sedaka and others of his ilk "owed less to Big Joe Turner than to Irving Berlin," though their music "often rocked, it seldom swung.")

Some songs were written less analytically: when one studio session wrapped and most of the musicians left, the Dixie Cups began to sing in English and Creole a street ditty they'd known from childhood; a producer told everybody to grab anything they could lay their hands on and bang out the distinctive chick-chick-chick, chick-chick rhythm of "Iko Iko," and a kind of thumb piano that Jeff Barry and Ellie Greenwich had brought back from their Jamaican honeymoon provided the song's bass line. Then there's the Latin influence on the pop music of this era, from the BOM-ba-bom Brazilian *baion* beat (in "There Goes My Baby") to Afro-Cuban rhythms and Mexican horns (both can be heard in "This Magic Moment").

The times they were a-changin' by the mid sixties, and if John Lennon and Paul McCartney declared Carole King and Gerry Goffin their favorite songwriters, Bob Dylan dismissed the Brill Building sound as "I'm hot for you and you're hot for me—ooka dooka dicka dee." But Leiber and Stoller and their progeny kept pop music on track during some of its darkest days. Rock 'n' roll exploded onto the scene in the '50s with Elvis, but in 1957-58, Elvis was drafted into the army, Jerry Lee Lewis was boycotted after marrying his 13 year-old third cousin, Buddy Holly was killed in a plane crash, and Chuck Berry was arrested for transporting a minor across state lines.

But to say the songs were pure confection is a misrepresentation—a lot of them were, but when the Leader of the Pack rides off to get killed on his motorcycle and Mary Weiss of the Shangri-Las sings "Look out! Look out! Look out!" you can hear the terror in her voice; no matter your age, you feel in your heart a teenager's intimation of mortality that's universal. Jeff Barry recalls coaching Weiss through the end of "The Leader of the Pack": "Look what happened to this guy. Here he is, he loves this girl. And just think about her: She

< 118 >

stands there and sees him pull away on his motorcycle. I got her all psyched up, and she was crying."

Years later, Mary Weiss recalls that "I had enough pain in me, at the time, to pull off anything. And to get into it, and sound—believable. It was very easy for me. The recording studio was the place that you could really release what you're feeling, without everybody looking at you." Everybody was listening, though. Talk about audience: "The Leader of the Pack" charted at number one on the Billboard Hot 100 on November 28, 1964. It's the best-known example of the teenage tragedy song (also called "tear jerker", "death disc" or "splatter platter"). On the surface, it sounds like a song for a girl audience, but it's really a song for guys: masculine self-pity has probably sold more records than any other emotion. Mainly, it's about thwarted love, and every member of every audience has felt that.

"The Leader of the Pack," as Jeff Barry said about another Shangri-Las song, is "a movie for the ear."

BESIDES, BETWEEN ELVIS AND THE BEATLES, rock wasn't dead—it just wasn't on TV. In the early sixties, the two worlds of image and sound were still trying to figure each other out. As Ken Emerson reports, when Joe Pasternak, who produced *Where the Boys Are*, scornfully dismissed Neil Sedaka and Howard Greenfield, asking Connie Francis of she really believed they could write a better song than Sammy Cahn (a favorite Sinatra lyricist and also a candidate to write the movie's theme), Francis replied, "Maybe not better, but it'll sell more records. It'll make the picture a hit no matter what the picture's like."

TV sets were popping up in every American living room then and would soon be in kitchens and bedrooms as well, and the savviest producers knew how to marry screen to song, though the history of music on TV is pretty much like the history of TV itself, a tale of the rare tour de force appearing at infrequent intervals among the embarrassing, the insulting, and, for the most part, the forgettable.

Figures who are sometimes ridiculed today, such as Ed Sullivan, often either were geniuses themselves or at least knew how to hire geniuses. When

< 119 >

the Beatles appeared on *The Ed Sullivan Show* in 1964, the television audience saw a set that was unadorned yet dramatic: three guitarists and three mikes in the foreground, the drummer and his kit simultaneously sublimated into the background and elevated on a riser above the others. "Sullivan allowed every trained monkey act and puppeteer to do something close to what they normally did," writes Austen, "with the TV professionals directing them to make it better fit the TV screen, and then some manipulative camera work to get it just right."

Sullivan also knew or at least learned how to use the audience. In Elvis's appearances on the show in 1956 and 1957, the cameras showed "the same Eisenhower-era company men and their wives that were always in the Sullivan audience," but by the time of the Beatles' first performance, the cameramen were showing screaming girls bunched together. After all, the essence of pop music is narcissism—you empathize with either the gang leader or his girl or both when you listen to "The Leader of the Pack," whereas nobody at a Mozart recital ever wished he were dying young and penniless in 18th century Vienna.

In *TV a Go-Go: Rock on TV from American Bandstand to American Idol*, Jake Austen puts his finger on the importance of "the receptive fan" to rock programming, especially when he notes that, during the Beatles' third appearance on the Sullivan show, "one screaming girl shows her intense, howling love for the Beatles then notices she is on TV. As she stares at herself on a monitor her excitement and screaming intensify."

Unfortunately, in 1971 CBS head of programming Fred Silverman decided to respond to the youth revolution and go for a younger and more urbane look by cancelling shows that were rural (*Beverly Hillbillies*, *Green Acres*, Hee Haw) or that he deemed old-fashioned (*Lassie*, *The Ed Sullivan Show*). And the Sullivan show *was* old-fashioned; by appealing to a multi-generational audience, it hearkened back to the variety stage shows of nineteenth-century America, with grandparents and teenagers alike watching magic acts but also Bo Diddley (Sullivan's first rock performer, in 1955). In contrast, Austen points out how dull rock acts appear on *Saturday Night Live* where "unambitious cameras" shoot whatever is going on and "spread-out musicians, under boring lighting schemes," blend into distracting sets which, though changed annually, always

< 120 >

suggest the same urban clutter. And, as opposed to Ed Sullivan's trick of making audience members themselves into performers, "audience reaction [on *SNL*] is never tangible and rarely documented."

How can you be Narcissus without a mirror?

Most rock 'n' roll doesn't work on TV for the simple reason that most rockers are, like the Brill Building songwriters, trained musicians from their youth as well as lifelong fans of their art, whereas TV executives are businessmen trying to guess what their audiences want and, as often as not, failing. When rock and TV made beautiful music together, it was usually because of a single mastermind who is easy to mock today, such as Ed Sullivan or such talk-show hosts as Mike Douglas, Merv Griffin, and Dinah Shore, all of whom had a sense of what Jake Austen calls "the entertainment omnibus," to use an antiquated term for a vehicle that carries passengers from all walks of life: "they saw how everything fit together, even it wasn't obviously related."

If you've ever been to a party where someone has brought one of those "salads" made of frozen dessert topping and instant pudding mix that are delicious for a bite or two yet leave a taste in your mouth that no amount of turkey and dressing can take away, you know what it's like to research this period. For while there are peaks in the relationship between music and television, there are many more valleys. Network television will never be more than it is, though what it is is so powerful in its numbing mediocrity that, with the exception of sports, it takes everything it touches down with it. The history of rock 'n' roll on TV would be devoted mainly to such valleys as the Monkees, the Partridge Family, rock 'n' roll cartoons, and reality TV.

Then again, some of the abominations are so horrible as to be wonderful, such as a post-Monkees show called *The Righteous Apples* in which a band by that name spends their down time solving hate crimes, including one masterminded by a racist South African abortion doctor who sterilizes black women. Another failed show called *Popstars* featured a band called Eden's Crush consisting of five young women who shared what Jake Austen describes as "dark-haired, dark-eyed, relatively fair-skinned looks that suggest ethnicity while still

< 121 >

adhering to European standards of beauty," the theory being that "American teens of all races would connect with a group that wasn't any race at all." But remember, audiences like performers who look like them: while *Seinfeld* and *Friends* ranked 59th and 118th recently in African-American homes, *American Idol* ruled because it features black performers.

Looking back over the fifty years in which a new art form was born and matured (and, some say, died), and thinking especially of the role played in rock 'n' roll history by such figures as Jerry Leiber, Mike Leiber, and Ed Sullivan, it's hard not to think to think of Serbian poet Vasko Popa's statement that poetry is written not by lovesick teenagers but by sly old tricksters. Actually, the art bus has seats for both: passionate youngsters as well as hardened vets who see how everything fits together. And while television shrinks and flattens the music, nonetheless it can deliver that music to an audience that wouldn't have it otherwise.

Paradoxically, TV creates an audience of millions by creating a million micro-audiences of two or three or, for the most part, one viewer each. Which is how we like it: Edward Bellamy's novel *Looking Backward* was written in the late nineteenth century, when real people lived communally and enjoyed music live, since there was no other way to experience it. Bellamy's book is set in the future, somewhere around our own time. In the utopia-to-come, citizens like you and me don't have to go all the way down to some band shell in a park to hear a concert; instead, live music is piped into their apartments so they can enjoy it alone.

Newer isn't better. That happens to be the truth, but it also sounds like the name of a band, maybe an alt-punk group. Maybe the best thing about music on television is that it reminds us how great live music is. I live two blocks from a club, and if Newer Isn't Better ever plays a gig there, I'm going.

< 122 >

A Bigger World:
Martha Reeves and the Vandellas' "Dancing in the Street"

ON A JULY DAY IN 1964, a twenty-two year-old singer named Martha Reeves takes a crosstown bus from her Detroit home to the Motown recording studio. It's been three years since she gave up her job with a dry cleaner, but she still lives at home with her parents and ten siblings. Motown execs don't have a song lined up for Reeves at the moment, but waiting for her is Maxine Powell, the "Miss Powell" who coaches Martha and the other singers on their public demeanor and helps them improve their stage acts. Even though she has already recorded two Top 40 numbers for Berry Gordy, Jr.'s hit factory, she's still more like a kid going to school

In Studio A, Marvin Gaye, who had some early successes of his own, is working on a song with two other men. When he sees Reeves, Gaye stops crooning and says, "Hey, man, try this on Martha."

She is reluctant to take on a song written for a male voice, but she idolizes Gaye, so she puts on a pair of headphones. A music track erupts; a blare of what sound like Mexican horns backed by a sledgehammer beat make it clear that this is a departure from the typically romantic Motown sound. Martha belts out the first words: "Calling out around the world. . . ." Two minutes and thirty-six seconds later, she has nailed the song in one take, though there is a second take as well (more on that later). The Vandellas are called in to sing backup, and an American classic is born.

As I was working on this chapter, I was in my doctor's examining room for a routine visit and got to talking about music with a couple of nurses who were in their late twenties. "You know a song called 'Dancing in the Street'?" I asked. And when they said no, I sang the first line. Instantly they began to snap their

< 123 >

fingers, bump their hips, and come back with the second line: "Are you ready for a brand new beat?"

Fifty years after the song was released, the two nurses were dancing to and singing a song they knew, even though they didn't know they knew it.

THIS SAME SUMMER, America is coming to a boil. Young Northerners swoop into rural Mississippi to register black voters; in June, three volunteers go missing and will later be found tortured and dead. Two days after "Dancing in the Streets" is released, a purported confrontation between U.S. and Vietnamese naval vessels takes place in the Gulf of Tonkin, leading to an expanded war in Vietnam. Demonstrations break out on university campuses. Malcolm X declares, "We want freedom by any means necessary," and daily, other dissident voices join his. Earlier that year, Cassius Clay defeats Sonny Liston to become heavyweight boxing champion and changes his name to Muhammad Ali after converting to the Nation of Islam.

Back in the studio, Ivy Jo Hunter, one of the three co-authors of "Dancing in the Street" (along with Marvin Gaye and William "Mickey" Stevenson), has bad news for Martha Reeves: her take was terrific, but—dang!—they'd forgotten to turn on the recorder. Reeves is miffed. She'll do it again, sure, but she really doesn't like to do second takes. So this time, there's an edge to her voice. When she finishes, she looks up at the control booth window, where the three men who wrote the song are congratulating each other as though something special has happened.

And it has. Reeves' voice sells the song, of course, but she was singing with some of the greatest musicians in the business. The Funk Brothers—a fluid group whose members included legendary bass player James Jamerson, guitarist Joe Messina (a rare white player), and percussionist Jack Ashford, whose tambourine smashes can be heard throughout "Dancing in the Street"—turned almost every song into a hit, despite or perhaps because of the primitive conditions under which they often worked.

Studio A was a small room with a hole in the wall cut through to a bathroom that served as an echo chamber. ("Don't flush while they're recording"

< 124 >

was a warning Reeves remembers hearing often.) Four microphones hung from the ceiling, meaning the engineers had only four tracks to work with. Two by fours were put down and covered with plywood. When a rhythmical stomp was called for, the first four people to show up with leather shoe soles (no rubber, please) were recruited for the task; today the floor is splintered from all that heavy treading. On another Reeves hit, "Nowhere to Run," one of the songwriters beat a chain with a hammer until his hand bled.

"Dancing in the Street" shot up the charts, peaking as the number two Billboard pop single, and it remains popular almost fifty years later. It begins with a horn fanfare that brings you to your feet. Then the title becomes a memorable hook that is repeated throughout by both lead and backup singers (with one important variation). The bridge, the different-sounding passage that interrupts the steady flow of verses, slips to a minor key in a way that still stuns artists. ("Mention 'Dancing in the Street' to any musician," writes Mark Kurlansky in his book on the song, "and he or she will often reply, 'That bridge!'")

Add it all up and you have to agree with Jon Landau, the music critic who became Bruce Springsteen's manager and who said, "The record is perfect."

WHICH DOESN'T EXACTLY MAKE IT the political anthem it may look like in retrospect. Berry Gordy, Jr. kept his music and musicians in what Mary Wilson of the Supremes called "the Motown bubble," steering clear of controversy and putting profit before politics. Reeves herself insisted it was no more than a "party song." And its co-writer, Mickey Stevenson, said that if the song had any meaning, it was that people of all kinds could get together and have fun.

I asked dozens of people who were in their teens in 1964 what the song meant to them, and the replies I got were studded with images of the era: jukeboxes, turntables, cars with tailfins, mom-and-pop soda shops, first kisses, stolen sips of beer and puffs on cigarettes, forty-cent banana splits, transistor radios (a huge technological advance, since it mean teens could take their music with them).

One guy said it was the song that he learned to dance to at church camp. Another said it told him, a farm kid at the time, that there was a bigger world

< 125 >

out there. A woman said she heard Martha and the Vandellas making a promise to her, a promise that distance didn't matter and that people would find a way to come together and celebrate life. That's a pop song's ultimate promise to its audience: that there's a home for you in the world, you can create that home for yourself, and the best place for you to do that is on the dance floor.

Not a single person I interviewed used the word "politics."

True, there is an eerie overlap between the song and the troubles of the day. Reeves had just finished performing the song in Detroit's Fox Theater on a July night in 1967 when her show had to be cancelled because the city was in flames following a crowd reaction to what was seen as the use of excessive police force at an unlicensed bar in a black neighborhood. (The rioting lasted for five days and is credited as the largest urban uprising of the Sixties.)

H. Rap Brown, then chairman of the not entirely accurately named Student Nonviolent Coordinating Committee, resented Gordy's lack of activism. "If Motown doesn't come around," he warned, "we are going to burn you down." Ironically, Brown co-opted Motown's hit that year as his theme song. He visited black neighborhoods and spoke from the roof of a car; often music spooled out of the car radio as a crowd formed, and often that music was "Dancing in the Street."

But "Dancing in the Street" is no "Marseillaise." A better comparison is to another 1964 song, Sam Cooke's "A Change is Gonna Come." That song's title suggests that it's a call for civil rights, but the lyrics are intensely personal: more than anything, the singer describes his aching loneliness. It's the flip side to "Dancing in the Street": Sam Cooke says he's sad because he doesn't have anybody, Martha Reeves tell every guy to grab a girl.

Both songs are deliciously ambiguous, and there is a tiny but significant detail that makes both the personal and the political readings of "Dancing in the Street" possible. It's the kind of thing that drives academic theoreticians wild with joy. The word "street" is singular in the title and in Reeve's lines, but when her backup singers respond, they say "dancing in the streets," which is different: "street" describes a block party, whereas "streets" suggest a whole city erupting. So the song can be taken either way, even though clearly the emphasis is on joy, and, well, dancing.

< 126 >

Oh, and something else happened in that studio in 1964 that gives the song its indelible quality. In a 2011 interview with co-writer Ivy Jo Hunter and Reeves, the singer mentioned how annoyed she was that they forgot to turn on the recorder and had to do another take, at which point Hunter grinned and said, "'Look at me. I'm sitting in a studio with an artist you don't want to upset. Do I say, 'Do it again,' or do I say the machine wasn't on?'" It takes forty-seven years, but at last Reeves finds out how she was tricked into singing her best and most famous song.

Reeves sounds irritated and edgier on the second take, though another way to put it is to simply say that her voice is more urgent. The message is powerful, after all, and Reeves delivers it forcefully. The message is that we all want to have a good time, but we're going to have even an better time if we invite everybody to the party.

< 127 >

"I Don't Play Guitar, I Play Amp": How Jimi Became Jimi

IN 1967, A GIRL I WAS INTERESTED IN told me she had two tickets to a show at Hunter College, and would I like to go? "Sure!" I said, because she was cute, and then, "Who's playing?" She shrugged and said, "I don't know. Some guy from England? My roommate got the tickets and can't go, and she didn't want to waste them."

That settled, and it being the late sixties, we got right to the next and more crucial issue: what drugs were we going to ingest? Neither of us had any acid. She had some grass, but toking up under the watchful eye of Hunter College security didn't seem like the best idea.

I had some mescaline, which I loved but figured might be a little too, ah, *primeval*, especially for a first date. The last time I'd tripped on mescaline was at a Vanilla Fudge concert with a bunch of guys. The Fudge's deconstructed covers of Motown classics ran the gamut from dirge-like to positively Wagnerian, and about halfway through I began to see that drummer Carmine Appice wasn't playing the drums, or just playing the drums, but playing the drums and butchering meat as well, the blood flying in arcs as he threw his arms in the air.

When the show was over, I told my friends I wanted to see the meat. They tried to talk me out of it, but evidently mescaline makes a even a shy person sure of himself, so I got onto the stage, which is when one of the roadies said, "The fuck you want?" I said, "Um, may I see the meat, please?" and he said, "Get the fuck outta here."

In my one experience with it, mescaline was stupid and fun. A lot of fun, actually. But it didn't seem like the best idea when I was trying to get a girl interested in me. "It was, like, far out," she's saying to her roommates, "but then the dude I was with ran off because he said he wanted to see the meat."

In the end, we decided to split one of her mother's diet pills. That may not

< 129 >

sound like much to you, but fifteen minutes before the show started, I was ready to unscrew every row of seats in the house with my belt buckle and re-install them again, though why that seemed necessary, I'm not sure.

Then the curtain went up on two pasty-looking Englishman and a black guy with a feather in his hat who began to play the loudest music I'd ever heard. Every strum of his strings sounded like guitar chords, sure, but also like Godzilla's feet pounding on my chest. When you're high, you're not sure whether what's affecting you is "you" or "it," so I looked around wildly to see how my fellow concertgoers were doing. To a person, they seemed aghast, at first, but by the third line of the first verse, their expressions were already changing into something like that on the face of St. Teresa in Bermini's statue, the one where her divine lover is thrusting his spear into her, and she's writhing in pain and ecstasy.

And then the guy with the hat pointed to his bass player and said, "Excuse me while I kiss this guy."

THAT SAME YEAR, A RECORD REVIEWER called Jimi Hendrix's music "robust" and" hellish" in the same sentence, which is like describing God as "outstanding" and "divine." "Robust" just doesn't cut it—that adjective might apply to a Sousa march, but not to such sulphorous anthems as "Manic Depression" and "Foxy Lady."

Hendrix's music was a hellfire that swept across global culture, alarming the Three Ps (parents, preachers, and politicians) and ravishing a youth ready, as youth always is, for something fresh.

Where'd all that sound and fury come from, though? The story begins with a tortured Seattle childhood and the death of a neglectful alcoholic mother at age thirty-three; the estranged father wouldn't let fifteen year-old Jimi and his younger brother Leon go to the funeral and instead gave them shots of Seagram's 7 whiskey, saying that's how men handled grief.

Young Jimi took up with the wrong crowd and, after some minor run-ins with the law, was given the choice of military service or jail. He soon found

< 130 >

himself in the Army's 101st Airborne Division, and he didn't turn out to be much of a paratrooper: Private Hendrix "requires excessive supervision at all times," read one supervisor's report. So he used his down time, which apparently was considerable, to indulge his obsession with the guitar.

How obsessed was he? So much so that he took a broom to elementary school and strummed it so constantly that a social worker worried about his mental health. His father found him a discarded ukelele with one string on it, and from there he worked his way through a series of pawnshop twangers until he could afford a decent instrument.

And he never stopped strumming. Following an early discharge from the Army, essentially Hendrix did nothing except play, starve (he claimed to live on orange peels and tomato paste at one point), learn from the many masters who took to a shy if driven pupil, and cycle in and out of group after group.

Apparently, every time young Jimi saw somebody play a lick he hadn't seen yet, he'd ask them to show him how it was done. Most maestros don't want to give away their trade secrets, but Jimi was as persistent about asking as he was about strumming, and as he bounced from one band to another, his toolbox grew and grew.

THERE ARE A LOT OF BETTER-THAN-AVERAGE GUITARISTS who remain nameless, however, so at one point, Jimi began to study another key component in the entertainer's curriculum: showmanship. In *Becoming Jimi Hendrix*, Steven Roby and Brad Schreiber describe one of his mentors, Gorgeous George Odell, as a "self-promoter with a sharpened sense of showmanship" and the importance of a distinctive appearance. In an era when even rock musicians cultivated a cookie cutter look and band members often wore matching outfits, Gorgeous George sported a silver wig and changed clothes as many as twelve times during a show; Hendrix's signature hats, headbands, scarves, and paisley shirts may owe more to that silver wig than one might think.

Even more important, Gorgeous George instilled in Jimi the necesiity for energy, commitment, flair, and especially the stamina to give the audience "a

< 131 >

complete performance, from beginning to end, of offering the audience a consistent level of entertainment." One colleague who knew both said that George "could put on a four-hour show in itself, and he knew about people and how to make them happy. Jimi got it from a cat that knew it as a second kind of nature."

Another of Jimi's teachers was Billy Davis, who played guitar for Hank Ballard and the Midnighters. "Jimi watched intently as Davis swung the guitar behnd his head and played it fiercely," write Roby and Schreiber, and "at times, Davis stepped up close to his amp and used the feedback to sustain a note." Rebuffed twice, teenaged Jimi finally not only got backstage to meet Davis but won him over: "After we talked for a while" says Davis, "he invited me back to his house so I could show him some of the things I did on the guitar, and for some reason I went twice. . . . Jimi introduced me to his dad and showed me this little cheap guitar he was playing, and I showed him some licks on my Stratocaster."

After all the lessons, though, Jimi remained Jimi. "Admired, hired, and fired" is the apt phrase Roby and Schreiber use for this period of Hendrix's life; he played rhythm 'n' blues covers in Little Richard's band and many others, but his penchant for "wrong" notes and impromptu solos got him the boot every time.

Maybe, though, the truth is simpler. Maybe the greatest guitar player of our times simply couldn't play, at least in the conventional sense. For one thing, he couldn't read music; for another, being left-handed, he taught himself to play by flipping the typical right-handed guitar upside down and playing the strings in reverse order. Jimi wouldn't play the music the way he was expected to, say Roby and Schneider, but Billy Davis, who should know, says simply, "He couldn't play the music right."

Until, of course, he could. One aspect of his musical growth is that he got better and better at improvising; as Miles Davis said, "If you hit a wrong note, it's the next note that you play that determines if its's good or bad." Another is that, over time, his ear got better and better, and for a rock musician, it's better to have a good ear than to be able to play charts. Jimi's wrenching version of "The Star-Spangled Banner" is note-perfect—except for the notes that he bends

< 132 >

like hot metal as his guitar wails all the anguish of the Vietnam war era better than any human voice could. Listen to it on YouTube: in Hendrix's hands, our national anthem is part metronomic bandroom standard and part wild, sobbing improvisation.

Of all the bandleaders who hired and fired Jimi, Little Richard alone appreciated Jimi's homemade genius. "He was the greatest guitar player I ever had," he says. "Not one of my men has ever come close to him. He would wander off stage playing his guitar. He was into his guitar, really wrapped up in it, and that's the way it should be. He put his heart into it. He never sounded like just one man. He put so much under me, I just had to sing hard." Jimi returned the compliment, telling a reporter that he wanted to make his guitar sound as wild as Little Richard's voice.

STILL, JIMI WAS UNEMPLOYABLE. Then came the cross-pollination that almost seems a necessary part of artistic evolution. For Melville, it was Shakespeare; for Picasso, it was African masks. Hendrix's leap forward came when he discovered Bob Dylan. When *Blonde on Blonde* came out in 1966, Jimi spent his last food dollars on the album; among other effects, Dylan's voice showed Hendrix that his could have an even greater effect if he avoided sounding like the crooners of the day.

Within a year, Hendrix was a star; within four, he was dead in London of what appears to have been an accidental overdose of sleeping pills and wine. I listen to his music almost every day, but I think, too, of the quiet, profound lesson he taught: follow your passion obsessively, so that when you encounter the thing or person that'll change your life, you'll be ready.

And add your own ingredient to the mix. In Hendrix's case, it was volume: after losing an early guitar duel duel to a bandmate with a bigger amp, he vowed never to enter the fray with any other than maximum power, and later he said "I don't play guitar. I play amplifier."

That's not exactly true. But when I saw Hendrix at Hunter College in 1967, he kicked off the show with "Foxy Lady," and its first chords fell like artillery

< 133 >

shells on an audience whose members, their ears perhaps more attuned to the acoustic caresses of Joan Baez or Peter, Paul and Mary, stared at each other in disbelief and then rapture.

By the way, I know that the last line of the first verse is "Excuse me while I kiss the sky." But regardless of what he said on stage—you need to remember that my ears were bleeding and I had ingested an entire half of a very powerful diet pill—Jimi pivoted and pointed at bassist Noel Redding, fingering him as "this guy" that he wanted the audience's permission to "kiss."

I may have been discovering Hendrix that night, but he'd played that song a hundred times in public before. And when he saw how happy it made the audience when they thought he was offering a biracial kiss between two guys instead of the dreamy "kiss the sky" which might have come from a Donovan song or a Beatles B-side, he made it part of his act.

< 134 >

"Everybody's Audience Was Hipper Than Mine": The Jewish Elvis

EVERYBODY LOVES SOME KIND of music. Well, not everybody: as a contributing editor to *Rolling Stone*, it's David Wild's business to ask the people he meets what kind of music they like, and everyone "from presidents to punks," as he puts it, has given him an answer. Except one person, but we'll get to that later.

Meanwhile, the music-loving world can be divided into two categories, those who like Neil Diamond and those who don't. But after that, it gets complicated: Wild believes that "at least half of the people who claim they don't like Neil Diamond actually, secretly, privately *do*," which is why his defense of the oft-maligned singer is called *He Is . . . I Say: How I Learned to Stop Worrying and Love Neil Diamond*. Actually, Wild has always been a huge fan and is, like all fans,, fond of adverbs and italics. He is also proud of his objectivity, as when he notes that the people who don't like Diamond's music are not only "one hundred percent wrong" but also "either utterly pretentious poseurs or totally vicious bastards."

That's okay with Neil, though, who seems proudly aware that he isn't everyone's cup of guitar-driven pop music with a shot of schmaltz and a sprinkle of Vegas sequins. "I don't fit in," he tells Wild in an interview. "You could put me in a rock show and I wouldn't fit in. You could put me in a country show and I wouldn't fit in."

Compared to such contemporaries as Simon and Garfunkel, Diamond says "their audience was much more intellectual, liberal, you know? Hipper. But then everybody's audience was hipper than mine. . . . What can I say? I was left with the rest of America."

Are you beginning to see why David Wild is crazy about this guy?

The "rest of America" is a lot of people, mainly older ones. Diamond got his

< 135 >

start in the Brill Building, writing "I'm A Believer" for the Monkees and other hits as well. His debut single "Solitary Man" was released in 1966, years after Brill Building contemporaries Neil Sedaka, Carole King, and the team of Jerry Leiber and Mike Stoller had scored huge hits in what was then the new teen market. But the late start may have given Diamond's career longevity beyond those of his peers. Wild quotes legendary guitarist and producer Chet Atkins as saying "a long apprenticeship is the most logical way to success. The only alternative is overnight stardom, but I can't give you a formula for that."

ANOTHER FACTOR IN DIAMOND'S DEVELOPMENT was surely the fifties Brooklyn he grew up in, a kind of Renaissance Florence located on Flatbush Avenue. It was a great locale for introspection: "We were indoors a lot," Diamond said in an interview. "The weather wasn't so good. It's not as though we were on surfboards all day."

An extraordinary number of future pop culture icons were huddled there against the cold and rain. Diamond graduated from Abraham Lincoln High, which gave the world Sedaka, King, Joseph Heller, and Mel Brooks, while earlier he had attended Erasmus High where Bernard Malamud, Barbara Stanwyck, Mae West, and Mickey Spillane had gone before him, as had the Barbra Streisand with who he would later sing "You Don't Bring Me Flowers."

And each of these greats knew that. As Diamond says, "Every school kid in Brooklyn learns at some point that George Gershwin was born in Brooklyn and that he became a very respected musical prodigy around the world. So there was a tradition there."

"Solitary Man" is the ultimate ode to masculine self-pity, but not the teenaged kind. True, nobody feels sorrier for himself than a teenager, but the singer has had it to here bein' where love's a small word, and a teenager hasn't lived long enough to have had it to here. "Solitary Man" is kick-ass self-pity, whereas "You Don't Bring Me Flowers" is the crybaby kind. What gives "Solitary Man" backbone are the trombone salvoes that lend a mariachi air, and it's hard to imagine teens of Diamond's day or any other saying, "Hey, trombones—far out, man!"

< 136 >

But to curl one's lip at "Solitary Man" is to dis one of the greatest pop songs of all time, one whose spare arrangement lets the emotions come through unfiltered. Would this were more the case: too many songs by the Jewish Elvis, like those of the Tupelo, Mississippi original, are overproduced.

Yet of musicians it must be said that by their hooks ye shall know them. A hook is a musical idea, often a short riff, passage, or phrase in pop, rock, hip-hop, and dance music designed to catch the attention of an audience and, beyond that, to "brand" the song. It's got to stand out, to be easily remembered. It can be repetitive—that helps—but it can be attention-grabbing in a single use, if it's powerful enough. When a really good hook does appear and vanish and come around again, the audience will, without even thinking about it, assign different meanings to it, and the song becomes richer and more fully dimensional.

Silly shouts make great hooks, as we've seen in "Tutti Frutti," but so do instrumental breaks: think of the theremin in "Good Vibrations" or the saxophone hook in Gerry Rafferty's "Baker Street." A good hip-hop hook is the refrain in "How I Could Just Kill a Man" by Cypress Hill and, later, Rage Against the Machine. What a horrible wish! And it won't leave your mind. Thanks to effective hooks, most people reading these words will be able to whistle the beginning of Beethoven's Symphony No. 5 as well as play a lively air guitar version of the Eagles' "Hotel California."

By this standard, Diamond is among the most memorable musicians ever. According to fellow singer-songwriter Robbie Robertson of the Band and also the producer of Diamond's 1976 *Beautiful Noise* album, "He thought up these melodies you couldn't get out of your head. And sometimes it was so aggravating that you couldn't get one of these songs to go away, but that just proved how infectious they really were."

In a sense, *He Is . . . I Said* is a 224-page petition to have Diamond admitted to the Rock and Roll Hall of Fame in Cleveland. True, rock is about sticking it to the man, and it's hard to stick it to the man when you're singing duets with Barbra Streisand. But rock has changed: the Rolling Stones aren't street-fighting men any more, and the Beatles never were. Even Madonna has been inducted into the Rock Hall.

< 137 >

Robbie Robertson also told Wild, "My theory is there was a musical vacuum out there between Elvis Presley and Frank Sinatra. And there was this huge audience that said, 'We've got to have something,' and they adopted Neil." If Neil is sitting with Elvis on one hand and Frank on the other, that's pretty good company.

Which brings us to the one person Wild interviewed who couldn't name anyone's music she liked, namely, Paris Hilton. Perhaps America's best known celebutante is either too busy to populate her own iPod or afraid that someone will find out she really is a part of "the rest of America." Paris, darling, if you're neither hip enough for Elvis nor hep enough for Frank, you just might find that Neil is the real deal. His audience might not be as trendy as what you're used to, but there's not a poseur or a vicious bastard in it.

THAT PETITION TO GET DIAMOND into the Rock and Roll Hall of Fame must have worked, because he was finally inducted in 2011. When an interviewer hinted that he might not be a real rocker, Diamond described rock 'n' roll's big-tent approach by saying, "I think any music that's made by the youngsters of the generations from the 1950s until the present is some form of rock music."

With characteristic modesty, he noted that "any club that has Chuck Berry and Little Richard and The Everly Brothers is a club that I want to be a part of," adding, "I've always looked at it like rock & roll was a circus. We're just clowns in that circus. We're doing our bit to entertain and make people smile."

Which is the way it has always worked at every show I've been to. I've never heard any member of any audience ask what kind of music is being played; that comes later, if at all. Audiences vote with their bodies, not their brains. You don't ask if this is rock or pop you're listening to or something else entirely. You bob your head, clap your hands, hoist your girlfriend on your shoulders, dance in the aisles, mosh, and pass out from sheer ecstasy. I bet the Rock Hall voters listen to music and read reviews, but they'd learn just as much by looking at fans' faces.

< 138 >

Everybody Who Heard Them
Started a Band:
The Velvet Underground, The Doors

AH, FAME. When Herman Melville died in 1891, a notice appeared in *The New York Times* titled "The Late Hiram Melville," and if that were not enough to make an old mariner spin in his grave, the subhead read "a tribute to his memory from one who knew him."

The Velvet Underground's luck hasn't been quite that bad, but almost. As auspicious beginnings go, the start of this band was distinctly in-. Their first album was rife with edgy sex and drug songs with titles that say it all, like "Heroin" and "Venus in Furs." Fronted by the German model and actress Nico, the album set the stage for the glam and punk movements that followed. It also played a part in the Czechoslovakian revolution in the '80s and continues to influence bands today.

But when *The Velvet Underground and Nico* appeared in 1967, not much happened, at least at the time. Yet as musician and producer Brian Eno said, "The first Velvet Undergroundh album only sold 10,000 copies, but everyone who bought it formed a band."

The band's history is inseparable from that of its best known member, Lou Reed. Raised on Long Island, Reed went to Syracuse University, where he was befriended and influenced by the poet Delmore Schwartz, whom he called "the unhappiest man I ever met in my life, as well as the smartest, until I met Andy Warhol."

The mercurial Reed gigged around Syracuse with fellow musicians until he was banned from the bar circuit for violent behavior, so he and his group would assume a name like Pasha and the Prophets and go back to work until they were discovered and had to change names again. After graduation, Reed took a job with the Pickwick International record label, where, in his own words, "There

< 139 >

were four of us locked in a room and they would say, 'Write ten California songs, ten Detroit songs.'"

Not long after, Reed met John Cale, a classically trained violist who had been born and raised in Wales. The two began writing together, and when Reed ran into former schoolmate and guitarist Sterling Morrison on the subway, they had the band's nucleus. With their first gig looming, Morrison remembered that another Syracuse friend had a kid sister, Maureen "Mo" Tucker, who had played drums in an all-girl group. And with that, the Velvet Underground was born.

Music critic Rob Jovanovic positions the Velvets in their time by noting first how little they had in common with the British Invasion groups, the folk rock movement led by Bob Dylan, and the new San Francisco sound, which included bands like The Mamas & The Papas and The Byrds. Especially the latter: Sterling Morrison said, "You had very sensitive and responsible young people suddenly attuned to certain cosmic questions that beckon us all and expressing these concerns through acoustic guitars and lilting harmonies and pale melodies. I hate these people." And to Reed, the whole San Francisco scene was "just tedious, a lie and untalented. They can't play and they certainly can't write."

By contrast, according to Jovanovic, the "cold, hard" sound of the Velvet Underground could only have come out of the "sleaze, dirt, and danger of Manhattan." No doubt the certainty on the part of some New York artists and intellectuals that they are superior to their counterparts in the provinces lay behind the disgust that the Velvets felt for West Coast bands. A trip to Los Angeles didn't help; Reed and Morrison erupted in rage when they found out that the fans they craved preferred the Jefferson Airplane and the Grateful Dead.

Besides, the antipathy between the East Coast hipsters and the flower power crowd was mutual; Cher walked out midway through a show where the band played with their backs to the audience, saying of their music, "It depressed me: it will replace nothing, except maybe suicide."

So what do audiences want? What didn't work in San Francisco worked fine for a hipper-than-thou New York club crowd.. After all, the band's con-

< 140 >

tempt was equal-opportunity in nature; they offered it freely to everyone, and the Greenwich Village crowd lapped it up.

In a sense, the Velvet Underground was practicing what Greil Marcus, in his book on the Doors, calls termite art, a term he takes from film critic Manny Farber. The idea is that there is a kind of painting, film, and music that "feels its way through walls . . . with no sign that the artist has any object in mind other than eating away the immediate boundaries of his art, and turning these boundaries into conditions of the next achievement." Unlike the Velvets, the Doors are known to today's listeners principally through the three-minute versions of their songs on oldie stations rather than the longer pieces from their albums and live shows.

Of such a Doors' song, "L.A. Woman," Marcus writes: "As the performance takes shape all four musicians sound as if they are so sure of the song they can trust it to keep going even if they seem to stop playing it. And they do seem to stop, over and over again, less playing the song than listening to it."

If you think that doesn't sound like the best way to woo listeners, you're right. Or at least it's not an approach designed to please fans who only want to hear radio hits. After a certain point, the story of the Doors becomes "the drama of a band at war with its audience," in which lead singer Jim Morrison and listeners exchange taunts that would bring a concert by Usher or Taylor Swift to a screeching halt.

Then again, in an interview with *Rolling Stone*, Morrison said,

> You give people what they want or what they think they want and they'll let you do anything. But if you go too fast for them and pull an unexpected move, you confuse them. When they go to a musical event, a concert, a play or whatever, they want to be turned on to feel like they've been on a trip, something out of the ordinary. But instead of making them feel like they're on a trip, that they're all together, if instead you hold a mirror up and show them what they're really like, what they really want, and show them that they're alone instead of all together, they're revolted and confused. And they'll act that way.

< 141 >

This is exactly what happens at the Singer Bowl in Queens, New York, on August 2, 1968, in the "bizarre, ugly seventeen minutes" it takes for the Doors to get through "The End," their deliberately unnerving song about a latter-day Oedipus who lives out a scenario that is both wish and nightmare. The trouble begins when the audience starts to call for "Light My Fire"—again.

"We just did that one," Morrison says. People begin to chant the song's lyrics, and when Morrison shushes them, somebody shouts, "Fuck you!" The dialogue spirals out of control, and the band can't start "The End" for two minutes, though when they do, a woman who, in Greil Marcus's words, "sounds like someone running through an asylum while orderlies with syringes try to bring her down" runs screaming through the house. Morrison makes up lyrics, becomes unintelligible, then silent. He becomes "a freak, the Elephant Man, the crowd thrilled at how grotesque he is, how crazy," until finally "the real music is coming from the crowd, a tangled skein of sound moving through the hall without a brain."

Doors drummer Jon Densmore notes that, as their popularity soared and the venues grew bigger, the band often acted as though there was no audience at all. Usually they knew the first three or four songs they'd play, but after that, as often as not the four musicians stopped the show and argued for minutes about what to play next, as though they were rehearsing and not playing to an arena filled with increasingly nettled fans. "The audiences began to change with our growing notoriety, and instead of a few thousand people coming to surrender to the trancelike music, we had ten thousand spectators with a 'show-me' attitude. You were egging them on, and they were egging you on. It became a vicious circle.

Densmore, like others, saw a connection between Morrison's performances and Artaud's Theater of Cruelty. "Ultimately the audience will go to the theatre as they go to the surgeon or the dentist," says Artaud, "with a sense of dread but also of necessity. A real theatrical experience shakes the calm of the senses, liberates the compressed unconscious and drives towards a kind of potential revolt."

Is that what a Velvet Unnderground concert was like? Well, yeah, but on a much less intense level. After a while, the Doors seemed to want to offend ev-

< 142 >

erybody. Of course, the reason why their audiences were so much bigger is that they had already built a huge following with innocuous pop tunes s like "Touch Me" and "Hello, I Love You," songs Sterling Morrison would have found "lilting" and "pale."

MEANWHILE, THE VEVETS WAS DISCOVERED by Andy Warhol, who became their nominal manager but did little more than lend his celebrity. Nico left after the first album to pursue her own career; then John Cale left and was replaced by Doug Yule. There had been tension between both of these original members and Lou Reed, fueled in part Reed's jealousy of each of them.

Sterling Morrison left the band to study for a PhD in medieval literature and, after that, become a tugboat captain (you read that right). Mo Tucker had five children and worked in the billing department for Walmart (you read that right, too), though she eventually returned to music. Reed has had the longest and successful post-Velvet career, though when you look at his photographs, you wonder how much pleasure he found in it—did that guy ever smile?

Then again, whatever Reed's about, it's not necessarily good times. In 1975 he issued *Metal Machine Music*, an hour of guitar feedback that Jovanovic calls "one of the most loathed rock albums of all time." Fans hated it, and critics, too: the review in *Cream* consisted entirely of the word "no" repeated 816 times. "Listening on headphones could send a listener crazy," says Jovanovic, but maybe that's the idea. In the liner notes, Reed wrote, "Most of you won't like this, and I don't blame you at all."

The Velvet Underground's appeal is that they offered an alternative to the happy musical pastels painted by the Beach Boys and the Beatles. Loneliness, paranoia, masochism: these are the themes of the New York band's grim canvases. Like all accomplished artists, Reed and the others dish up a variety of offerings, though if popular music has a sunny and a scary side, the Velvet Underground definitely spends most of its time in the shadows. Lennon and McCartney say that love is all you need, but evidently a healthy dose of terror and boredom need to be on the menu as well.

Unlike many music writers, Jovanovic is able to describe the band's sound

< 143 >

in precise yet non-technical language; his song-by-song descriptions alone are worth the price of his book. Raw and amateurish at times and worldly and sophisticated at others, the Velvet Underground always sounded like a bigger group than it was. Songs like "Sunday Mornings" and "Sweet Jane" are as tightly layered and pretty as the San Francisco songs the band purported to hate, while in "White Light / White Heat" and "All Tomorrow's Parties," the instruments appear to neglect or even war with each other.

How did just four people do all that, asks Jonathan Richman in the tribute song that uses the band's name as its title, and the refrain asks, "How in the world are they making that sound / Velvet Underground." No wonder this band's audience is made up of more aspiring musicians than any other. All a kid needs is a guitar and an amp and the desire, as Lou Reed said, "to do that rock and roll thing that's on a level with *The Brothers Karamazov.*" Such a kid might listen to the Velvets, look at a few of his like-minded friends, and think, if they did it, so can we.

You can hear the influence of the Velvet Underground in the work of David Bowie, Roxy Music, the Cars, the Strokes, Nirvana, Joy Division, Sonic Youth, Beck and many more, just as the effect of each of these artists or groups has rippled out into an ever-expanding ocean of music.

Rare among rock bands, though, they played an unparalleled part in late twentieth-century European history. Every social movement has its sound track; civil rights marchers stepped solemnly to gospel and skittered giddily to James Brown's calls for change, just as Hendrix and the Stones supplied background music for the war in Vietnam. The Velvet Underground became part of political history when a young Czechoslovakian playwright named Václav Havel, whose plays would soon be banned by the invading Soviets, visited New York in 1968 and was given a copy of *The Velvet Underground & Nico*, which he brought back to Prague. The record was copied and passed around; it heavily influenced a band called The Plastic People of the Universe, who were arrested and put on trial. That farcical proceeding brought Czechoslovakian dissidents together, and in this way began the movement that eventually saw the resignation of Communist leaders and the election of Havel as president.

< 144 >

Thanks to movies, television, *New Yorker* cartoons, and this nation's beleaguered English departments, most literate people know who Moby Dick is, even though Melville's classic novel has probably sold fewer copies in a hundred years than any single title by Stephen King. A minority of music fans today know about the Velvet Underground; when I asked a class of eighteen undergraduates if they knew who the Velvets were, only five raised their hands. But because of the way musical tides ebb and flow these days, it's almost certain that the others listen to a lot of music shaped in one way or another by Lou Reed and company.

By the way, the five students who could identify the Velvet Underground are all in bands.

< 145 >

Great Song. Who Wrote It?
Doc Pomus and Townes Van Zandt

SINGER-SONGWRITER JOE ELY WAS DRIVING down a dusty road outside of Lubbock, Texas one day on 1971 when he saw a hard-luck case thumbing rides or at least trying to. As the stranger had a guitar with him, and since Ely had done his share of hitching, he stopped and gave the fellow a lift. As he dropped him off, the stranger opened his backpack. "But there weren't any clothes in there," says Ely, "not a stitch. Instead there were about twenty-five albums, neatly stacked." The stranger gave Ely a copy, they packed up a six-pack and drank a couple, and said farewell.

The stranger was Townes Van Zandt, and the album was *Our Mother the Mountain*, which Ely listened to once in amazement and then again and again with his friend, fellow songsmith and performer Jimmy Dale Gilmore. "Townes was a like a combination of Hank Williams and Bob Dylan," Gilmore recalls, and later, musician Steve Earle would say that "Townes Van Zandt's the best songwriter in the world, and I'll stand on Bob Dylan's coffee table in my cowboy boots and say that."

He reminds others of John Keats, who also wrote hard and died young. And Thomas Chatterton, the suicidal poet who was an icon of doomed genius to the English Romantics as much as Van Zandt was to his generation of Texas musicians. And Van Gogh: another songwriter, Guy Clark, called Van Zandt "the Van Gogh of country music," a compliment the artist deflected by saying "Actually, Guy said that because I have no ear."

The son of a fourth-generation oil family, Van Zandt was a crooked branch on a tree filled with congressmen, soldiers, and lawyers. His exasperated parents sent him to a military boarding school, where, as his roommate recalled, "Townes could probably get into trouble faster than anyone I've ever seen."

In later life, he was such a fuck-up that only one character in his circle

< 147 >

of deadbeats, stumblebums, and honky-tonk angels comes across as quirkier. That would be yet another Texas songwriter, Blaze Foley, who liked to sleep in dumpsters and even had a preference for those emblazoned with the initials BFI, which stood for the name of the manufacturer, Browning-Ferris Industries, though Foley insisted they meant "Blaze Foley Inside."

Foley had a thing for duct tape, and when he died, his friends hatched a plan to kidnap his body and wrap it mummy style. When Van Zandt talked them out of it, one of the would-be pranksters said "You know it's pretty scary when Townes Van Zandt is the voice of reason."

Yet he was charismatic to a degree that was all but unnatural. Among the dozens of crunchy stories in John Kruth's *To Live's to Fly: The Ballad of the Late, Great Townes Van Zandt* is that of how one of the many women who was obsessed with him, who was named Bidy, went to see a therapist, but all Bidy could talk about was Townes. Townes this, Townes that: no matter how the therapist, who was a woman, tried to swing the talk back to Bidy's problems, it was all Townes, all the time.

So finally the therapist says, "Look, who is this Townes Van Zandt?" And Bidy, says, well, you can catch him up at such and such a roadhouse this Friday. So the therapist goes to the gig. And at their next session, Bidy says something like, "I think I'm ready to talk about my childhood now," and the therapist says, "Wait, we can get to that—tell me more about Townes."

In another story, Townes lived at one low point in an awful run-down cabin with his dog Geraldine. Even though he had four or five albums out, he had no money. He famously got paid in cash after gigs and then would walk around giving it away to homeless people, pulling out a wad and spilling twenties and fifties that blew down the street like autumn leaves. So Geraldine would go and kill a possum many mornings and leave it on the steps; Townes would make up a fricassee and sell the skin for two bucks. When he married his third wife, Jeanene, she walked out one morning and saw a dead possum and screamed. So Townes comes out and says, "Hey— that means Geraldine likes you!"

It comes as no surprise to learn that Van Zandt was eventually diagnosed as bipolar. Yet out of his highs and lows come songs—"Flyin' Shoes," "Dead Flowers," the "Pancho and Lefty" that Willie Nelson and Merle Haggard made

< 148 >

famous—that work better on the troubled mind than any upbeat ditty could. "His sad songs had that wonderful capacity to make a depressed person actually feel better," said yet another of the hundreds of people who adored him.

So what went wrong? Why doesn't Townes Van Zandt have the stature of Dylan or Willie Nelson? In a word, his career was massively mishandled. Van Zandt had only one interest, and that was to get the song right and then go on to the next one. His producers mangled his work, drowning spare voice-and-guitar pieces in lush strings and syrupy orchestral arrangements. Too late, one producer said, "If it were today, I wouldn't have budged Townes once inch off the dime. . . . What we needed was not to adjust the artist's work, but to develop a marketing strategy. You don't adjust their work. The minute you do, it's been infected." The people who know his songs love them as fiercely as his friends loved him, but inept producers stood between him and the audience he should have had.

Later in this book, I'll give examples of producers who helped artists to be more than they would have been on their own. But sometimes, if the audience isn't there, it's not the artist's fault.

And you could add to this misstep the fact that Van Zandt was an indifferent performer as well, missing shows or showing up drunk and singing off-key. Too many late nights and too much booze did him in, and his heart gave out when he was 54. To the end, all he cared about was the songs, which remain some of the greatest in the American songbook.

IN CONTRAST TO THE ENIGMATIC LONER that was Townes Van Zandt, there's a second kind of artist, the social networker as represented by Doc Pomus: a Monet, say, who had tons of friends in the Paris art world, as opposed to Van Zandt's Van Gogh.

Not that Doc didn't have his problems: crippled by polio, he used crutches from his childhood forward and, always overweight, ended his days in a wheelchair. Born Jerome Felder, he quickly acquired a bluesier stage name. Doc jump-started his career in a legendary way: as a teenager, he used to frequent a bar named George's in Greenwich Village, and one night in 1943, he struggled

< 149 >

up in front of the mike and shouted out Big Joe Turner's "Piney Brown" as the increasingly amazed musicians behind him laid out a slow, undulating blues.

Is there any teenaged geek who hasn't dreamed of jumping up on stage and blowing the audience away? The Jack Black character does this in *High Fidelity*, and Napoleon Dynamite wows the girls with his ultra-smooth dance moves in the film of the same name.

But Doc Pomus actually did it.

Before long, he was a hit at black clubs in every borough, as unlikely as that seems. But as Alex Halberstadt says *Lonely Avenue: The Unlikely Life and Times of Doc Pomus*, "ever since he was a kid he knew instinctively that being a fat Jewish paralytic made him something others reviled and feared: a thing, a nigger. Now he belonged."

Fast-forward twelve years, though, and you find Doc doing the same thing: he's working all the time, he's still wowing audiences at the clubs, but he's thirty now, and the grind is getting him down. But whereas Townes Van Zandt burrowed into his own head and made art of the angels and demons he found there, Doc began to look around him. One of his first moves was to forge a partnership with pianist Mort Shuman; before long the two of them were pumping out the hits. Their first was "Teenager in Love"—long after his teen years had ended, Doc remembered the sting of rejection, and the song became a chart-topper for Dion and the Belmonts.

Like his contemporary Sam Cooke, Doc had a gift for making songs out of what happened in front of him: "Save the Last Dance For Me," for example, comes from Doc's memory of his wedding day, as he sat with his crutches and watched his brother Raoul whirl the new bride around the floor.

Now imagine the recording session: Ahmet Ertegun is producing the song for the Drifters, and just before lead singer Ben E. King steps up to the mike, Ertegun tells King the story of the fat cripple watching another man dancing with his pretty new wife. King's eyes moisten, and he fights tears as he gives one of the most moving performances of his life.

In other words, Doc Pomus knew how to get over himself and let others bring out the best in him in a way that was impossible for an artist like Townes Van Zandt. Doc's audience was vastly bigger than Townes'. In his case, the lush

< 150 >

strings and syrupy orchestral arrangements worked out just fine. Townes' soulful ballads and the Drifters' two-and-a-half-minute pop operas are apples and oranges, of course, but as the man says, it's all fruit.

But his career wasn't a cakewalk, either: by the late sixties, the Beatles, the Stones, and Bob Dylan had killed off the three-chord pop song, and once again Doc found himself foundering.

He never stopped working at his chancy craft, though, and once again, the dice started to roll his way. By the time Elvis died in 1977, he was already being treated as a self-parodying has-been by the media. Upon his death, he became an icon; his sales soared, and the dozens of songs that Doc had co-written for him (including "Little Sister," "His Latest Flame," "Suspicion," and "Viva Las Vegas") insured a steady flow of good-sized paychecks for the rest of Doc's life.

Near the end, Doc got the recognition he deserved from younger artists, including the blocked Bob Dylan, who came by in 1986 to seek advice on getting the music to flow again, and, yes, Lou Reed, a neighbor who dropped by frequently. Until shortly before his death in 1991, he still had weekly workshops for aspiring songwriters; guests like Tom Waits pitched in to show the youngsters how they could make their ideas better by bouncing them off other people.

Most artists are somewhere between the loner and the networker. To one degree or another, most alternate between the isolation of the woodshed and the chatter of the coffee shop. Here are two musicians who, using entirely different methods, wrote the songs we can take to heart on a rainy day or jump up and dance to, even though we might not know who wrote them.

< 151 >

Song Man:
Will Hodgkinson's Failed Quest
and What We Can Learn From It

"Stay uncommercial. There's a lot of money in it,'" said Jerome Kern, who did just fine following his own advice. And if turning one's back to the commercial side of show biz is the way to go, then, by Kern's standards, Will Hodgkinson should be a millionaire.

In an earlier book called *Guitar Man*, the thirty-something English music journalist tells how he used his connections to get guitar lessons from Roger McGuinn of the Byrds and alt-rocker PJ Harvey, among others, with the goal in mind of learning the instrument well enough to perform before a live audience in six months' time.

Now, in *Song Man*, Hodgkinson takes the inevitable next step: having (sort of) mastered the guitar, he follows a trail trodden by countless no-talents as he sets out on a quest to write a hit single and, in the words of one of the many endearing failures he comes across in this engaging chronicle, seal himself inside a bubble of fame and money, never mix with normal people again, and have "a porter on the door of the building, because the last thing I want is for an axe murderer to come and chop me up in my sleep."

This is a tall order, but then Hodgkinson is nothing if not ambitious, though in that polite, self-deprecating way that makes English ambition so much easier to stomach than our go-for-the-throat American variety.

And he does record his single, though if it's something less than a hit, perhaps that's because he made the mistake of throwing out the rules before he learned what they are. Jimi Hendrix is reported to have said, "Learn everything, forget everything, and play." At least Hodgkinson got the last two steps right.

Not that he didn't begin with plenty of pluck, though it doesn't take long for him to discover that his search won't be an easy one. First of all, many of

< 153 >

the songs he likes best were written before he was born, during a period when "music was just better . . . because people were still excited by the freshness of rock 'n' roll," which was, after all, only part of the global cultural revolution that gave us today's world. Yet "the Beatles wrote songs that always appear to have existed. Like all the best ideas, you cannot imagine a world without them."

So how did young men barely out of their teens write songs of such deep yearning, such profound understanding of the human condition? Since he couldn't interview the late George Harrison, who ostensibly wrote "Something" for then-wife Pattie Boyd, he goes to the muse herself. (hough Harrison is on record as saying "Everybody presumed I wrote 'Something' about Pattie, but actually when I wrote it I was thinking of Ray Charles"),

Boyd isn't much help, and Hodgkinson concludes that "Something" is poignant precisely because "it is vague. A muse escapes definition, and George doesn't pinpoint anything about Pattie Boyd; as the title suggests, his fixation on her is based on nothing more than something." Still, he can't help but be dissatisfied at so early a stage in his quest, though when he vents his frustration to a co-worker, she tells him, "George Harrison's song is about something in the way she moves. . . . Never does he sing about 'something in the way she deconstructs post-modernist theory and underlines a new approach towards moral relativism.'" So much for the academic approach.

Meanwhile, Hodgkinson needs all the help he can get. His song "Mystery Fox" sounds so bad ("Mystery Fox / Get out of your box / It's time for me / To chase you up that tree, o mystery fox") that you begin to think he's setting himself up for failure so he can prove that great songs can only be written by the Beatles of this world. When he sings it at a wedding, one of the guests proclaims, "'That was the worst thing I ever heard in my life.'"

But then he has other songs. Even better, he has all those contacts in the business as well as a musically gifted wife to help him achieve his goal, for it is a truth universally acknowledged that an obsessive yet good-natured doofus will have an exasperated but genuinely affectionate spouse to help him over all the scratches in that big vinyl LP we call life.

Hodgkinson's wife NJ has a strong singing voice, not to mention tons of patience with his at-home composing sessions, though at one point she says,

< 154 >

"I just can't bear it any more. . . . It's torture. There is no tune. You can't sing. You're completely out of tune. There's nothing. Nothing! Sorry, I don't mean to be rude to you . . . but I'm really tired and I've had a hard day and, if you keep playing that song, I think I might cry." Ever sensitive to the constructive criticism of his biggest fan, Hodgkinson replies, "So you don't like it?"

IF YOU CRAVE AN ABSOLUTELY PAINFUL listening experience, you can do no better than to listen to *The Most Wanted Song / The Most Unwanted Song*, a CD by the team of Komar & Melamid with Dave Soldier. The three men appear on the cover sporting mad-scientist lab coats with haircuts to match. One of them is holding a calculator, and not one of those fancy Texas Instrument models engineers use, either, but a four-function job that you'd get for a couple of bucks at the drug store.

In a quest to write the world's most popular song as well as its opposite, these geniuses polled roughly 500 people to find out what instruments, vocal qualities, and themes people either loved or detested. In his liner notes to the CD, Dave Soldier summarizes their findings:

> The most favored ensemble, determined from a rating by participants of their favorite instruments in combination, comprises a moderately sized group (three to ten instruments) consisting of guitar, piano, saxophone, bass, drums, violin, cello, synthesizer, with low male and female vocals singing in rock/r&b style. The favorite lyrics narrate a love story. . . . Most participants desire music of moderate duration (approximately 5 minutes), moderate pitch range, moderate tempo, and moderate to loud volume, and display a profound dislike of the alternatives.

On the other hand,

> the most unwanted music is over 25 minutes long, veers wildly between loud and quiet sections, between fast and slow tempos,

< 155 >

and features timbres of extremely high and low pitch, with each dichotomy presented in abrupt transition. The most unwanted orchestra was determined to be large, and features the accordion and bagpipe (which tie at 13% as the most unwanted instrument), banjo, flute, tuba, harp, organ, synthesizer (the only instrument that appears in both the most wanted and most unwanted ensembles). An operatic soprano raps and sings atonal music, advertising jingles, political slogans, and "elevator" music, and a children's choir sings jingles and holiday songs. The most unwanted subjects for lyrics are cowboys and holidays.

The men wrote lyrics, hired musicians, and recorded both the best and the worst song; both are on the CD.

It's the only CD I own that I've never listened to all the way through, not even once. The problem is that the scientists asked a potential audience what they wanted to hear, but as Steve Jobs said, "It's not the customer's job to know what they want." People didn't tell him they wanted a phone that did this and that, yet somehow he came up with the iPhone, and when he did, everybody said, "Yes, that's it -- I want one of those!"

Music works the same way. I know I should listen to the most unwanted song again as I write this piece, but no promise of reward or threat of punishment would induce me to do so. So painful was the experience that I only made it through a few minutes the first and only time I listened. As a measure of how horrible it is, I can only report Dave Soldier's estimate that "fewer than 200 individuals of the world's total population would enjoy this piece."

Yet the most wanted song is not especially wantable. It's the kind of song you might hear as you're tilted back in the dentist's chair or making your way down the aisle of an airplane. It's not even Muzak. It's just melody and rhythm set slightly below the level of mere pleasantness. It's not really anything.

THE PROBLEM IS THAT THERE IS A HIDDEN curriculum of songwriting that works something like this: yes, there are rules, but nobody knows what they

< 156 >

are, and nobody can explain how you learn them. Almost all of the masters that Hodgkinson seeks help from—Keith Richards, Ray Davies of the Kinks, the Hal David who wrote all of those great Dionne Warwick songs with Burt Bacharach—they all use the "r" word, but no one seems to be able to tell him what a single one of those rules is.

Oh, they have terrific stories. Andrew Lloyd Webber tells Hodgkinson that initially "Do-Re-Mi" went "Do *is* a deer, a female deer, / Re *is* a drop of golden sun," and so on, and it wasn't until someone told Richard Rodgers to drop the verb that the song became what it is today. "Very often somebody else will suggest the slightest alteration to your song that actually changes everything," notes Sir Andrew.

And Ray Davies tells of the moment he was liberated as a songwriter, which is when he listens to a live recording of John Lee Hooker's "Tupelo, Mississippi" and hears a car horn in the background, realizing then that songs had imperfections in them because they were made by imperfect people—like himself, say.

Davies is one of the several interviewees who, in their own way, reinforce Jimi Hendrix's learn everything / forget everything advice. "It's actually impossible to tell someone how to write a song," he says, though when Hodgkinson points out timidly that Davies is teaching a songwriting course at the moment, the artist says that "doing it is the key. We all pick up our own methods along the way." There are only twelve notes, after all. And as Hodgkinson says, "even John Coltrane failed to discover the key of H."

In *A Man Called Destruction*, her biography of Alex Chilton, Holly George-Warren tells the story of a composition of a hit song that, with a few changes, is probably the story of how a thousand songs were written. Chilton was the sixteen year-old lead singer of the Box Tops, who scored hugely with "The Letter" in 1967; it went to number one on the Billbooard chart and stayed there four weeks.

The record company wanted a quick follow-up, so they booked the band in a studio at 10:00 on a Saturday morning. It was up to songwriter Dan Penn and keyboard player Spooner Oldham to come up with a hit. Penn and Oldham agree to meet the Friday evening before and write till they had a winner. Each

< 157 >

man brings ten songs to the writing session . One's got to be a hit, right? Or they can mash up two songs and make a hit on the spot.

There they are on Friday afternoon, writing and playing and playing and writing. Nothing. Ten p.m., eleven p.m. midnight . . . nothing. Finally, at 4:30 a.m—and remember, the band is coming in at 10:00—they throw in the towel. Completely disconsolate, they go to a barbecue joint across the street from the studion and order some food.. Spooner Oldham puts his head down on the table and says, "I could just cry like a baby."

Dan Penn jumps up and says, "That's it! That's the song!" He throws a bunch of bills on the table, and by the time they cross the street and reach the studio, they've already got the first verse: "When I think about the good love you gave me / I cry like a bee-beh. . . ." The result is "Cry Like a Baby," the Box Tops' second big hit.

In other words, Penn and Oldham "just did it," in Ray Davies' words. As he makes way among the dozens of songwriters he talked to for this book, Hodgkinson learns that part of "doing it" is learning from one's betters. Thus Gaz Coombes of Supergrass: "'The entire career of Supergrass has been an attempt to copy Neil Young and David Bowie. Having failed to do that, we came up with our own sound.'"

And Andy Partridge of XTC calls himself a "'human mincing machine,'" saying "I shove in the Kinks at one end, and by the time it's come out of the mincer, it's all mangled up with my personality. And warning: this Kinks tune may contain elements of Beatle once it's been through my mincing machine. And now that I'm poking around a bit, what are these orange bits I see? Oh crikey, it's The Beach Boys!"

Ultimately, Hodgkinson realizes, "the history of creativity is the history of mistakes. We try to copy our heroes and it comes out differently as we apply, consciously or not, our own imagination and personality to what we are doing."

Perhaps this explains why so many of the sixties and seventies groups that Hodgkinson loves were not able to write exciting new songs even though they kept recording and touring. How can you make those all-important mistakes when, as ex-Rolling Stones manager Andrew Loog Oldham tells him, "Those people don't even have to press the buttons on elevators"any more? When your

< 158 >

life's perfect, you've got staff to brush away those grains of sand from which oysters make pearls. Or, as Oldham observes, "not being able to pay some chick child support is a whole different thing from not *wanting* to pay some chick child support."

Echoing Jerome Kern on staying uncommercial, Neil Young once said, "I know that the sacrifice of success breeds longevity. Being willing to give up success in the short run ensures a long run. If you're really doing what you want to do." In this way, writes Greil Marcus in *The Shape of Things to Come: Prophecy and the American Voice*, Young "scatters terrible concept albums among dissonant masterpieces and craven, comfort-food crowd pleasers."

OKAY, WE CAN'T ALL BE Don Gibson, who wrote "I Can't Stop Loving You" and "Oh Lonesome Me" on the same day in 1957. But how did Hodgkinson fail so miserably at songwriting when he had the best in the business behind him?

Maybe he failed to respect the rawness of rock 'n' roll. His approach is cerebral, whereas rock is visceral. You don't charm or titillate, you grab: Gregg Allman says of his early days on with the Allman Brothers Band, "I realized that if we did things right, we could grab people with the first eight bars of a song, and we wouldn't have to worry about the rest of the night. The key was getting them right away."

Too, Hodgkinson seems to make the mistake that plagues novices in every field, namely, wanting to Make a Statement. "Rock 'n roll may be most of all a language that, it declares, can say anything," says Greil Marcus: it can "divine all truths, reveal all mysteries, and escape all restrictions." But rock says all that without really saying anything. We non-musicians learn the words to songs—that's all we can learn—but Marcus quotes guitarist and critic Robert Ray as saying, "What's interesting about rock & roll is that the truly radical aspect occurs at the level of *sound*. 'Tutti Frutti' is far more radical than Lennon's 'Woman Is the Nigger of the World,' and the sound of Bob Dylan's voice changed more people's ideas about the world than his political message did." Sure, there's always a social explanation for any art work, says Albert Camus, "only it doesn't explain anything important."

< 159 >

Think of how slippery song lyrics are and how we bend them to our will, reading a song one way and then, when we grow older or a different context presents itself, in a way that's totally different. A good song sets that up for you. Take Sting's "Every Breath You Take" as an example. The intent seems romantic, but there's an aspect that's creepy, even menacing. Do we really want someone to love us that much? Well, yes and no.

Or take Bob Marley's "I Shot the Sheriff." Now no one should murder anyone, much less an officer of the law, so it's a little surprising to encounter song lyrics that amount to a murderer's confession. But when we begin to narrate the song to ourselves, notice how the story changes.

First, like a lot of criminals, the killer says he committed a crime, yeah, but not exactly the one he's accused of: "I shot the sheriff / But I didn't shoot no deputy."

Second, he may have been simply defending himself: "I swear it was in self defense." And here context enters in: it's hard not to think that, given the political situation in Jamaica in the '70s, the shooter actually might have been defending himself from a vigilante sheriff. "Sheriff John Brown always hated me," he says.

Besides, the alleged killer, for whom our sympathy grows as the song goes on, was trying to leave his old life; "I started out of town," he sings, and suddenly he sees the sheriff "aiming to shoot me down."

Maybe it was self defense! But even so, "If I am guilty, I will pay." In the end, the song is a plea bargain: I did something bad, though not as bad as they say, and I'll serve whatever reasonable sentence I get. He could be completely innocent, though. Or completely guilty.

In both the Sting and the Bob Marley songs, a lot of our enjoyment comes from our getting not one but many stories; the conflicting narratives engage each other in an argument that never ends.

One of Mary Wells' story-songs demonstrates the power of metaphor, which allows a listener to believe that statement that's being made and its opposite at the same time. "Two Lovers" describes a devoted boyfriend and then another who is callous and indifferent. The trick, of course, is that they're both the same guy. But if you're a young man, it's almost impossible to listen to "Two

< 160 >

Lovers" and not think of yourself as the Other Man, the one who'll make Mary happy and deserve her kisses.

Another mistake is to try to be *too* original. Novices often want to throw off every constraint and leap into new territory, but audiences are more conservative. Even when new territory's in sight, smart artists will use familiar elements as a base camp: you set up your tent, get a fire going, and then walk out through the ice and hope you don't (or do) run into the Abominable Snowman. "The bridge from the music to the third verse is when you want to be different," says Gregg Allman, "but you don't want to go all the way from A to Z. You want something that contrasts things a little—kind of like matching a shirt with a pair of pants."

Before he enrolled in the Writing Seminars at Johns Hopkins University, novelist John Barth studied jazz at Julliard. Barth's musical background helps explain why he channeled Fielding, Sterne, Smollett, Cervantes, Rabelais, Voltaire and other masters of the picaresque novel to arrive at the narrative voice for his masterpiece, *The Sot-Weed Factor*. "At heart I'm still an arranger", Barth once told an interviewer. "My chiefest literary pleasure is to take a received melody"—a classical myth, a Biblical scrap, a worn-out literary convention or style—"and, improvising like a jazz musician within its constraints, re-orchestrate it to present purpose."

Isn't that what songwriters do as well? An interviewer once praised Sting for composing such original songs as "Roxanne" and "Every Breath You Take," and here's what Sting said in reply: "I don't think there's such a thing as composition in pop music. I think what we do is collate. It's like folk music. It makes copyright a bit interesting and difficult. I'm a good collator."

Put it all together and you've got a world-beater of a song, one that gives you everything an audience could possibly want, not only in music but in life itself. Why did Sinatra have the impact that other singers didn't, and why did the Beatles spur Beatlemania—why is there no Gerry and the Pacemakers-mania? It's because their work was fully dimensional. Those songs contain every emotion we've ever felt, and they hint at mysteries we can't articulate; in other words, you get the whole roller coaster ride.

Or think of love. If you've found the person you want to spend your life

< 161 >

with, it's because you spent years trying out relationships with other people who didn't quite give you everything you needed. And if you haven't found that person yet, you're still selecting, dating, rejecting, being rejected, and so on, all in an attempt to find that the best one.

We love the music we love and the people we love because they bring out the best in us. That's why music is generational: Sinatra was right for my parents, the Beatles for my contemporaries, and the young people I pass on the sidewalk with earbuds in are listening to the music *that makes them feel most like their best selves.*

I had a student who had only one tattoo, which was of a Red Hot Chili Peppers album cover; that band gave him such power that he devoted a significant amount of his very limited skin surface to their cover art!

Same thing with love: you've been in a relationship with someone who held you down; aren't you happier with the person who makes you feel as though you can do anything? Amd doesn't a great song make you feel exactly the same way?

ALL ART CONSISTS OF THE DELIBERATE transformed by the accidental. In this case, the deliberate resides in all that woodshedding advocated by Hodgkinson's interview subjects, all that mastering of the great songs that have already been written, and the accidental is the random changes that come from our own imaginations and personalities as well as the suggestions made by such collaborators as the anonymous person who told Richard Rodgers to take the "is" out of of "Do-Re-Mi." That's not going to happen if, as cult folk/rock songwriter Bridget St. John tells Hodgkinson, "you're part of a big publicity machine that is controlling every part of your image."

For better or worse, Hodgkinson never gets that far in his quest for success, mainly because he can't find a way to spend as much time in the woodshed as great songwriting requires. He has to pay the bills, after all, and his band mates are dodgy at best. They do manage to book studio time and record Hodgkinson's compostions. Wisely, though, nobody quits his day job.

< 162 >

Want to hear how the songs turn out? You can go to Hodgkinson's page on MySpace.com and listen to them, though it's a pleasure best pursued in solitude: ten seconds after I tuned in, my wife leapt to her feet and, echoing the moment in the book when NJ tells her husband that she's had it up to here, said, "Turn that off right now."

The songs are, um, horrible. The band sounds like a bunch of eighth graders trying to play Doors covers on instruments somebody left on the curb for the solid waste truck. And the vocals are so hysterical and constricted that one imagines Hodgkinson being chased through the studio as the shade of Jim Morrison tries to strangle him with a pair of his signature black leather trousers. This isn't garage rock. It's garage-sale rock, if that.

I hope it's apparent at this point that this is an essay about bad music, not a bad writer. The truth is that I have a major crush on Will Hodgkinson. Like the figure at the center of every major religion, he has sacrificed himself so that the rest of us may be saved. I know so much more about what makes audiences happy now, even if I know a little too much about music that I never want to hear again.

But then you knew those songs wouldn't be any good. As the music plays and the dog crawls under the bed and the baby wails and your wife grabs her car keys, I hope you will join me in hoisting a pint in praise of Will Hodgkinson. For by summoning the courage to post his songs on line, he proves precisely the point of this charming little book, which can be summed up by the joke in which the tourist asks the woman carrying a violin case how to get to Carnegie Hall, and the musician answers, "Practice, practice, practice." Hodgkinson and company put many hours into their art. It wasn't enough.

< 163 >

Why There'll Never Be Another Willie Nelson

TALLAHASSEE—Anyone who has ever walked through a pawn shop has seen better-looking acoustic guitars than the one that hung around Willie Nelson's neck at his recent concert at a nightclub called the Moon. The instrument looked as though it had taken a direct hit from a small-bore shotgun and been taped together well enough to produce passable sounds.

But the notes that emerged were studio-perfect. Nelson is known for his sublimely adenoidal voice and catchy pop-country lyrics, but he is also one of the most inventive guitarists on stage today.

And in the musical world of pampered slowpokes, Willie takes the stage when he says he will. A good-sized crowd milled around in front of the Moon that evening, enjoying the sweet air of April, when someone from the club stuck his head out the door and shouted, "Y'all get on in! Willie's starting in five minutes and finishing at 9:45—sharp!"

Five minutes later, Willie walked out, trademark grin flashing under a black cowboy hat. By the second song, he had hurled the hat into the crowd and donned a red bandanna, an article of clothing that has come and gone in American pop culture, though working people everywhere still use them to mop their sweaty brows. In his Rambo phase, Sylvester Stallone sported a bandanna, as did Bruce Springsteen when *Born in the U. S. A.* was high in the charts. But Willie still wears his, and though from time to time he tossed the bandanna of the moment into the crowd before grabbing another one, throughout he looked less like a country-music star and more like the guy who has come to your house to jump-start a balky air conditioner or patch the roof.

As he played, Willie picked out different audience members and wiggled his fingers at them like a fond grandpa. Willie's grin is so cherubic that it's not hard to imagine what he looks like in his baby pictures.

< 165 >

The truth is that, as long as he continues to perform, Willie Nelson will occupy a permanent position between that of precocious youth and revered veteran. Although he first stepped on stage at age 4 and wrote his first songs when he was 7, his first commercial success was as a tunesmith writing songs for stars like Patsy Cline and Faron Young. As Adam Gopnik writes in *The New Yorker*, Willie didn't become known as a performer until middle age and thus never had to fight to hang on to a fickle audience, a struggle that more pop stars have lost than won.

There are people Willie's age who look as though they've looked that way their whole lives, as though they were jowly and wore glasses and business attire as a child, as though their own mothers called them "Mr. Cooper" and "Mrs. Thorndyke." In contrast, Willie—has anyone ever called him "Mr. Nelson"?—looks like all of his ages at once. Lay him on his side and saw him in half and you'll find the infant, the schoolboy, the young knockabout, the husband (several times, actually) and father settling into middle and then old age, and finally the Willie he is now. Narcissism is a great aid as far as an audience's identification with artists goes, and that why we all like Willie—when we look into him, we see ourselves.

And maybe we're more than a little grateful hat he's paid some dues that were never charged to our account. Willie's domestic battles are legendary; one story has him coming home drunk and being sewn up in the bed sheets by an angry wife. His run-ins with the law are a matter of record, as is his fight with the I. R. S. over unpaid taxes. But just as he strikes the observer as neither young nor old, Willie seems neither proud nor ashamed of his offenses. He doesn't hide them: when asked, he tells the stories on himself in detail and shrugs as if to say, well, we all have a past, don't we?

And while the past may be a nice place to visit, who wants to live there? As soon as Willie finished a classic like "Blue Skies" or "Funny How Time Slips Away," he slipped into a blues or swing tune or a flamenco-tinged ballad, often by another song writer. If he swallowed a line now and then or sang a note off-key, well, nobody's perfect.

Besides, that's what he has been doing from the very beginning, as evidenced by CD *Crazy: The Demo Sessions*, recorded in the 1960s but only re-

< 166 >

leased in 2003. Throughout, there were constant reminders of his guitar skills as he caressed an instrument that looked as though it had been used for target practice, toying with tempos and ringing chord changes that sounded more like the gypsy riffs of Django Reinhardt than American country.

Then, at 9:46 p.m. on the dot, Willie thanked everyone for coming, asked "Y'all got time for a couple more?" and concluded with a medley of up-tempo spirituals.

Willie Nelson is a one-man Mount Rushmore of American music, a craggy-faced superstar who stays that way by acting like the guy you called because you need some help around the house. He'll be 82 the year this book is published. He's still touring. But for a working man who still has to make his way through a lot of bandannas, it's what you have to do to get the job done.

< 167 >

The Road to Excess:
Led Zeppelin and Queen

In Led Zeppelin's heyday, which was the early '70s, I noticed that certain women of my acquaintance seemed to shake with a near-visceral disgust when the band's name was mentioned. Now I know why. At first, as with any tale of success, the story of the band captivates, and then slowly it begins to horrify. Not everyone in it is a villain, but enough of the main characters become so grotesque over time that it's hard to avoid a sickly feeling that becomes worse the more you know. As a group, the musicians and their entourage are like star athletes who turn up in the headlines as thugs. You can't forget the thrills they gave you, but you'll never feel the same about them again.

In the beginning, the four musicians were like any other hardworking lads besotted with a new sound. There was singer Robert Plant, a blues enthusiast who could go on for hours about his favorite American roots musicians when the rest of the band just wanted to party. Guitarist Jimmy Page, who came from the same tiny area outside London as guitar geniuses Eric Clapton and Jeff Beck, was one of the most in-demand session players before he helped form the group. Page's studio work sometimes had him playing next to the third member, John Paul Jones, a virtuoso on several instruments and a skilled arranger as well. Percussion was supplied by John Bonham, the loudest, fastest drummer of his and perhaps any era.

Planty, Pagey, Jonesy, Bonzo, as they called each other: like thousands of other young Englishmen of that day, they devoured the blues that American musicians took for granted, but then they took their fandom one step further and transformed the sounds of Howlin' Wolf, Robert Johnson, and Blind Willie McTell into something the world had never heard before.

In this they were added by Granty, that is, Peter Grant, the physical giant who became their manager and helped create a new business model that,

< 169 >

in addition to the band's talent and passion, is the other half of the formula that rocketed Led Zeppelin toward unimaginable riches as well as unspeakable decadence. Whereas earlier business people disdained pop music and tried to wring the most out of bands before discarding them, the new crowd went all in to nurture and guide the groups rather than exploiting them.

Unless it's happened to you, it's impossible to know what it's like to be a pimply kid eating beans on toast one day and be a millionaire the next, with men in suits and sunglasses handing you the keys to luxury automobiles and packs of nubile women fighting to lick the skin from your body. The Led Zeps became gods before they became men. As Jimmy Page reports, when someone said, "I grew up to Led Zeppelin," he'd say, "So did I."

No wonder it all went to their heads. The sex and drugs were non-stop, as is to be expected. What appalls here is the violence. John Bonham, Peter Grant, and tour manager Richard Cole veer out of control again and again. In *Led Zeppelin: The Oral History of the World's Greatest Rock Band*, Barney Hoskyns quotes a journalist says, "I've never seen anyone behave worse in my life than Bonham and Cole. I once saw them beat a guy senseless for no reason and then drop money on his face."

True, cocaine and alcohol, especially in combination, make people do things they wouldn't do otherwise, but I've never read a musical history that uses the words "sociopath" and "psychopath" as much as this one. (The title of the English version of Hoskyn's book is the more appropriate *Trampled Under Foot: The Power and Excess of Led Zeppelin*.)

Not everyone was in on the mayhem, of course; in Hoskyns' account, Robert Plant and John Paul Jones come off as decent chaps overall. And when he wasn't leading the havoc, Peter Grant was an extraordinarily successful manager. Part of his strategy was to keep the world's most outrageous band a relative secret by not issuing singles or appearing on television or cultivating the press.

That way, as legendary groupie Bebe Buell recalls, "You didn't hear Led Zeppelin on the radio; you heard *about* them from the boys in your class. . . . I don't know if the music was designed to give boys power and sexual prowess, but I do know that when the boys listened to it, they would become extremely cocky and full of themselves."

< 170 >

In the end, the songs speak for themselves: the permanent appeal of "Black Dog," "Immigrant Song," and "Whole Lotta Love" make Led Zeppelin, along with the Beatles, the Stones, and Pink Floyd, one of the rare bands with intergenerational appeal.

Still, now I know why no woman ever asked me, "Who's your favorite Led Zep?"

IF YOU'VE EVER ASKED YOURSELF, "What world-famous pop star named Farrokh Bulsara was born into a Parsee family in Zanzibar?" then look no further. That and every other fact of Freddie Mercury's over-the-top life is now related in a biography by Lesley-Ann Jones whose *Mercury: An Intimate Biography of Freddie Mercury* clumsily yet fittingly names him twice. Some readers may be reminded of the 2008 documentary *Anvil! The Story of Anvil*, but whereas that band fizzled, her subject bestrode the music world like a god. If it had been up to him, no doubt Mercury would have found a way to work in his name a third time.

If you never exactly thought of him as Zanzibarian, that's because Mercury went out of his way to keep his origins a secret. His early years can't have been easy: when he was eight, his parents send him to boarding school in India. As a teenager there, he formed his first band, the Hectics, but when his grades slipped, he returned to Zanzibar to finish high school. After he moved to England and became a success, relatives and schoolmates complained that the former Bucky Bulsara (so nicknamed because of protruding front teeth) wanted nothing to do with them.

In London, his great pal was the Reginald Kenneth Dwight who also took on the name of a Roman god when he became Elton Hercules John. The similarities don't stop there: both were devoted to their mother, both studied piano at an early age, both were bothered by their appearance and developed an outlandish look to disguise self-perceived ugliness. And each, writes Jones, "was confused to say the least about his sexuality."

Fortunately, Mercury was anchored throughout his entire career by bandmates who would have appeared able and intelligent in any profession, much

< 171 >

less the anarchic one of rock 'n' roll. The other three members of Queen were honors students at different universities; one contemporary says "they were probably the smartest band in the business." Mainly, though, in the words of another, "they genuinely liked each other's company" and in that way avoided the rifts that fractured many another group.

Not that they were choirboys. One album-release party that "could only be described as an orgy" featured "dwarfs and drag queens, fire-eaters and female mud-wrestlers, strippers and snakes, steel bands, voodoo dancers, Zulu dancers, hookers, groupies and grotesques, some performing unimaginable and possibly illegal acts on each other." As if that were not enough, Jones encourages readers to flex their powers of imagination to vein-popping intensity as she reports offhandedly that "one model arrived on a salver of raw liver." You can get a gauzy notion of what all this looked like by peeking into Harry Doherty's *40 Years of Queen*, a coffee-table book described as "an official publication . . . approved at every stage by the band," meaning its prose is fairly tame, though its lavish photos give some idea of the group's nothing-succeeds-like-excess lifestyle.

Happily, all that hoopla was met and matched in the band's actual performances. A lot of groups are short-lived because their partying skills exceed their musical ability, but Queen was over the top in every arena. As *Crossroad* goes to press, a Queen reunion tour fronted by Adam Lambert and led by guitarist Brian May is in its second year on the road, and *New York Times* critic Jon Pareles notes that "modesty was never part of Queen's appeal. Queen piled on everything it could: umpteen vocal overdubs by Mercury, umpteen-plus guitar layers by Mr. May, and a gathering melodrama in each song that was inseparable from the way Mercury's voice could rise through octaves without thinning out." In terms of genre, Mr. Pareles suggests, why stop with just one? "The band's songs merged hard rock with music-hall, blues-rooted guitar drive and oompah absurdity, along with a streak of Gilbert & Sullivan."

Freddie, meanwhile, was spending many of his nights prowling the gay districts of the world's capitals. In 1981, there were reports of the first cases of a rare form of skin cancer found in otherwise healthy male homosexuals, and within a few years, AIDS had become a recognized epidemic. He may have

< 172 >

been infected before the disease had been identified; at any rate, he was diagnosed with AIDS in 1987 and died in 1991, though he and the band continued to work together to the very end.

Lesley-Ann Jones toured with Queen and had unrivaled access to them and their circle; her best quality as a journalist is the way she spotlights the canny assessments of industry insiders, such as the record executive who described their sound as "the purest ice cream poured over a real rock 'n' roll foundation." Of course, showbiz excess works best the first time, and after that, the law of diminishing returns kicks in. Writing of the 2014 Queen appearance at Madison Square Garden, Mr. Pareles criticizes the band's self-indulgence, noting that there was "a long, sagging midconcert stretch of unaccompanied solos, and it took the show some time to recover momentum afterward." Of course, that just reminds one how well those stunts worked with audiences back in the '70s.

Future fans may or may not decide that "Bohemian Rhapsody" is little more than a six-minute oddity, but few groups have seen their hits cross over the way Queen has: "We Will Rock You" was adopted as an anthem by both the New York Yankees and the Manchester United football club, and "We Are the Champions" seems destined to be sung in sports arenas forever.

The word "fanatic" doesn't come to mind when you think of Queen's audience the way it does when you think of, say, the Red Hot Chili Peppers and see a floppy-haired kid in surfer shorts flailing away on an air guitar. What you see instead is drag queens and stevedores alike dipping their spoons into that bottomless sundae of ice cream and power chords.

< 173 >

The Kids Aren't All Right:
Husker Dü and the Meaning of Punk

As the Florida legislature debated whether or not to require school boards to prohibit students from wearing saggy pants, I was having lunch with an older friend. "I don't get it," he said. "Why do they insist on showing everybody their underwear?" "Because you don't get it," I replied. "Huh?" said my friend. "I don't get it!" "Yeah, and that's why," I said.

We could have gone on like Abbott and Costello forever, but the point is that the young are always going to their best to provoke, irritate, and outrage the elderly, even if the elderly are not that much older than they are. By the mid seventies, Elvis, the Beatles, and the Stones were looking positively patriarchal to a new generation of musicians. In contrast to the clean story lines and sentiment of classic rock lyrics, punk bands offered rage; instead of established chord progressions and elaborate instrumentation, the punks offered volume, speed, and distortion. Whereas big bands like the Moody Blues and Roxy Music made music meant to fill huge arenas, a punk group might be three grubby guys in the corner of a dingy club somewhere.

And as the Sex Pistols proved, they didn't even have to know how to play their instruments.

What remains unsettling about punk is the metric a live band uses to measure its success. Whereas Billy Joel or Tom Jones might say a show had gone well because of the ovations they received or the quantity of intimate wear that had piled up on stage, a punk group would insist the audience give as good as it got, returning every curse and sneer tenfold. After a while, of course, punk became big box-office itself, but during its underground days, the bands bullied their audiences until the audiences fought back.

In this account of his life as a punk warlord taking on the establishment, Bob Mould writes of one concert this way: "I walked to the microphone and let

< 175 >

loose with twenty seconds of foul language, which only made the crowd hotter. Objects rained down on the stage: drink containers, sandwiches filled with stones, and bags filled with (I think) mud."

Simon and Garfunkel would walked off stage at this point, but not Mould: "I would be in the middle of a song and see an object heading toward me. . . . I had time to react, so I either caught the objects or blithely spun to the side to avoid being hit. I loved it."

Mould was born into a family with an angry, abusive father; before long, he was looking for a way out of his tiny upstate New York town, where he was also struggling with the fact that he found himself drawn to boys. Together, a rocky home life and the felt need to hide his sexuality turned Mould toward "a type of obsessive-compulsive disorder—not the hand-washing kind, but one based around routine, ritual, and numbers."

Obviously there were a lot of moving parts in young Bob's life, and they all came together one day when he saw a Ramones album; the musicians looked like thugs, and the songs were loud, fast, and deadpan. Within a few years, Mould and two other musicians formed the seminal punk band Husker Dü. Taking their name from a Danish board game, Husker Dü wasn't always popular; Mould recalls one bar where Native Americans and local ranchers started to mix it up but then joined forces to brawl with the musicians.

Then again, Mould was the kind of bandleader who didn't like to give the audience a choice. Typically, he writes of one gig, "we set the stage ablaze that evening. By that time we'd gotten really good at pile driving as many songs into the set as possible, and this breathless approach left crowds a bit bewildered. No time to talk, think, or react. Good."

Readers who expect *See a Little Light* to be a tell-all memoir like Keith Richards' *Life* will be disappointed. It's more of a job manual, as befits a book by a musician who describes his touring life of consisting of little more than a car, a guitar, and a bottle of water. Mould imparts his business philosophy: "don't promise what you can't deliver, know what you're worth, and show up on time." He espouses what he calls the hot potato theory: "It's like inspiration is a hot potato you pull out of the oven and then toss to someone else. So we listen, we

< 176 >

become fans, we become inspired, we create, and somehow the work we create eventually finds its way back to the ones who inspired us."

He also tells aspiring punkers how to get by. In a world where bigger acts like Metallica have two identical sets of full staging, including washers and dryers, and fly the entire production from show to show, one planeload of equipment leapfrogging the other, Mould and his musician friends found ways to pinch pennies.

Once they were recording in the same studio as Whitney Houston, who ordered huge deli platters that she never touched; when Whitney went home for the day, they sent an engineer upstairs to filch her cold cuts. He offers more personal advice as well; after a successful career in Husker Dü and other bands and as a solo artist, he grew tired "of not being gay," as he puts it, and here tells others "you can't come out soon enough" as well as "it's never too late to come out."

Bob Mould is middle-aged and happy now; in the last lines of *See a Little Light*, he says, "Finally, I am able to enjoy life as it happens. In the thirty-plus years since he co-founded Husker Dü, punk got mainstreamed, though before that, it was succeeded by rap, which has since entered the mainstream itself. Both genres have left indelible stamps on music and couture as well; most white bar bands still dress the way Husker Dü did, and rappers have paved the way for, among other fashion statements, saggy pants.

The Florida legislature did pass its anti-droopy drawers bill. But just as *Everything Falls Apart* (Husker Dü's first album), there's always a *New Day Rising* (its fourth). Mark my word: those crazy kids out there are planning something, and not even a guy with as focused a mind as Bob Mould knows what it is.

< 177 >

Skateboards, Heroin, and Why Grunge Matters

AMONG MUSICIANS, DRUMMERS are a breed apart. On the one hand, the drummer is the timekeeper, the one who counts off the song and keeps the other band members on the beat. On the other, the drummer sits behind everyone else and usually doesn't write songs or sing them, so often he's "only the drummer."

Actually, Dave Grohl was in the habit of saying "I'm only the drummer" as a way of sidestepping conversations about the band Nirvana following the suicide of lead singer Kurt Cobain in 1994. By all accounts, though, he's one of the best in the business; if you look up Grohl on YouTube, you get a sense of just how good he is. But he's also known as the Nicest Man in Rock.

That probably presented a problem for biographer Paul Brannigan: it's hard to write about nice guys. Wisely, Brannigan writes what turns out to be a rich history of recent pop music as it moves from punk and hardcore to grunge to indie bands, many of which, like Nirvana, ended up signing with major labels. For his part, Grohl flits in and out of this world like Candide, landing on his feet and making new friends at every turn.

Students of that period will find much to dwell if they read Brannigan, but there's a second group that may also learn a lot, and that's parents of, shall we say, overly active boys. Grohl describes himself and others like him as "kids who grew up in the suburbs listening to rock 'n' roll records, doing petty crime and drugs, just little vandals from the middle of nowhere."

A lot of these scamps grew up to be lawyers, college professors, and, in this case, a member of such acclaimed bands as Nirvana and the Foo Fighters, although Mr. and Mrs. Grohl couldn't have foreseen that at the time. Looking back on his childhood in a suburb of Washington, DC, Grohl says his teachers "always said the same thing: 'David would be a great student if he could just

< 179 >

stay in his . . . seat.'" When teenaged Dave had to get permission to drop out of high school and go on the road with the band Scream, his mother's reaction was, "Hallelujah . . . because, of all the things he's done brilliantly in his life, school was never one of them."

That happy kid still seems to be part of Grohl's persona. When he gushes about the tour van being like "a traveling tree-house," he sounds like Huck Finn setting out down the Mississippi on his raft. And when he gets his first big check for his work with Nirvana, Grohl buys himself a BB gun because he didn't have one as a child.

Nirvana's overnight rise from obscurity to international acclaim and its violent end tested Grohl's sanguine outlook during what he later called "a tornado of insanity." Lost for a while, he distracted himself by making a fifteen-song tape, playing all the instruments and doing the vocals himself. When record companies heard the tape and started calling, Grohl recruited four other musicians and formed the Foo Fighters; not long ago, their seventh studio album, *Wasting Light*, debuted at the top of the *Billboard* chart.

In 2009, as the Foo Fighters warmed up on the South Lawn of the White House to play for the Obamas and guests at a Fourth of July barbecue, Grohl is reported to have looked around and said, "Well, well, well. Who'd have thunk?" Not his teachers back in Springfield, Virginia, that's for sure.

GROHL IS A ONE-OF-A-KIND poster boy for happiness in the world of grunge, a type of rock music that emerged in the eighties around the Seattle area, and it came from what director and screenwriter Cameron Crowe calls "the whole coffee-culture, 'two or three jobs, one of which is your band' lifestyle." Actually, Mark Yarm's *Everybody Loves Our Town: An Oral History of Grunge* has a lot more to say about lifestyle than it does about music. Its real subjects are youth, drugs—way too many drugs—and how bands soar and crash. Mainly, though, it's about youth.

That whole mid-1980s Seattle scene sounds a lot like what high school would be like if there were no classes and everybody smoked pot all day. People in their mid-twenties were officially old. You didn't have to know how to

< 180 >

play an instrument to be in a band, just own one. And when you got kicked out, you formed what Jason Everman, an early member of Nirvana, calls a "revenge band." No wonder so many sprang up so quickly.

Pearl Jam, Soundgarden, Nirvana, and Alice in Chains were part of grunge, but so were Coffin Break, Cat Butt, and Spluii Numa. The different bands were united in their desire to sound like a band they liked or, more often, to not sound like one they hated.

The anti-establishment vibe may explain why the bands seem to have shared a certain lack of hygiene as well; Megan Jacobs, who was a receptionist and then a vice president (not an atypical career arc for that time and place) at the Sub Pop record label, which broke many of the big grunge names, recalls that "we would rate bands on how much they smelled." The worst offender was the girl band Babes in Toyland, who proved that women can be as malodorous as men if they just put their minds to it. (Courtney Love played with the Babes briefly before being kicked out, forming Hole, and marrying Kurt Cobain.)

Excess was always in good taste. Matt Lukin of Mudhoney says "there's nothing funnier than a drunk naked guy, if you're the drunk guy," which he often was. Musician and booking agent Danny Bland recalls that "we were magnets for trouble, and we liked it that way," and Buzz Osborne of the Melvins remembers that "when I drank, I'd break out in felonies or break out in bandages, one of the two."

Mainly, though, everybody had fun. As Osborne says, "It wasn't so much making trouble as discovering the world, like Mickey Mantle showing up in New York City the first time."

What is grunge, though? The best non-technical definition comes from Candlebox singer Kevin Martin, who says, "In Seattle, it's rain, there's not a lot of punk rock, there's what I call dirgy rock—slow, down-tuned, heavy—which is what everybody called grunge." A journalist named Jeff Gilbert provides a more technical summation: grunge is "complaining set to a drop D tuning," meaning the bottom or E string on a guitar is tuned down a whole step.

That smudging of the traditional guitar sound is consistent with grunge bands' contempt for what they saw as corporate music. Then again, it's not uncommon for musical iconoclasts to mess with a slick sound. In his memoir

< 181 >

Chronicles, Bob Dylan writes about his youthful adoration of Brylcreemed teen idol Ricky Nelson, whose studio polish couldn't have been more different from Dylan's slurs and snarls. Similarly, a lot of these musicians say their first crushes were on stagey bands like Cheap Trick and Kiss, but like Michelangelo, who deliberately left chisel marks on statues, the kids from Seattle liked to rough up the surface of their art.

Their disavowal of a corporate sound notwithstanding, obviously a lot of these groups achieved enormous success, which means they took on their fair share of the problems all young rockers have. Pot turned to cocaine and cocaine turned to heroin; an accurate picture of that time would have to be strewn with dirty needles, revolving-door visits to rehab centers, and far too many young corpses. The iconic grunge death, of course, didn't involve an overdose but the suicide by shotgun of Nirvana's Kurt Cobain in 1994.

WHILE IT'S EASY TO POINT fingers, the problem for all these youngsters who got in over their heads is that, in their teens and twenties, they became rock stars before they had a chance to become human beings. As Courtney Love says,

> I have this thing, me and my manager call it the Rocket. It's what happened to Kurt, it's what happened to me. It's what happened to Eminem. It's what happened to Britney Spears. Instead of just going up in steps—you're an apprentice with a mentor, you learn your craft, you go up to the next level and the next level—you disappear into the Rocket. You have to fight centrifugal force. *Who's our friend? Who's not our friend? Who do we fire? What do we do? What's gross? What's not?*

And Cobain's bandmate Krist Novoselic recalls,

> We were these young people from southwest Washington, ill-equipped. We didn't have the emotional support and the experi-

< 182 >

ence at all to deal with this. And we were just whisked away—whisked, whisked up into it, and it went up and up and up and up, like the spaceship *Challenger*. And then it exploded. It's like, [drummer Dave Grohl] and I landed, right? But Kurt didn't.

If you lived in Seattle in those days and are eager to relive them, you'll want to read Yarm's history, as you will if you simply like grunge. Yarm dives deeply, which means his scope is limited at the surface level.

But it would be a mistake not to view grunge as part of the continuum of music as a whole. In his brilliant, sweeping history *Yeah! Yeah! Yeah! The Story of Pop Music from Bill Haley to Beyoncé*, Bob Stanley mentions that "great pop strain of big men on the brink, tough guys choking back the tears, brought to their knees and reduced to falsetto shrieks" and then takes us from Frankie Laine to Del Shannon to Bruce Springsteen. Then Kurt Cobain of Nirvana comes along and erases Springsteen's blue-collar romanticism. After Cobain's death, the grunge of Nirvana and other Seattle groups breeds with other genres and leads indirectly to bands like the Red Hot Chili Peppers, whose "ultra-masculine mix of funk, hip hop, and metal," in Stanley's words, made them the biggest-selling rock group in the world

Yarm interviewed more than 250 people for *Everybody Loves Our Town* ; most of the quotes are just a few sentences long, and the language is unfiltered. It's pure street talk, for the most part, which means it has all the crunchy bits but the longueurs as well; sometimes twenty pages go by without you learning more than who quarreled with whom.

And then you come across words like these from Jerry Cantrell, guitarist and singer for Alice in Chains: "I never had a whole lot of money and stuff. But when my mom passed away, I got a little money that she left to keep me jamming. So I just totally went crazy. I bought a bunch of amps, did a lot of drugs, and was an idiot, but fortunately it turned out okay."

That nutshells the whole grunge scene right there, and it's why, the drowsy-making passages notwithstanding, I came away from this book with a big smile on my face. Lots of it is like a gray day in western Washington; you've been kicked out of yet another band, and your girlfriend is spending far too

< 183 >

much time with the drummer from the Melvins or 7 Year Bitch or the Screaming Trees. In the end, though, "Everybody Loves Our Town" made me want to be young, stupid, and lucky again.

Mainly, it made me want to be young.

< 184 >

Ebony vs. Ivory:
The Re-Segregation of Rock 'n' Roll

THERE WAS BLACK, THERE WAS WHITE, and then there was black and white. There was jazz and rock and hip hop, and then there was—what? All along, there was pandemonium, fevered mingling, one tribe swapping their pretty beads and shiny mirrors for the pelts and dried fish of another, and for that we should be grateful. Or at least resigned, because American culture has one great theme, race, and one great art form, pop music, and the two are and will always be inseparable, will always be the twin helices of our national DNA.

I was born in the last days of World War II, when the phrase "civil rights" wouldn't have meant much to anybody, at least not in Baton Rouge, Louisiana. The races mixed freely, but only up to a point, and entirely unself-consciously. Everybody knew where to go, what to do, and how to do it, and this knowledge was so thoroughly ingrained that it was another twenty years before any of us even thought about going somewhere our grandparents hadn't been and doing something new and doing it in a way that hadn't been done as far back in one's family as one could remember.

The day began with the arrival of Dot, my "black mama," and Alphonse, the Haitian yardman. My mother was a schoolteacher and my father a college professor, but we lived on a working farm, so my brother and I were feeding chickens or watering horses as Dot began cooking and cleaning and Alphonse sharpened his tools. The schools we attended were segregated, but at the end of the day and on weekends we played with black children, such as Siebel and David, whose parents worked on the much larger Burden plantation down the road. Siebel was close to my age, and often he and I listened to the radio and danced, if you call yelling, throwing our arms in the air, and rubbing our fannies together dancing. Moving from the all-white world of school to a mixed

< 185 >

one before and after was effortless; I certainly didn't question it, and nobody else seemed to notice, either.

Each different kind of music had its place, too. My parents favored classical music, but, in what I'm sure was an effort to hook my brother and me on "good" music, they tended to choose works of a syrupy or bombastic nature: *Scheherazade*, "Bolero," the toreador song from *Carmen*, *Peter and the Wolf*, "The William Tell Overture." We listened dutifully, even making up our own lyrics to songs we couldn't understand, though when the older folks weren't around, my brother, who was four years older than I was, would put on the jazz disks he had somehow managed to slip into the house.

His need for secrecy didn't have a racial basis; by that time, the idea that black music was subversive had come and gone. Fats Waller may have raised a few eyebrows, but Gershwin made jazz respectable, which meant that, if white bands played it and it was okay to listen to them, then it must be okay to listen to black bands as well. Besides Benny Goodman's band was mixed-race, and it played at Carnegie Hall. Still, who wants to listen to his parents' music? If you're a kid and you're not trying to define yourself through music that your parents would find different, possibly incomprehensible, and maybe even repulsive, you're not doing your job.

But if my parents had caught my brother and me listening to Art Blakey and the Jazz Messengers and found all that riffing outrageous, they hadn't heard anything yet. I'm not sure of even the inexact date, but it must have been either in late 1955 or early the following year that I switched on my little green plastic Westinghouse radio in the room my brother and I shared and heard a voice say, "AWOPBOPALOOMOPALOPBAMBOOM!" Who was it? *What* was it? What did it mean?

Later, when I figured out that there were more little green radios in the world than mine and that I wasn't the only one who loved this new music, I asked myself, who is this for? Who is the audience? And did this singer—what was his name again?—even have an audience in mind, or did he just get up in front of a microphone and start screaming?

He made me feel as though I could do anything.

< 186 >

*

As KEITH RICHARDS OF THE ROLLING STONES said, Little Richard's "Tutti Frutti" is the song that turned the world from monochrome to technicolor, and certainly the backdrop in 1955 was pale, indeed. According to Billboard charts, the hits that year were, first, Perez Prado's "Cherry Pink And Apple Blossom White," followed by Bill Haley & His Comets with "Rock Around The Clock," then Mitch Miller's "The Yellow Rose Of Texas," Roger Williams' "Autumn Leaves," and, at number five, Les Baxter's "Unchained Melody."

True, "Rock Around the Clock" marks a milestone in rock history: Haley, a country performer, is credited with, not the first rock 'n' roll record (that title has many claimants) but, in the cautious wording of Wikipedia's multi-headed scribe, "the first recording to be universally acknowledged" as a rock 'n' roll record. Compared to the syncopated Little Richard and Chuck Berry songs that would soon be on the charts, the plodding "Rock Around the Clock" betrays its country origins, yet it sounds like a revolutionary anthem in contrast to the other four hits of the year, mainly syrupy instrumental wallpaper, soothing sounds for grownups whose musical ideals were identical to those of the engineers who picked tunes for department store elevators and dentists' waiting rooms.

As far as what the lyrics meant, well, they meant nothing—and everything. In *Blue Monday: Fats Domino and the Lost Dawn of Rock 'n' Roll*, Rick Coleman notes that many early rock singers used nonsense syllables that mimic traditional African drum patterns meant to be tuneful rather than merely rhythmic. The start of "Tutti Frutti" is the most dramatic instance, but Jesse Hill's "Ooo Poo Pah Doo" and Smiley Lewis's "Tee-Nah-Nah" are other examples.

With its twenty-four-hour party atmosphere as well as its rich gumbo of languages, New Orleans is the perfect breeding ground for nonsense. In "Jock-a-Mo," Sugar Boy Crawford says, "If you don't like what the big chief say / You got to jockamo feena nay." In online forums, the literal-minded ask "what do these lines mean?" and even "what language are they in?" What they mean is that somebody out there is dancing and snapping his fingers, like a kid. Every audience is childlike at heart, and children aren't cerebral, they're visceral: they're here to play.

< 187 >

Later, the la-la-las in many of Sam Cooke's songs became an extension of the idea, though the yeah, yeah, yeah of the Beatles is the best known example of syllables taking the places of actual words. In fact, the studio engineers who recorded "She Loves You" thought the repeated yeahs were substitutes for the real lyrics that the Beatles would surely produce when the session began.

Had the engineers known more about the hybrid nature of rock 'n' roll, they wouldn't have been so surprised. The original members of the Rock and Roll Hall of Fame are Elvis, Chuck Berry, Little Richard, Fats Domino, Jerry Lee Lewis, Sam Cooke, James Brown, the Everly Brothers, Buddy Holly, and Ray Charles. Six black musicians, five white: talk about a potpourri.

And the influence went both ways: the Beatles may have covered the Marvelettes' "Please Mr. Postman" early on, but, as Gerald Early writes in *One Nation Under a Groove*, what made Motown possible was not that Elvis covered rhythm and blues hits but that Fats Domino covered a country and western tune, "Blueberry Hill." According to Rick Coleman, Domino was upset when Hank Williams died, saying, "That country music tells a story; that's just like rhythm and blues. Look at Hank Williams—he was twenty-nine when he died, and the songs he wrote, man!" He went on to record three of Williams's songs, including his signature "Jambalaya."

Not long ago, I heard Little Richard in concert, and he began by announcing "I am the beautiful Little Richard, and you can see that I am telling you the truth!" He kicked off his show with "Good Golly Miss Molly" and then went into "Blueberry Hill," alternating throughout between his own hits and standards by Ray Charles, Hank Williams, Bob Seger, and such less-knowns as his fellow Specialty Records artist Larry Williams ("Bony Maronie"). Little Richard sang spirituals ("I Saw the Light"), country songs ("Jambalaya" again), and even "The Itsy Bitsy Spider."

Not long after, I spoke by phone with Willie Ruth Howard, Little Richard's cousin, whom I was interviewing for my book on the singer, and she told me her favorite performance ever was when Little Richard sang, not one of his own hits, but Hank Williams' "I'm So Lonesome I Could Cry."

< 188 >

*

To the pioneer performers, then, the most influential music of our times was as black and white as the eighty eight keys on a piano. After that, though, what happened? In an essay entitled "A Paler Shade of White: How Indie Rock Lost Its Soul" which appeared in the October 22, 2007 issue of *The New Yorker*, music critic Sasha Frere-Jones analyzes the re-segregation of American music with unusual acuity and insight. He juxtaposes two concerts by the Canadian band Arcade Fire, a name which, judging from how often my students mention it, is about as popular as a band can get these days. The first concert, writes Frere-Jones, was "ragged but full of brio," and he recalls spending the evening happily pressed against the stage. But by the second concert, the band's limitations couldn't be hidden any longer: "I was weary after six songs," he writes, because "if there is a trace of soul, blues, reggae, or funk in Arcade Fire, it must be philosophical; it certainly isn't audible." What was missing was "a bit of swing, some empty space, and palpable bass frequencies—in other words, attributes of African-American popular music."

After all, rock 'n' roll is "the most miscegenated popular music ever to have existed." Why, then, did rock undergo a "racial re-sorting in the nineteen-nineties"? To answer that question, Frere-Jones goes back to the nineteen twenties, when folk music was being recorded for the first time and it was not always clear where the songs came from, as I point out in my chapters on "John Henry" and "The House of the Rising Sun." It's a given that African slave hollers shaped the rising and falling patterns of blues singing, but scholars now believe that such modes as the call-and-response singing integral to the African-American church may have been brought over by illiterate Scots who learned scripture by singing back lines as their pastor read them aloud.

It's easy to see how listeners might think that a song which sprang from a forest appears to have fallen from a single tree. After all, if arrangers do as complete a makeover of a song as Burdon, Price, and their bandmates did with "The House of the Rising Sun," their artistry will erase the path they took to find and claim the song in the first place.

What baby boomer can claim not to blushed upon learning that the Stones'

< 189 >

"Love in Vain" or Cream's "Crossroad" were actually written (or at least record-ed) decades earlier by Robert Johnson? The borrowing (or theft) by white mu-sicians from black ones is well-documented, but what's interesting is how the flow went in the other direction as well: it was a milestone in English rock when Mick Jagger and Keith Richards met on a train between Dartford and London in 1960 and Jagger lent Richards an LP by Muddy Waters, as Sasha Frere-Jones points out, but before long, Otis Redding was covering the Stones' satisfaction, just as Little Richard included such "white"standards as "Baby Face" and "By the Light of the Silvery Moon" on his early albums.

Sure, the recording industry was racist: industry execs hustled to have Pat Boone and Bill Haley cover Little Richard's songs, though while the blander versions outdid the originals initially, music lovers caught on fast, and soon the Georgia Peach was outselling his pale imitators. And if the industry wanted to hide the fact that rock 'n' roll came from such pioneers as Little Richard and Fats Domino (who said modestly of his role, "Well, I wouldn't want to say that I started it, but I don't remember anyone else before me playing that kind of stuff"), white musicians were often more frank: "A lot of people seem to think I started this business," said Elvis as early as 1957. "But rock 'n' roll was here a long time before I came along. Nobody can sing that kind of music like colored people. Let's face it: I can't sing it like Fats Domino can. I know that." But as I say earlier, if Elvis hadn't wriggled his hips on television (everybody, or at least the teenaged viewers, knew what Ed Sullivan was hiding when he had his cam-eramen shoot the singer from the waist up), we'd all still be doing the foxtrot.

BECAUSE IT WAS ON THE DANCE FLOOR, and not just in the music, that the rac-es really came together. The rock audience, and certainly the rhythm 'n' blues audience, is by definition out of its seat and shuffling, shagging, hot-stepping, or simply shaking as though in the throes of a shared seizure. Rick Coleman re-counts incidents ranging from the ridiculous to the sublime, an example of the former being the 1956 show in Houston where blacks where allowed to dance but not whites, though when white teenagers hit the dance floor, it was decided that only whites could dance; "I won't play if Negroes can't dance," said Domino

< 190 >

in a rare outspoken moment, though when teens of every shade began to bop together, police stopped the show, provoking a riot. Another time, the sheriff in a Mississippi town tried to put back up a rope that had been knocked down by segregated dancers who were gyrating a little too hard. The mayor stopped him, though, saying, "Everybody here knows each other."

In a refracted image of this scene, Buddy Holly and the Crickets were booked into the Apollo Theatre in 1957 by a promoter who assumed they were a black group. They won over the audience anyway, though not initially, as portrayed in the 1978 movie *The Buddy Holly Story*; they were booed their first time on stage and needed to perform twice more before the applause came. Later, rock impresario Bill Graham introduced audiences at the Fillmore and the Fillmore West to such white groups Jefferson Airplane, Janis Joplin, and the Grateful Dead, but also to artists like Otis Redding, Chuck Berry, and Santana, often on the same stage.

For all that, the most successful musicians in the next several decades were white, Michael Jackson being the notable exception. All that changed with the 1992 release of Dr. Dre's *The Chronic*, featuring Snoop Doggy Dogg. "You could argue that Dr. Dre and Snoop were the most important pop musicians since Bob Dylan and the Beatles," argues Sasha Frere-Jones, and while he clearly means that they "upended established paradigms" and gave lasting expression to a form of hip-hop that, at this point, seems destined to outlast competing genres, including rock itself, he may as well have said that hip-hop gave African-American music such a mammoth presence that "white" music had to skedaddle into the enforced purity of indie rock. Commercially successful groups such as the Flaming Lips and Wilco, writes Frere-Jones, drew on psychedelia, country rock, and the Beach Boys, whose Brian Wilson is "indie rock's muse." And so "in the past few years, I've spent too many evenings at indie concerts waiting in vain for vigor, for rhythm, for a musical effect that could justify all the preciousness" and sabotage the "lassitude and monotony that so many indie acts seem to confuse with authenticity and significance."

What's bad for "white" music, though, is clearly good for "black." As Frere-Jones points out, black musicians are now as visible and influential as white ones. As such, they're pressured to create distinctive sounds, ones that rely on

< 191 >

no other artist or genre; they're aided in this by a 2004 federal appeals court decision that using as few as three notes from another work could be a copyright violation, thus making the sampling of another artist a practice forbidden to all but the wealthiest rappers. Meanwhile, the indie rock that most young white kids listen to these days is missing something, for "the uneasy, and sometimes inappropriate, borrowings and imitations that set rock and roll in motion gave popular music a heat and intensity that can't be duplicated today, and the loss isn't just musical; it's also about risk." A sentence or two follow, but Frere-Jones ends essentially on that enigmatic note.

So what does he mean by "risk"? Usually that word suggests a step into the unknown, but it seems to me now that the greatest risk would be to make that a backward step into a world where the races partied together. The time when black and white kids danced to the same music was brief and it was tense, but it existed. Besides, in racial terms, all times are tense: the race issue of the day centers on Hispanic immigration and its myriad nuances involving drivers licenses, health care, bilingualism, and so on. But that's just today, and it's just Hispanic: can the Chinese version be far behind?

In *The New Yorker* issue following the one in which Frere-Jones' essay appeared, several writers mentioned indie rock songs with African-American roots, though none did noticeable damage to his portrait of a fragmented musical landscape. One reader pointed out how hard it would be today for a white group to steal a black song, as Led Zeppelin did when they turned Willie Dixon's "You Need Love" into their first hit single, "Whole Lotta Love," given the extent to which black music has become overtly political. Indeed, this is the point Nelson George argues in the final pages of *Hip Hop America*, where he points out that hip hop remains viable because the nation's problems—poverty, dysfunctional schools, drug addiction, the rift between classes—are as marked as ever. "This is all terrible for the social fabric of the nation," writes George, "but it is prime fodder for the makers and consumers of edgy, aggressive culture."

In other words, the audience is big, it's getting bigger, and it wants different things. There's too much money to be made out of social rot, and so much money that the music that stood on its own two dancin' feet in the days of Little

< 192 >

Richard and Fats Domino is now seen a gateway to even more lucrative enterprises: the rapper Jay-Z, who is also rapper and president and CEO of Def Jam Recordings and Roc-A-Fella Records, notes in an interview in the November 29, 2007 issue of *Rolling Stone*, that the new music business is "all about brands. It ain't just about music anymore. Music is a great foundation for so many other things. We have to make money in different ways."

Jay-Z then seems unfazed by the interviewer's quote from comedian Chris Rock, who notes that "Stevie Wonder's records would have been shitty if he had to run a clothing company and cologne line." Besides, as the always-perceptive Kelefa Sanneh notes in a December 30, 2007 *New York Times* article about declining hip-hop sales, "Because hip-hop is so intensely self-aware, and self-reflexive, it came to be known as big-money music, a genre obsessed with its own success. If we are now entering an age of diminished commercial expectations, that will inevitably change how hip-hop sounds, too." It could be that no one has to kill this golden goose; unless buyers suddenly clamor for rap songs about the joys of cocooning in years to come, rappers might find themselves on the same low-cal economic diet as the rest of us.

So the pop music that was the engine in a car full of teenagers is now an accessory, like the hood ornament or custom license plate on a car with a single kid at the wheel. Niche marketing is all. Once fragmentation was something that happened; now it's something that's planned for. A profile in the September 2, 2007 *New York Times Magazine* of Rick Rubin, co-head of Columbia Records, describes how the label assembled a group of twenty college students in an attempt to "take the pulse of the elusive music audience." Contrast this corporate approach to taste-making with Little Richard and a bunch of session musicians goofing around in a New Orleans studio until they came up with "Tutti Frutti," the song that made rock 'n' roll what it is today. Too, imagine any work of genius written according to a corporate model: if, in the eighteen fifties, Harper and Brothers had polled readers on what they wanted in a book, *Moby-Dick* would be shorter, wouldn't have Ahab as a central character, and

< 193 >

would likely end with a victory party on the deck of the *Pequod* complete with fruity drinks and hula girls.

If record companies cater primarily to niche audiences, there will be an additional effect beyond the obvious one of fragmentation. Yes, the niche audience will get more and more of what it wants, and that's the idea: happy customers, wealthy companies. But the downside is that the audience will cut itself off from anything new and interesting, a song or even an entire musical genre that may turn out to be more engaging than the programmed choices on their iPod. In a revealing article titled "Muslim Singer With a Country Twang" (*New York Times*, November 13, 2007), a Nashville music reviewer is asked to listen to the songs of Kareem Salaama, a singer born in Ponca City, OK of Egyptian parents, and points out that, Salaama's artistry notwithstanding, songs expressing divergent viewpoints on such matters as war are no longer played on country radio and that the last African-American star was Charley Pride decades ago, adding, "Culturally, it is a homogenous genre. That makes for some boring music, and it would also make it difficult for someone like Kareem to break through."

And it also makes it difficult for music to grow and change the way it always has. David Brooks writes in a *Times* piece called "The Segmented Society" that in the seventies, artists like the Rolling Stones and Springsteen drew on a range of influences to produce songs that might be tinged by country, soul, blues, or all three, and the result was gigantic followings and huge arena shows. But at some point "the era of integration gave way to the era of fragmentation," notes Brooks. "There are many bands that can fill 5,000-seat theaters, but almost no new groups with the broad following of the Rolling Stones, Springsteen or U2."

Fragmentation of the musical audience is an example of "long tail" marketing as described by Chris Anderson in *The Long Tail: Why the Future of Business is Selling Less of More*, a study of the effect of such long tail companies as eBay as opposed to old-fashioned "big dog" ones like Sears. Once again, the effect is not merely on the music: as David Brooks says, "It seems that whatever story I cover, people are anxious about fragmentation and longing for cohesion. This is the one driving fear behind the inequality and immigration debates, behind worries of polarization and behind the entire Obama candidacy."

< 194 >

Yet it is this longing for cohesion that I see as the light, however dim, at the end of David Brooks' tunnel. If audiences want cohesion that much, the corporations will find a way to sell it to them. The technology will change first, and the music will follow.

MEANWHILE, THOUGH, THE LONGER ONE looks at a world fragmented by mass marketing into increasingly narrow niches, the more one is reminded of Edward Bellamy's 1888 novel *Looking Backward*, the story of a man from 1887 who awakens in 2000 from a trance to find himself in a high-tech utopia. On a typical evening, the hero expresses a desire to go down to the band box in the park and listen to some live music, but his kindly guide explains that that's not necessary any more, that there are pipes connecting the band to a listening room in every home. This means that citizens can listen to a concert simply by flipping a wall switch, but in a world of such ease, asks Bellamy, who is going to put on a suit or a pretty dress and stroll out arm in arm to enjoy the music, sure, but also watch children at play, see that the leaves are turning, chat with one's neighbors? Bellamy was disillusioned with an increasingly competitive industrial society, and he wasn't the only one: as many as 165 Bellamy Clubs sprang up in cities all over the country so that readers could discuss his ideas, maybe swing America back to a culture where people gathered on sidewalks to swap ideas and talk politics, culture, music.

That idea didn't take. We can look backward; we just can't go there any more. We have no choice but to live in our time, knowing that it will be different five years from now—five minutes from now, as far as that goes. All pop phenomena pass, and tomorrow's teenagers will gasp with laughter when they see images of today's kids with their low-rider jeans and backward baseball caps, their iPods throbbing with hip hop. Something else will take the place of all that, and no one can even come close to predicting what that something else is any more than they could have predicted the sound and look of Little Richard or the Beatles. To paraphrase what Steve Jobs said Apple customers, it's not the audience's job to know what it wants.

If I had a ballot, I'd vote for a world that has a lot less targeting and a good

< 195 >

deal more chance in it, more risk. In his brilliant study *Searching for Robert Johnson*, Peter Guralnick goes back to a time even before the era of rock 'n' roll, the day of the itinerant bluesman; he quotes Johnson's fellow musician Johnny Shines, who says:

> See, Robert was a guy, you could wake him up anytime and he was ready to *go*. Say, for instance, you had come from Memphis and go to Helena, and we'd play there all night probably and lay down to sleep the next morning, and you hear a train. You say, "Robert, I hear a train; let's catch it." He wouldn't exchange no words with you; he's just ready to go. It's really, I mean if a person lives in an exploratory world, then this is the best thing that ever happened to him.

I wrote at the beginning of my black playmates Siebel and David, boys I raced with, fought with, laughed with, climbed trees and built forts with, danced with. They dropped off my radar and I off theirs at some point, but years after I had left Baton Rouge to begin my adult life, I came back once to visit my parents and read in *The Morning Advocate* that Siebel had been shot to death by his stepdaughter; he'd had too much to drink and begun hitting family members with an iron chair, and then the bullet stopped him. By this time, I was a tenured professor with a wife, a child of my own, two cars, a mortgage. The professor in his corduroy, the dead man on the kitchen floor: you can't imagine two more different endings. But for the longest time, it seems, we were the best of friends.

< 196 >

Sharon Jones,
or Why Soul Music Is Forever

BACK IN THE DAY, ARETHA AND OTIS topped the soul charts, and then the music turned in a different direction. Today, Sharon Jones and the Dap-Kings have their hands on the wheel, and they want to steer listeners to a new place on the musical spectrum that looks and sounds very much like an old one.

Jones and the band are the biggest act for indie Daptone Records, an artist-run company on the model of the Stax label that produced much of the best soul music of the '60s. Currently, Daptone promotes the work of nine groups, and the Dap-Kings played on the late Amy Winehouse's *Back to Black* album and backed her on her U.S. tour. In their suits and sunglasses, the eight Dap-Kings are as visually hip as they are musically tight—"soul nerds to the core," cackled Jones in a recent phone interview.

Most of the Dap-Kings' success is due to Jones herself, though, whose high-energy performances have fans lining up for tickets wherever she appears. Born in Augusta, Georgia in 1956, Jones moved to New York as a youngster and now makes her home there.

Following a rocky beginning in the music business, however, Jones worked at Rikers Island as a corrections officer. I asked her in a telephone interview whether that meant "prison guard," and Jones replied, "That's right, baby—with the keys and everything!" And before she began to record and tour with the Dap-Kings, she had a 16-year stint as a wedding singer. "My band was an unusual wedding band because I was in it," Jones said of the otherwise all-white aggregation. "But I was the one who got Uncle Sid up out of his chair. I got Aunt Minnie up on stage and dancing with me."

These days, audiences can catch Jones making her movie debut in *The Great Debaters*, in a performance so hot-blooded it'll take away the breath of any viewer quick enough to catch it. She's only on screen for a few seconds,

< 197 >

which may be just as well. The movie, which recounts the struggles of a black college debate team in Depression-era Texas, alternates between the earnest and the melodramatic, and if Jones's role were any bigger, she might have stolen the show from producer and director Denzel Washington, who also stars in the film.

The opening scenes of *The Great Debaters* feature a juke joint in full-tilt boogie mode; dancers wave their arms in the air as a house band churns out the songs. But it all looks like a movie until the camera pans past Lila, the singer, who is clearly in the grip of something other than the director's off-screen guidance. As Lila, Sharon Jones swings her shoulders to the back beat, but her eyes dart wildly. The music has gotten way beyond itself; those eyes brim with surprise and even fear. When Lila isn't singing, her mouth hangs open, and she pants like a leopard about to tear out your willing heart.

Which is pretty much what Sharon Jones looks and sounds like when she appears as herself with the Dap-Kings, as she did in 2008 on the campus of Florida State University, where guitar player and MC Binky Griptite introduced Jones "as the brightest star in the Daptone universe" just before she began to power through the night like a supernova. Menacing and seductive, she brought young men onto a tiny stage, flirted with them, and sent them away with a queenly wave of her hand. There wasn't room on the floor to dance, though a pandemic of fierce pogo-ing shook the club past midnight. And from time to time Jones, who has obviously seen a James Brown show or two, kicked off her heels and did all the dancing for everybody.

In person as well as on *The Great Debaters* sound track, Jones also tackles the spiritual side of soul, as she does on such songs as "Answer Me" from her album *100 Days, 100 Nights*, where she also plays a mean piano. "It's all God's music to me," says Jones, though. "I've been going to the Baptist church since I was born. I tithe. How could what I do be wrong? I pray and read my Bible every day, and then I get on stage and sing."

As Dap-Kings bassist and band leader Gabe Roth says, "Sharon can reach anybody because she cut her teeth doing weddings. She was paid for making sure that everyone had a good time." When asked if she liked to tour, Jones replied, "I love it. I get depressed when I stay home." Jones is caring for an ailing

< 198 >

mother, and she said, "I've lost 24 four family members and friends in the last year. Thank God the good outweighs the bad!"

Besides updating classic soul grooves, Jones's goal is to "just be comfortable. I'm not married. I'm past my childbearing years. I'm tired of renting. I want a house. I want the simple things in life." In the meantime, she confides that "I'm glad they didn't ask me who I was wearing on the red carpet [at the *Great Debaters* premier in New York]. I would have had to say K-Mart, Wal-Mart—all those marts!"

Like the other artists at Daptone, Jones wants to reinvent yesterday's sweet soul music for a new generation. And recent changes in the music business are making that goal possible: as audiences turn away from disappointing major label offerings and choose music based on blogs and word of mouth, the Daptone artists stand as much a chance as anyone.

Music critic Bryan Borzykowski points out that Jones is "different and genuine—two things lacking in pretty much every huge album the majors release—so she'll do just fine on an indie." He goes on to say that "there's definitely more success in her future—maybe even a top 40 hit—but I think it'll be driven by the fans rather than major label marketing."

Pop music's horizon is broader than ever now. Where once there was a single audience for pop music, now there are countless smaller ones. There's a place on everybody's iPod for a new sound, even if it happens to be an old one. Sharon Jones says her mission is to make sure that sound is soulful.

< 199 >

"A Fictitious Head of State from a Place Nobody Knows": Bob Dylan

IF YOU WANTED TO FIND OUT THE TRUTH about Bob Dylan, the last thing you might want to do is interview him. Between 1962 and 2004, he gave more than 200 interviews, and it's hard to imagine that he hasn't done dozens since, each more baffling and enigmatic than the last.

That said, it's easy to see why this notorious shape-shifter would deliberately try to exasperate his more blockheaded questioners, such as the journalist in 1965 who said "for those of us well over thirty, could you label yourself and perhaps tell us what your role is?" (It's a sign of the innocence of those days that a writer of the same period described Dylan as appearing "tieless.")

Too often in interviews, Dylan sounds like a self-parody, explaining how this or that "cat" is or isn't "uptight" or "groovy" or that something either is or is not "where it's at." At other times, he is plainly nettled, arguing "I'll bet Tony Bennett doesn't have to go through this kind of thing" and telling the same interviewer, when asked if he'd grown up wanting to be president, "No. When I was boy, Harry Truman was president; who'd want to be Harry Truman?" The problem, of course, is that most of his interviewers saw themselves as normal and Dylan as more than a little odd, which is hardly his view. When asked if it wasn't weird to be at an awards ceremony with Gregory Peck, the musician says, "Well, listen, everything's weird. You tell me something that's not weird."

If you read enough of his interviews, though—in *Bob Dylan: The Essential Interviews*, Jonathan Cott collects thirty-one of them, which is plenty—suddenly the method beneath his madness becomes clear. It's obvious that he is keeping his mind free and his art agile by rejecting every label, saying he doesn't know what rock and roll is, for example, and even what the words "homosexual" and "junkie" mean. Beyond that, often he seems either to be actually

< 201 >

riffing his way toward another song or at least keeping in the air the playfulness that fuels the single most inventive musical mind of our time, as when he gives an account of his life that includes his getting a job "as a Chinaman" and moving in with a schoolteacher who invented a refrigerator that turned newspaper into lettuce.

And there is the occasional nugget of clarity, as when Dylan describes his compositional method in homey terms:

> It's like this painter who lives around here—he paints the area in a radius of twenty miles, he paints bright strong pictures. He might take a barn from twenty miles away, and hook it up with a brook right next door, then with a car ten miles away, and with the sky on some certain day, and the light on the trees from another certain day. A person passing by will be painted alongside someone ten miles away. And in the end he'll have this composite picture of something which you can't say exists in his mind. It's not that he started off willfully painting this picture from all his experience. . . . That's more or less what I do.

Most of the time, though, he prefers to gyre and gimble in the wabe. "I have an idea that it's easier to be disconnected than to be connected," says our greatest master of reinvention, which is why, after one questioner begins by noting "I don't know whether to do a serious interview or carry on in that absurdist way we talked last night," Dylan tells the simple truth when he replies, "It'll be the same thing anyway, man."

When nineteen year-old Bob Dylan arrived in New York in 1961, the record companies were still run by middle-aged men whose tastes ran to Tommy Dorsey and Benny Goodman. In his high school yearbook, Dylan had said his goal was to join Little Richard's band, and he and the Georgia Peach share a trait indispensable to show business success, which is to sound like no other entertainer before or after them. Few executives understood what Dylan was up to, but the John Hammond who signed him to Columbia Records did. As Hammond said, "I understand sincerity."

< 202 >

Now Dylan's audience can hear what Hammond heard with the release of two new sets of recordings. Columbia Records released *The Bootleg Series Volume 9—The Witmark Demos* in conjunction with Columbia/Legacy's release of the artist's first eight albums in a box set titled *Bob Dylan—The Original Mono Recordings*. Both sets have been long sought after by collectors; the Witmark demos saw their commercial release nearly five decades after they were first recorded, and the mono recordings returned to the marketplace for the first time on CD as well as vinyl.

The 47-song Witmark demos (so called after M. Witmark & Sons, Dylan's first publishing company) present the unfiltered Dylan, the man with nothing but his guitar and harmonica and occasionally a piano on which he chunks out the chords guitar-style; on "Mr. Tambourine Man," there's the distinct sound of a foot keeping time. In the absence of production values, it's easier to see how the songwriter's genius first showed itself as he took existing musical templates, stripped them to their bare essentials, and reloaded them with new information: the ramblin' man song ("Don't Think Twice, It's All Right"), the protest tune ("Blowin' in the Wind"), the say-hello-to-my-baby song ("Girl From the North Country"), the Old World ballad ("Seven Curses").

Here is where Dylan parted company with the other folksong writers of his day. Realizing that to continue with the traditional melodies would be an artistic dead end, he began to write the songs that, as he says in his says in his 2004 autobiography *Chronicles, Volume One*, established him as "a fictitious head of state from a place nobody knows." These are the songs that appear on the eight albums from *Bob Dylan* (1962) to *John Wesley Harding* (1968) that comprise the new mono recordings.

In his liner notes to the mono box set, Greil Marcus fans the flame of the recent mono resurgence, complaining that stereo "meant the guitar over here and the voice over there, with the feeling that neither were quite there at all." Whereas with mono, "there was something concrete in that single sound, something that made the songs into facts, the way Little Richard's 'Ready Teddy' is a fact before it is anything else: something you can't argue away."

The full frontal power of mono meant "there was something that made the song into events, the story they told happening as you listened: another kind

< 203 >

of fact, even if the events were of the kind that might turn out differently every time you put the record on."

Marcus blames the "cult of stereo" on *Playboy*,

> where the gleaming components of amplifier, pre-amp, receiver, turntable, and wood-paneled speakers were offered as part of what was not quite yet called a lifestyle, a way of showing off your refined taste, your money, and your one-step-aheadness, right along with your clothes—your *sartorial* style—your liquor—your *pre-prandial libations*—and your line: *Baby, you haven't heard Brubeck until you've heard him on this.*

To Marcus, stereo is part of some big-city pussy hound's sleight of hand, one more *pas seul* in the rake's progress toward soulless boinking. Whereas there's nothing tricky about mono: "it got your attention," Marcus says. "It hit you in the face."

In one of the best critical books on American culture, Marcus descibes what he calls "the old, weird America," which is essentially Walt Whitman's country, a low-tech landscape populated by peddlers, grifters, schoolmarms, bent cops, hoboes, and riverboat gamblers, a place where dreams are more important than plans, where people make do, where your neighbor might be a millionaire tomorrow or an inmate at the razor-wire motel. It's Bob Dylan's world, the one he came from and the one he keeps alive in his songs. In a word, it's the world of monophonic sound, a form of sound reproduction that you can call either "primitive" or "elemental," a blunt-force delivery system so basic and engaging that it doesn't need improving, which just means that engineers are going to get out their tool kits and try.

Dylan's audience will have the ultimate say, but if Greil Marcus is right, mono may be all the artillery the head of an invisible empire needs.

< 204 >

What Producers Do
and Why We All Need One

WE DIDN'T HAVE A TV IN OUR HOUSE until I was twelve. When we finally got one, I was in thrall: coming home after a day of filling out math worksheets, listening to "book reports," and playing dodge ball, I poured myself a bowl of sugary cereal and headed west to a black and white land of sheriffs, deputies, buckaroos, jaspers, painted but still-virtuous women, and snakes of both the human and herpetological kind. I was in heaven.

My parents, on the other hand, were bewildered. Until I clued them in with as much eye-rolling middle-school sarcasm as I could muster, they thought that all programming was local. And for a while, at least, I'm fairly sure that my father thought there was a direct connection between our set and the WBRZ studio in downtown Baton Rouge and that content was delivered through a pipe, perhaps, sort of the way we got our water.

I can't blame them, though. The first time I heard Little Richard on the radio, I was pretty sure it was just him and me. He said everything I needed to hear, even though I didn't know I needed to hear it; it was though he picked up the phone and said, "David? This is Richard. Sit down, son, and listen to this."

As a journalist, the deeper I got into the world of music, the more I understood the key figures who connected artist and audience, the lyricists, A & R men, and engineers who opened the valve and sent a flood of music to a thirsty farm boy. More than anything, I learned to honor the person who played the part of the producer, whether that was an official title or just a role played by a father or other relative. He or she might be an executive in an office high over Manhattan or the person who makes sure you have a good breakfast and come right home after school to practice. Either way, the producer is the yoke, the linchpin, the indispensable bond between musician and audience.

< 205 >

As I approach the end of *Crossroad*, I want to look at the producers in the way I have artists and audiences and provide a bigger picture of the music world by examining the different types and noting how their presence matters.

OR THEIR ABSENCE. Let's start with a whole cityful of musicians that could have used some guidance in the worst way.

As the once-great Ottoman Empire crumbled, it was known as "the sick man of Europe," a phrase attributed to Czar Nicholas I of Russia, though the exact source is unknown. Today we may say something analogous about Detroit, a city that's lost almost two-thirds of its population in recent decades. The trouble began with the 1967 riots that left 40 dead and thousands of stores burned or looted, and even today Detroit's murder rate remains among the highest in the country.

Ah, but we all know that great art comes from the forge of pain and suffering, don't we? The Harry Lime character played by Orson Welles in *The Thin Man* famously said that bloody Renaissance Italy produced Leonardo and Michelangelo, whereas peaceful Switzerland's principal contribution to civilization is the cuckoo clock. Closer to home, there's the blues tradition that came from Mississippi plantations where slavery was all but a fact, even though the law had abolished it decades earlier.

By that token, Detroit should have produced some memorable art over the years. And it has, even if none of the artists are up there with Michelangelo or Son House. But so far it hasn't manage to come up with the kind of work that emerged from New York and Los Angeles in the same period. The city did better in terms of music over the last fifty years than it did in urban renewal, but that's not saying much.

Many a book author has had the experience of realizing that the end result is going to be completely different from what was initially foreseen; an example is the biography of Robert Frost by Lawrance Thompson, who came to hate his subject and said as much.

And one wonders if that isn't the case with *Detroit Rock City*, the definitive study of the Motor City's musical triumphs and misfires, if Steve Miller

< 206 >

(the journalist and author, not the rock musician of the same name) didn't start kicking through the rubble in hopes of nuggets that he would never find. On the surface, the book promises to hold up a vibrant musical culture that produced works we'll be listening to years from now, but that never happens. What we get instead is a picture of what is needed to create and maintain an artistic community—in a word, people in charge who know what they're doing. That makes *Detroit Rock City* worth reading in a perverse way, because the picture is a negative image, one that depicts what's necessary to make art by depicting its opposite.

In the beginning (that is, the late sixties), there was MC5 and Iggy and the Stooges, two bands remembered today more for their raucous performances than their music. MC5 guitarist Wayne Kramer strikes an ominous chord when he says "the decline of the MC5 and the parallel decline of Detroit is not a mystery to me. . . . A lot of other people were in desperate situations as well. And some of them had guns."

Part of the problem is that, with almost all the Detroit bands, no one was minding the store. Iggy Pop recalls, "We had no idea about a career at all. What was very important was how we wanted to look and how we wanted to sound and what we wanted to do. . . . I always believed that if you do that superbly, the career would take care of itself."

Not so, as it turned out. No one managed or produced the Stooges the way Brian Epstein did the Beatles or Andrew Loog Oldham the Rolling Stones in their early years. Deals were made and scores settled in back alleys, not board rooms; singer Scott Richardson reports that when another band thought he was trying to poach Iggy for his, a couple of the rival musicians put a knife to his throat and told him to lay off.

That doesn't mean there were no success stories, although the acts from this period who made it onto a national stage—Bob Seger, Ted Nugent, Grand Funk Railroad—aren't on anyone's top ten list of influential musicians.

Still, the Detroit bands who are remembered today had good people at the top, such as Bob Ezrin, who produced Alice Cooper. That group's lead singer (the Vincent Damon Furnier who fronted the Alice Cooper band originally but took its name as his own when he launched a solo career) says that Ezrin

< 207 >

listened to their music and said he would produce their album but that they had to relearn everything and develop a "signature."

Told that no one in the band knew what he meant, Ezrin explained: "When you hear the Doors, you know it's the Doors, and when you hear the Beatles, you know it's the Beatles. When you hear Alice Cooper, you could be any psychedelic band."

So the musicians set up in a barn north of Detroit and practiced ten hours a day until they developed a distinctive sound. For better or worse, their nearest neighbors were the inmates of a psychiatric hospital, and when they roared their approval, the band knew (or at least told themselves) that they had a good song.

The young Detroit musicians who just wanted to get together and jam found audiences, played gigs, and even made a little money. But without guidance, most of them were not able to move up to the next level. By equating creativity with anarchy, they put a limit on how creative they could be.

The counterintuitive truth about an artistic signature is that, if it becomes popular, it allows the artist to grow and try new things. Jim Morrison of the Doors said, "You give people what they want or what they think they want and they'll let you do anything." The Doors were known for angering and confusing their audiences; Morrison himself snarled at his fans and baited them as savagely as any Detroit lead singer might. The difference, of course, is that the Doors had already established themselves with bouncy pop hits like "Hello, I Love You" and "Light My Fire," so they could afford to be offensive. As a result, the band appealed to heartland teens but also to listeners who were looking for something edgier.

Back in Detroit, far too many musicians seemed more dedicated to survival rather than growth. One's eyes glaze over in the middle third of this book as the scuzziness accumulates. There's little music in Miller's pages, plenty of drug use and violence. As lifestyles go, the musicians of late-twentieth century Detroit make the English Romantics look like a firm of CPAs.

Perhaps not surprisingly, many Detroit old-timers seem nostalgic for those overdose days. The literal last word goes to singer Rachel Nagy of the aptly named Detroit Cobras who praises recent changes in other midwestern cities

< 208 >

but adds, "I don't really know if I want to see that happen in Detroit. Detroit is Detroit. It's this beautiful place where you sacrifice your safety for a shitload of freedom."

If freedom is your only goal, fine. But if you want the life of the successful artist who has an impact on the lives of others, you might want to recall the words of Flaubert, who advised other artists to "be regular and orderly in your life like a bourgeois, so that you may be violent and original in your work."

Oh, and find somebody who knows how to run things better than you do.

Someone like legendary producer Ahmet Ertegun, say.

The night he heard Duke Ellington play live, Ertegun started down the path that ended in his becoming one of the greatest recording executives in music history. "It was nothing like hearing the records," he said later. "The engineers at the time were afraid that too much bass or too much drums would crack the grooves on the 78s, so they recorded them very low. And when you heard these bands in person, it was explosive. . . . I'd never heard music with that kind of strength."

Well, not yet, at least, considering he was only 10 years old at the time. The year was 1933; Ellington was playing at the London Palladium, and Ahmet's older brother, Nesuhi, took him to the show. (Their diplomat father was Turkish ambassador to the Court of St. James.)

Then again, young or old, Ahmet Ertegun seemed to be out late every night. The genius that led him to sign such artists as Aretha Franklin, Ray Charles, Crosby, Stills, Nash and Young, and the Rolling Stones doesn't seem to be a matter of being in the right place at the right time but of being everywhere all the time. A variation on such phrases as "Ahmet stayed out all night again" or "he changed out of the suit he'd worn to the clubs and went right to the board meeting" occur countless times in Robert Greenfield's *The Last Sultan: The Life and Times of Ahmet Ertegun* an almost diary-like account of the glitzy life that Ertegun led his death in 2006.

Mr. Greenfield is also the author of the deliciously drug-addled *Exile on Main Street: A Season in Hell With the Rolling Stones*, Mr. Greenfield's account

< 209 >

of life in Villa Nellcôte in the south of France during the summer of 1971, when the band made some of its best music amid excesses that were extravagant even by the Rolling Stones' own debauched standards.

If *The Last Sultan* doesn't titillate as much (it doesn't titillate at all, really), that's because the guys who made the music and the guy who recorded it lived rather different lives. Ertegun drank as much as any other club-goer and bounced a number of women other than his wife, Mica, on his knee, but he never let fun get in the way of business.

Ertegun founded Atlantic Records in 1947 with his friend and fellow jazz and blues lover Herb Abramson, though the major shareholder was the Ertegun family dentist, Vahdi Sabit. On the original three-page contract, the name "Horizon Records, Inc." is crossed out and replaced by "Atlantic Recording Corporation." Ertegun explained: "The name Atlantic was probably about our eightieth choice, because every name we came up with . . . had already been taken. . . . It wasn't a name we were crazy about—it was so generic. There are so many Atlantics, A&P and all that, but finally we said, who cares what we call it?"

The company's first records were not big sellers, largely because the partners had no idea of their potential audience. The discs include a recording of *This Is My Beloved*, a book of slightly erotic poetry that was popular with soldiers during World War II but a dud to veterans who had apparently returned to all the romance they could handle. Atlantic recorded Shakespeare's *Romeo and Juliet*, thinking "every university would buy at least one copy," in Ertegun's words, but "they were not interested in buying any." The company also tried a set of "trick-track children's records" that allowed a phonograph to randomly select tracks so that a set of four sides could tell 256 different stories, but that tanked, too. (Ertegun and Abramson must not have read kids to sleep at night or they would have known that children like to hear the same story over and over.)

Eventually, Atlantic found its niche with such bluesy pieces as "Drinkin' Wine Spo-Dee-O-Dee" by Stick McGhee, which went to No. 2 on the Juke Box chart in April 1949, and anything by Ruth Brown, who cut nearly 100 sides for the label between 1949 and 1961, making it possible for Atlantic to borrow

< 210 >

Yankee Stadium's nickname and become "The House That Ruth Built." Blind Willie McTell was signed, and so was Professor Longhair.

Then, in 1952, Ertegun and Abramson signed their greatest artist ever, a man born Ray Charles Robinson but known to posterity as "The Father of Soul" and "The High Priest" and to millions simply as Ray Charles. Within six months, Atlantic released two songs that would change music forever: Big Joe Turner's "Shake, Rattle and Roll," one of the first rock 'n' roll songs, and Charles's "I Got a Woman," a chart topper that established soul.

The shift in the Atlantic sound was due in part to the arrival of Jerry Wexler, filling the spot left when Herb Abramson, who had completed his dental studies on the government's nickel, was called to serve in the Army Dental Corps in Germany. (Who knew that early rock 'n' roll was so tightly connected with dentistry?) Brilliant and self-educated, Wexler was a cub reporter for *Billboard* when that magazine decided to change the name of its Race Records chart and Wexler proposed "rhythm and blues." The name stuck, but it wasn't long before Wexler decided that he would rather make records than write about them.

Wexler became the perfect partner for Ahmet Ertegun because the two were so different. Rock duos are notoriously opposed: Lennon was acid to McCartney's honey, and Jagger and Richards don't get along to this day, though they somehow keep making millions together. In Mr. Greenfield's terse summary, Wexler, who died in 2008, was a hipster, and Ertegun was hip. A self-described child of the Depression, Wexler was fearful, angry, liable to fly off the handle at the slightest provocation. Ertegun was born with a sense of entitlement; he had nothing to prove, and, as Mr. Greenfield said, he was "always cool."

Was he ever. Ertegun could play plenty of angles, but his primary occupation was simply being out and about. David Geffen, the record executive and film producer, recalls asking Ertegun how to make money in music only to have the older man stand up and shuffle across the floor. After Mr. Geffen says twice that he doesn't get it, Ertegun finally says: "If you're lucky, you bump into a genius and that makes you rich in the music business!"

Then again, Ertegun must have encountered thousands of non-starters in his nightly prowls. His focus was on the geniuses, and once he found them,

< 211 >

he gave them free rein. Rather than try to shape his artists' work to meet the desires of some perceived audience, as other executives did, Ertegun trusted the instincts of his artists as he trusted his own. The most forceful he may have been was when he advised Mick Jagger to break with the heroin-addicted Marianne Faithfull, but even here he sounds more like a wise uncle than a boss: "I've seen a lot of heartbreak with junkies. Believe me, old friend, it wrecks the lives of everyone around them as well."

It didn't hurt that Ertegun had a commanding presence. As Graham Nash recalls: "This guy could make wallpaper turn around and look at him. Every time he walked into a room, it didn't matter who else was there. Elvis could have been there and everyone would have been looking at Ahmet."

To Robert Plant he was "this absolutely elite gentleman, the master of serenity, as much at home with the backstage cavorting of Led Zeppelin as he was with the politesse of high society. . . . He was, to me, an oasis and a model—how to be settled in the midst of all this madness, how to know when to get excited and when not."

Mr. Plant also said: "We had some memorable nights together; I wish I could remember them." And that brings up one startling aspect of Ertegun's life, which is how little it startles. Late in the book, there is a reference to Ertegun's "always unbridled sexual appetites," but in an age of tell-all biographies, this one tells very little. Just before the end, there are a couple of pages on Ertegun's fondness for putting his hands up women's skirts, but his wife says, "I couldn't care less." Apparently Mr. Greenfield figures that if she doesn't care, why should we? Like its subject, *The Last Sultan* is all business.

"YOU OUGHTA WRITE about surfing!" blurted out Dennis Wilson in 1961 when he heard big brother Brian wondering out loud about subjects for his songs, and with that, pop music took a sharp turn and headed for the beach. In this way, writes Peter Ames Carlin, the Beach Boys join Melville, Twain, Hemingway, Kerouac, and others who patterned their work on "the impulse to break free from buttoned-down society," though one imagines that, given the group's seductively tinny guitar sounds and tight harmonies that peaked with Brian's

< 212 >

trademark falsetto, the Beach Boys could have sung about stamp collecting and still sold records by the millions.

Nothing came to them that easy, of course; the story of how dad-turned-manager Murry Wilson's clobbered the self-esteem of his oldest, most talented, and tragically thin-skinned son is well-known, and one approaches yet another re-telling with a certain jitteriness. But Carlin's *Catch a Wave: The Rise, Fall & Redemption of the Beach Boys' Brian Wilson* joins that elite rank of music biographies (Bob Spitz's *The Beatles* is another notable example) that doesn't simply clock a band's rise to fame but actually shows how its members developed their signature sound, and there is no doubt that Murry's insistence on dogmatic commercialism kept the boys' songs grounded "in the same public schools, libraries, hamburger stands, and city beaches where the vast majority of working-to-middle-class kids found love, heartbreak, and meaning."

But his incessant bullying broke Brian: it isn't long after the Beach Boys fire Murry (who immediately takes over a sound-alike band called the Sunrays) that Carlin is referring to Brian as "veering between humor, eccentricity, genius, and incipient insanity."

By then, Brian is spending most of his time in seclusion, having been replaced on the road by Bruce Johnston, who looked like the bandleader and even hit his high notes well enough to fool fans. By 1982, Brian's weight had ballooned to 340 pounds, yet he still hadn't found the courage to release *Smile*, the ground-breaking album he and Van Dyke Parks wrote and recorded most of in 1966 and 1967.

In Bob Stanley's brilliant survey of the golden age of pop music, there is a quick portrait of the enigmatic Brian, who carried the whole band's weight on his shoulders and paid a price for doing so. Dozens of writers have tried to explain Wilson's fragile genius and failed, whereas Stanley says his emotions simply "seemed to come out without any filter for what was deemed cool, or appropriate, or even musically acceptable"

Seemingly "unaware of any concept of roots credibility," Wilson was "pop's own Charlie Brown," a naïve bear of a man who wore his heart where everyone could see it and were welcome to it, too. Stanley describes Wilson leaving a 2004 London performance to a standing ovation and catching his shirt on

< 213 >

something: "Everyone wanted to run on stage and help him, wanted to help Brian Wilson. After what seemed an age he noticed what was wrong, but not before he had appeared, in front of two thousand people, as a lost little boy, Charlie Brown aged sixty-five, bumbling and bemused."

Carlin's account ends at that same event, the triumphant premiere of *Smile* in London's Royal Festival Hall on February 20, 2004, giving the story a graceful curve that begins with a gifted musician's descent into hell and ends with his release.

Still, a question remains. Without a doubt, Murry Wilson made Brian and the band a success. But would they have gone even farther without him?

MICHAEL JACKSON HAD TROUBLES with his producer/father as well. According to Nelson George, Jackson is pop culture's Rorshach text: the third member of pop's Holy Trinity, Jackson attracts more variant readings than Elvis and the Beatles combined. Putting aside his controversial personal life, you can begin with his radical changes in appearance over the years as he became a slave to plastic surgery and skin lightening. In this respect, at least, the most charitable approach is that of a nine year-old fan George spoke to in 2009 who had decided that there were two Michael Jacksons, one black and one white, and that the boy, "himself a dark brown," loved both.

If the lives of most celebrities are complicated, Jackson's was a three-ring circus, a zoo, and a nightmare all rolled up into one. Nelson George is a veteran music journalist whose book is a brief take on Michael Jackson's artistic career alone; the allegations about child abuse and addiction are either mentioned only briefly or ignored. But George does hit on several key incidents that helped to create the most widely-known international celebrity of our time, a person described on countless blogs and web sites as being as great as a god and as evil as Satan himself.

The first great musical influence on Michael was his father Joe, an "undeniable yet unlikeable hero," in George's words, a taskmaster who drilled the Jackson 5 relentlessly and imparted a rigorous work ethic but beat the boys as

< 214 >

well. "My father would kill me, just tear me up," Michael recalled.

Mother Katherine's influence was rather different. A devout Jehovah's Witness, she believed that heavenly reward was not as important as the idea of an earth repopulated by the righteous, a doctrine that shows up in lyrics and videos that portray Michael as a redeemer capable of transforming humanity.

Then there's *The Wiz*, the ill-fated remake of *The Wizard of Oz* that took twenty year-old Michael to New York at the height of the disco era. At night he was a regular at Studio 54 and other clubs, where he received an education in both fashion and dance moves that influenced him for the rest of his life. And it was on the set of *The Wiz* that Michael worked for the first time with legendary producer Quincy Jones, who became a second father to him, a nurturing one this time who turned the young singer into a mature artist.

A single month in 1984 marks a peak in Michael Jackson's career in more than one way. In February, he won an unprecedented eight Grammys, including producer of the year (shared with Quincy Jones), record of the year for "Billie Jean," and album of the year for *Thriller*. Yet a few weeks earlier, his hair caught fire while he was filming a Pepsi commercial. Friends and business associates alike say this is when Michael began taking the painkillers to which he would become addicted and that would kill him.

Earlier, he'd had a nose job and began the lightening that would eventually turn his skin bizarrely pale. After the fire, the changes intensified. And as George notes in perhaps his book's most chilling sentence, "once he had altered his face and lost contact with his original features, there was no turning back".

George makes a valuable distinction between pop songs, which stay within the boundaries of melody and only break out towards the end; rhythm 'n' blues tunes, in which the performer sings in and around the melody; and soul music, which has often has a deliberately rough edge. Within pop's confines, Michael Jackson achieved a genius of sorts in which he balances calculated commerce with what George calls the artist's "playful nightmares."

Eventually, the nightmares took over. After Joe Jackson and Quincy Jones, Michael made the worst possible choice for a third father: himself. No doubt he thought he was old enough to step into the role, but George explains the switch

< 215 >

another way in one of the book's most astute asides.

> It's often been observed that for athletes the legs are the first to
> go. They don't run as fast, jump as high, or fool others as easily
> with clever footwork. I think a similar thing is true of pop stars. As
> they age, they don't move as swiftly or as gracefully onstage, and
> their understanding of dance music erodes. When pop stars are
> young, making music, creating danceable music for peers, comes
> easily, because they are their own audience as much as fans are.
> Ray Charles, James Brown, Stevie Wonder, Prince, and Michael
> Jackson, men who made some of the greatest jams of their era,
> found their commercial fortunes begin to ebb as soon as they lost
> touch with the dance floor.

Quincy Jones was Michael's primary producer from age nineteen to twen-ty-nine; when Michael replaced him with himself, the dance jams began to shade into more emotional performances. Meanwhile, the artist's life, like his facial features, become a parody of itself.

In a sense, the nine year-old boy who said there were two Michael Jacksons was right. A loyalist to the end, Nelson George concludes that "great art is a projection of an individual's highest, most evolved self." Lucky the fan who, in a case like this, can focus on the art and not the all too frail human vessel whence it sprang.

AH, PARENTS. If you're one, the slouchy photo on the cover of her memoir of a teenaged Cyndi Lauper in tank top and platform heels is likely to trigger an automatic "Go to your room, young lady!" Not that that would have worked: she was mouthy then and is mouthy now, and if the many and detailed events of this memoir are to be believed, when Authority wags its stern finger in her face, even today she responds with a finger, though a different one, of her own.

As a youngster, she had plenty of reasons to be rebellious, including a creepy stepdad whom she fled when she was seventeen. She bounced from job

< 216 >

to job and lover to lover like a richocheting bullet, and when she finally says, "at the time, I didn't know that what I might have had was ADD," you buy her self-diagnosis.

She alway had a big voice, though, and as she bounced from band to band as well, it just got bigger, expressing itself best in one of the greatest pop songs of our time, "Girls Just Wanna Have Fun." Early on, record executives said they were going to make her into the next Streisand and have her sing ballads, but Lauper told them she was a rocker instead. Actually, what she remembers saying was, "I can't take enough medication to stay still that long, okay?" By then, she'd been around the music business enough to know that your first hit defined you, and for someone who sizzled the way she did, a dreamy love song might have meant donning a mask she could never take off.

The original "Girls Just Want to Have Fun" was written by a man and portrays women as trampy airheads. Initially, Lauper is simply put off, but her producer keeps urging her to rework the song in her own terms, and as she begins to think about what women really want, the word "anthem"comes to mind. She changes the key and adds a reggae bounce as well as a guitar riff from "Feel So Good," the catchy tune by Shirley and Lee.

Then girl-group pioneer Ellie Greenwich, who wrote and produced "Be My Baby" and Leader of the Pack," is brought in. The first thing she does is take Lauper into the studio hallway and have her chant what will become the song's hook: "Girls / They want / Want to have fun."

A Buddy Holly hiccup is thrown in on the word "fun," and by the time it's ready to record, says Lauper, her most famous song is "a combination of a Bob Marley blues approach to reggae, some Elvis Costello, a little Elvis Presley, Buddy Holly, Frankie Lymon, some Ronnie Spector, and of course Shirley and Lee." By standing on the shoulders of giants as well as staying true to her own sense of what it means to be a woman and an artist, Lauper comes through with a breakout hit that lodges at #2 on the Billboard Hot 100 for two weeks and nets her two Grammy nominations as well.

Cyndi Lauper never had the career of Madonna, whom the press pitched as her rival, even though the two like and admire each other. She fought a constant battle against sexism in the industry, and not just with crass business-

< 217 >

men: when Bob Dylan said, "I would have you in my band—and that's saying something, because I don't like chicks in bands," she had to explain that his "compliment" was an insult.

There were more hits, of course, such as "Time After Time" and "True Colors." And Lauper opened doors for performers like Lady Gaga. In 2010, Lady Gaga performed at a human rights dinner. Barack Obama introduced her by saying it was a privilege to open for her, and when Lauper teased him later, Obama, ever the diplomat, said, "She took all your moves! You're the original."

It's too bad she never got back into the studio with Ellie Greenwich and put together that magic cocktail of borrowings and influences. Yet who would not want to be remembered for just one great song—in this case, perhaps *the* perfect pop song?

There are YouTube videos of Lauper in the Buenos Aires airport in 2011, entertaining a group of stranded passengers with an impromptu version of "Girls Just Wanna Have Fun." The big voice hasn't aged a bit, and the crowd, most of whom look as though they hadn't been born when her 1983 hit came out, sing along delightedly as they celebrate a great tune and an even greater truth: there are two halves to the human race, and each is as entitled to pleasure as the other.

HERE'S A QUIZ FOR YOU: name the four performers who won an Oscar for acting and also had a number-one musical album. Okay, Sinatra is a gimme, and it won't surprise you to learn that Bing Crosby and Barbara Streisand are also on the list. [468] But that fourth name might be a little harder to come up with, so let's range back and forth over the last half-century of the entertainment business, as producer and music industry executive Clive Davis does in his autobiography, and give that last bit of show-biz trivia time to bob to the surface.

If the sixties were the golden age of rock 'n' roll, the last decade has been a peak period for books on that era. You could assemble a good-sized library on Elvis, the Beatles, the Rolling Stones and Bob Dylan alone, and there are plenty of volumes on or by (or both) artists as diverse as James Brown, Fats Domino, the Doors, Aretha Franklin, Jimi Hendrix, Tina Turner, and Neil

< 218 >

Young, to name just a few. There are invaluable books on some of essential if less visible figures in the music industry as well, like songwriters Doc Pomus and the team of Jerry Leiber and Mike Stoller. Two years ago, a biography appeared of Ahmet Ertegun, who founded Atlantic Records and who, along with Motown's Berry Gordy, Jr., might be said to rival Davis's range and influence in contemporary music.

Until now, though, no one has written a book that reveals as much about the industry as Davis's book does. In his self-portrayal, he comes across as the nicest guy in the world, but make no mistake about it: this is one mogul who loves his successes, acknowledges his screw-ups, and remembers every slight, often shedding crocodile tears as he points to yet another artist who might have had a career if only he'd listened to the old square from Brooklyn who knew what an audience wanted, what separated a song that sizzled from one that didn't.

Davis's parents died when he was still a teenager. Neither were college grads, but he attended New York University on a full scholarship and went on to Harvard Law School. His first job was with a firm that handled entertainment law, and that led to a position with Columbia Records. At the time, Columbia's stars included Dinah Shore and Rosemary Clooney, and in Davis's account, he and his associates sound like the executives in *Mad Men* trying to come to terms with a culture that was turning from martinis and fedoras to pot and Afros.

His colleague Mitch Miller called rock 'n' roll "musical baby food," which boosted the perception that Columbia was hostile to a sound that was defining a new type of American known as the teenager, a kid who had no interest in being a younger version of his parents but instead wanted his own money, car, clothes, and music. Davis didn't see rock 'n' roll as the end of civilization, as many of his peers did. As he says, it "just wasn't for me."

But he recognized good product, even if his lawyer's sensibilities sometimes got in the way. One of his early showdowns with an artist came when he had to tell Bob Dylan that the label wouldn't allow "Talkin' John Birch Society Blues" on his second album because the lyrics claim that all Birchers espoused "Hitler's views," which meant any member of the group could sue for slander.

< 219 >

"What *is* this?" Dylan exclaimed. "What do you *mean* I can't come out with this song?" Davis laid out his liberal credentials, including the fact that he had worked for Adlai Stevenson's campaign. Predictably, Dylan was unimpressed, though in later years he either forgave the affront or simply forgot about it.

Everyone knows what happened next. The Beatles toured America in 1964, and the musical world turned on its head.

In one of those weird alchemical exchanges that delight cultural historians, the boys from Liverpool, like the Rolling Stones and other English bands, discovered the music of America's black singer-songwriters, covering songs by Chuck Berry, Fats Domino, and Little Richard until they were savvy enough to write their own; in effect, they imported American-based music back to America, where an eager generation of kids with cash in their pockets snapped up 45s and LPs as fast as they rolled into the record store. The Beatles had signed with Capital Records, though, and while Columbia had a few English groups on Epic, its sister label, the problem was obvious. As Davis puts it, "we were very thin in the music of tomorrow."

"I knew what the problems were," he says, "but I didn't yet know how to fix them." He makes a few tentative moves, but his Saul of Tarsus moment doesn't come until a few years later when he attends the Monterey Pop Festival, where his v-necked tennis sweater and white pants set him apart as a fashion rebel among all those dashikis and caftans.

Then, on June 17, 1964, he hears an unsigned band called Big Brother and the Holding Company, whose singer, Janis Joplin, delivers a version of Big Mama Thornton's "Ball and Chain" that is now regarded, in Davis's words, as "not merely one of Janis's greatest moments onstage, but as one of the classic performances in rock history. It was simply overwhelming." [

Goodbye, Dinah; see you, Rosemary. Janis was "hypnotic," Davis writes. "Mesmerizing. She had a voice like no other—raspy, pleading, dominating, aggressive, vulnerable, the most expressive white female soul singer anybody had could have ever seen."(Her performance is available on YouTube, where, at roughly the 3:30 point in the clip, someone who appears to be Mama Cass Elliot is caught looking at Janis in open-mouthed wonder.) "This is a social and musical revolution," he thinks, "how could it be that none of us in the East

< 220 >

knew that this was taking place?" And then "this has got to be my moment, I thought. I've got to sign this band."

Despite their differences, Davis quickly established a rapport with Joplin, even if their relationship didn't start out quite the way she wanted. Band manager Albert Grossman told Davis that Joplin wanted to "ball" him to make their relationship more meaningful. The bemused executive demurred, and evidently their pact was sealed with nothing more than a firm handshake, although a male member of the band did attend the signing naked.

Davis couldn't have done better than to start this new phase of his career with Janis Joplin. For one thing, she listened to him. The original version of one of her biggest hits, "Piece of My Heart," ran longer than four minutes, which meant its radio play would be limited; too, the chorus wasn't repeated often enough to become the irresistible hook in the version we know today.

Davis put it to Joplin plainly. Without a hit single, the album might sell two or three hundred thousand copies; with a radio hit, it would do twice that, maybe more. Deep-dyed in her generation's skepticism toward The Man, Joplin wasn't pleased with the suggestion, but she went along. "Piece of My Heart" went to number twelve on the charts, and the *Cheap Thrills* album rose to number one, selling more than a million copies.

And that's what producers do. Referring to legendary producer Jimmy Iovine, Gwen Stefani refers to "Jimmy jail"—the purgatory Iovine sends his artists to again and again "to write that last track, that career-changing track," Ms. Stefani says in an interview. As painful as that jail can be, Mr. Iovine's nose for hits is usually right. "The good news is, he's Jimmy," Ms. Stefani said. "The bad news is, he's Jimmy."

The interaction between producer Davis and performer Joplin set up a template that not only determined the rest of Davis's career but also his account of it. From this point on, his memoir is largely the story of artists who ignored his advice and those who took it. As he explains it, if Laura Nyro, Loudon Wainwright III, Gil Scott-Heron, Jeff Healey, Taylor Dayne, and Curtis Stigers haven't had the same careers as Simon and Garfunkel, Santana, the Grateful Dead, Rod Stewart, Dionne Warwick, Whitney Houston, and Bruce Springsteen, it's because the members of the first group didn't listen to

< 221 >

suggestions offered by Davis that might have given propelled them to the stardom of the second.

Most of his suggestions had to do with one thing: songwriting. In Davis's retelling, Nyro and company thought of themselves as pure artists; they didn't want to write with others, and they didn't want to sing songs someone else had written.

In a telling anecdote, he recalls bumping into John Lennon in a coffee shop and asking him what new music he liked. Apparently the former Beatle had forgotten that he and his then-novice bandmates got their start by aping their betters as he replied, "Clive, let me ask you a question. Do you think Picasso went to the galleries to see what was being painted before he put a brush to canvas?"

The answer, of course, is yes: Picasso's earlier paintings are shaped by artists as diverse as Paul Cézanne and the African maskmakers, and even in late life he incorporated the work of Velazquez, Delacroix, and Manet into his own. If you put any Beatles song up against a solo effort by John Lennon, you see why collaboration is a good thing.

Davis is unfailingly polite as he tells his tales of artists who disagreed with him and always wishes them well (evidently their tepid sales are punishment enough), although he does it so often that, after a while, you begin to suspect that he's enjoying himself a little too much.

He is also frank about the times he was fired, which led to his becoming founder and president of Arista Records and, later, J Records. He mentions his rare artistic misstep, as when he turned down Tom Petty and instead chose Dwight Tilley (who?).

It's hard to imagine a better insider account of popular music during its fifty-year peak than this one, especially as that era is essentially over. The way music delivered is changing so radically that it won't take fifty years for someone to write the next installment. As recently as a year ago, music executives were saying that the future lies in digital subscription, but already download services like iTunes are beginning to appear antiquated as more and more listeners turn to free streaming sites like Pandora, Spotify, and YouTube.

< 222 >

Is all that music meant for the ages? Hardly. Not long ago, I had lunch with Otis Redding's daughter; when I said her father's songs would still be sung a hundred years from now, she said, "Yes, but in ten years, can you imagine anyone singing a song by _____," and she named one of Davis's artists.

As far as schlock goes, Davis has a lot to answer for—Kelly Clarkson, for example. (To be fair, Davis points out that Clarkson is not a very good listener.) And recently, when I asked singer-songwriter Richard Thompson what he thought of Davis's re-launching of Carlos Santana's career by pairing the musical pioneer with younger artists like Matchbox Twenty vocalist Rob Thomas, Thompson stiffened visibly and said, "I wish Carlos had chosen to remain a bit poorer!"

But in the end, wealth is the point. Davis trumpets his musicians' artistry on every page, though if you want to know how many units of what album shipped when, he'll tell you that as well. True, he gave the world Janis Joplin, but he also made a lot of money along the way. Ultimately, he and his artists made their millions through collaboration. It's difficult to express here what only the book can convey, which is that Davis's successes were built on working with musicians, usually over hundreds of hours of studio time, rather than dictating to them. The important thing for the individual singer or band is not to agree to every proposition; it's to listen to it.

Oh, and the fourth artist to have both an Oscar and a number one album is Jamie Foxx, whom Davis signed to J Records in 2004. Surprised? Don't be. Foxx may not be in the same category as Sinatra, but somewhere along the line, he learned the most important lesson a producer can teach, which is that, if you really want to reach your audience, and somebody who knows the business better than you do says he has a suggestion, hear him out.

< 223 >

Epilog:
Attack of the Killer Turntables

When the two Voyager spacecraft were launched in 1977, included on board were phonograph records made of gold-plated copper that contained sounds and images intended to convey the diversity of Earth culture. Given the relatively tiny size of the two Voyagers as they sail through the vastness of interstellar space, it's unlikely that an alien civilization will ever encounter them, much less delve into their contents. And if spidery life forms from some other solar system are able to queue up the one-of-a-kind LPs and actually play them, you and I won't know about it: Voyager 1 isn't expected to reach the vicinity of another star for 40,000 years or so.

Still, you want to put your best foot forward, and one can only imagine the wrangling that took place as the committee chose the records' contents; as we have seen, it's impossible to tell an audience what it will like. In the end, the musical selections included pieces by Mozart, Beethoven, Stravinksy and Chuck Berry. Not long after the first probe was launched, a character played by Steve Martin on a *Saturday Night Live* episode reported that aliens had indeed played one of the records and sent back an urgent four-word response: "Send more Chuck Berry."

Sure, it was just a comedy sketch, but it gives one hope that other civilizations will get along just fine with ours. In most movie and television treatments, the aliens are a crew of scaly lizard-like conquistadors (think *V for Visitors* or *Independence Day*) who want to enslave us or plunder our resources or just eat us à la carte.

But what if all they really want to do is bop to the beat of "Johnny B. Goode" (the Berry tune chosen for the Voyager record)? Okay, but now ask yourself, you middle-aged highbrow aging hippie: What if the Voyager probes had been launched in 2007, say, and the aliens ended up listening to Eminem or Snoop

< 225 >

Dog and Dr. Dre instead? Would rap have convinced them that we Earthlings are (or were—remember, this is 40,000 years from now) a bunch of materialistic, thuggish, wildly self-centered misogynists ? Which brings up an uneasy question, namely: Are we ? Wildly self-centered, at least?

THE SERIOUS POINT LURKING in all this is that, yes, music matters here on Earth, as it might in other planetary systems as well. What we like about it, how it moves us individually and in groups as we sing along with and dance to it, how it intersects with the rest of our world, and, not incidentally, how we go about making it and selling it—all this tells us something important about ourselves. And how music changes does, too.

We're at a milestone in the history of pop music, which makes it high time to look at the recent changes that have taken place in music and in our culture in general. 2012 marked the fiftieth anniversary of the founding of the Beatles, the Rolling Stones and the Beach Boys, among other bands. But it was also the threshold of other anniversaries that are just as resonant: The Cuban Missile Crisis turned now fifty years old, and a year later, we noted the fiftieth anniversary of JFK's assassination.

It's also worth noting that no less than six James Bond movies appeared between 1960 and 1969, fitting reminders of an era in which popular culture and politics not only collided but reached critical mass, setting off chain reactions that still shape our lives today. With the advantage of hindsight, we can see how art forms like movies and music are inseparable from the society that shapes and is shaped by them. Often my college students write nostalgically of the fabled Sixties, a period they never knew. They say they "miss" the music, the drugs and the sex, although how they could pull on more powerful weed and have more sex than they're having now is a mystery to me.

A lot of them are particularly irritated about having missed the music when it was new. As time passes, ever younger music fans shift the goalposts of musical memory: "Why couldn't I be around in the '70s?" complained "HeyGray-Day", writing in an interactive internet nook, after hearing for the first time the

< 226 >

Grateful Dead's "Look Out of Any Window" from the 1970 *American Beauty* album. "All the music today is absolute shit. And this is coming from a 16-year-old girl. I'm done with all this techno pop LMFAO Flo Rida Jennifer Lopez crap that is the new norm. I want to hear songs like these on the radio. Please."

Some of these young fans don't know how troubled that time was. There were be-ins, sure, but there were also very edgy sit-ins at Southern lunch counters. There were light shows when Janis Joplin and the Grateful Dead and the Byrds played the Fillmore and the Avalon, but at the same time, napalm was falling over Khe Sanh and Con Thien in Vietnam. Yes, the Beatles and the Stones brought a new sound, not to mention new hairstyles. But JFK is still dead, and so is the optimistic spirit he took with him to his grave. Nostalgia always tilts toward happy; that's just human nature.

For that reason, maybe it's better the students don't know.

Of all the things that happened roughly fifty years ago, which was the one that marked a dividing line not just between time periods but between one way of viewing the world and a totally divergent outlook? Some might vote for Marilyn Monroe's death at the age of 36; that punched a hole in the shimmering aura of American entertainment culture bigger than any that had been punched before.

But the JFK assassination wins by far. The best description of the difference his murder caused appears in a 1983 *Rolling Stone* essay by novelist Don DeLillo called "American Blood: A Journey through the Labyrinth of Dallas and JFK." Before Dallas, writes DeLillo, Americans saw the world as a coherent narrative—a Western, essentially, with good guys and bad guys, lone-gunman killers and Gary Cooper-style sheriffs to oppose them.

But by the time the rifle fire had stopped echoing in Dealey Plaza, the world had changed. America suddenly entered a moment of "randomness," says DeLillo, that continues to this day. On the afternoon of November 22, 1963, this country woke violently from the sweet sleep of the postwar period, an idyll of good jobs and stable family life that came after a conflict in which white-hatted American virtue trounced villainy.

Until the JFK assassination, life did seem like a Western movie or TV show

< 227 >

in many ways: you lived in your town and didn't think too much about what was going on elsewhere, because our leaders were good and strong people who knew how to take care of all that for us.

Then one day "a stranger walks out of the shadows," as DeLillo puts it, "a disaffected man, a drifter with three first names and an Okie look about him, tight-lipped and squinting." According to the old scenario, the sheriff gets rid of the scalawag and life goes on. No Texas tough guys stopped Lee Harvey Oswald, however.

Whatever else happened next, starting roughly fifty years ago, one thing we can be sure of is that the music changed. Music used to be entertainment, and its lyrics were romantic, clever or downright vapid. A lot of that persisted after November 1963, but popular music, and especially music for the young, quickly got heavy, political and sometimes downright philosophical.

Starting with "He Was a Friend of Mine," about the Kennedy assassination itself, folk and folk-rock emerged thanks to Bob Dylan, Phil Ochs and many others. It went electric, rock went mainstream, and soon millions were listening to songs like "Eve of Destruction", "For What It's Worth," and "Ohio." Even the Beatles got serious (after getting stoned), and Jimi Hendrix covered Dylan's cryptic "All Along the Watchtower." We had come a very long way in a very short time from the Andrews Sisters' "Three Little Fishes" singing "boop boop dittum dottum wattum choo,", and even from Elvis's "Heartbreak Hotel."

The elders, straining to keep up with a musical culture that was not only louder and more electric, but that was now supposed to even mean something, didn't know what to make of it. Being born to be wild was different to them from asking how much is that doggie in the window. The vaunted generation gap of the time had more to do with shifting musical tastes, the mores they reflected and advanced, than it probably did with anything else.

Mainstream gagsters had some fun with all this. From time to time on episodes of *My Favorite Martian* which ran from 1963 to 1966, "Martian" Ray Walston would produce a tiny box and play from it a snippet of "Martian music"—which was just a rapid-fire fritzing of dissonant buzzes and popping sounds—pronouncing it beautiful. Mere human Bill Bixby reacted with total bewilderment, which the audience was supposed to understand as code for a

< 228 >

typical adult reaction to something like the Byrds' synthesizer-inflected "Eight Miles High."

There were arguments within the subculture, too, and occasionally within the music itself. Don McLean's popular 1971 song "American Pie," ruing "the day the music died," in fact excoriated first the Beatles and then Roger Mc-Guinn and the Byrds for polluting rock 'n' roll with synthesizers and heavy lyrical themes:

Helter skelter in a summer swelter
The birds flew off with a fallout shelter
Eight miles high and falling fast
It landed foul on the grass

Those arguments and those changes now seem to most of us to be so mild as to be nearly imperceptible. Change has always happened more rapidly than our ability to understand it, which is but one of reasons why life is so much fun.

But changes in what an increasing number of scholars are calling technoculture are taking place today at warp speed. "Technoculture" isn't in most dictionaries yet, but it will be, if only because it explodes what we thought was an unravelable chicken-or-egg argument about the relationship between the music itself and the package it comes in. Do we like the music of, say, the Who because of the music itself, or do we like the music because of the wildly effusive personality of the entire act?

This question no longer means the same thing in the post-JFK era. The reason is that the relationship between the music and its delivery system is vastly different from the way it was only a few decades ago.

ANY OF US CAN LOOK at that world through any number of lenses, but since more people love music nowadays than they do religion, say, or science, it suggests that if you want to understand how most of us approach life in the 21st century, you ask a deejay, not a philosopher.

Let me explain. There's a nightclub three blocks from my house where I've

< 229 >

heard everybody from Bonnie Raitt and the Neville Brothers to Los Lobos and Warren Zevon. I've seen live performances of nearly every kind of music that presently exists, from classical to gamelan to rap. An exception until recently was electronic dance music, which can take the form of house, techno, dubstep or trance. So when I heard that Bassnectar, a DJ whose real name is Lorin Ashton, was appearing at my neighborhood club, I bought a ticket.

The night of the show, the noise level was painful before I even entered the building. As a Southern man, I'm culturally obliged to lean against a wall whenever I see one, but the vibrations were so intense that every solid piece of the structure pulsed as though it were electrified. The ticket taker I spoke to said that Bassnectar would be using the club's already considerable sound system but adding his own monster amps on top of them to bring the sound to the level of unbearability.

On stage, Bassnectar moved from laptop to turntable to spin his beats as screens flashed geometric patterns as gaudy as the sound was loud. On the floor, muscular, shirtless young men and young women in shorts and bikini tops bobbed up and down. They weren't mouthing lyrics—there were none—but chopping the air the way fans do in sports stadiums. Apparently there's a significant risk of dehydration at events like this, so two ambulances were parked outside next to the entrance. When I later asked the EMT guys if this was common practice, one said, "Only for these shows."

The club was more crowded for this show than I'd ever seen it before. No wonder promoters are trying to move in on what is a fairly straightforward operation: one person, a turntable, and whatever else you feel like adding. The whole show is portable and relatively worry-free; you don't have to house and feed a six-man horn section and hope that one of them doesn't get mugged in an alley or shot by a jealous husband.

You don't even need a single actual musical instrument. The headline of an article Ben Sisario in the *New York Times* says it all: "Electronic Dance Concerts Turn Up the Volume, Tempting Investors." I'm thinking of buying shares in a company that makes earplugs.

As we moved to the smart-phone era from what sociologist Zygmunt Bauman in his brilliant study *Liquid Modernity* calls the days of Fordism (think

< 230 >

assembly lines and socket wrenches), the soundtrack changed as well. Roger McGuinn once speculated that the underlying rhythm of popular music in any given era mimics that of the most sophisticated new transportation device of the day; that's why he adapted the synthesizer to make the Byrds' music sound like space-age travel.

But it's a generational thing as well. To my ears, Chuck Berry sounded about right with his V-8 Ford chasing Maybelline, and so did Bill Haley's "Rock Around The Clock," Elvis's "That's All Right (Mama)," and, above all, Little Richard's "Tutti Frutti." All that stuff went at least 70 miles per hour in a big-hog Chrysler or Plymouth on a hilly country road.

That was then, and this is now. They weren't around in my day, but even my students know the difference. One wrote in a recent paper that "no one genre or artist can be blamed for stupid music,"that the fault lies with the "mass media market machine" that turns music and other media into "an exact science solely for the enjoyment of the masses." That's because, she added, "in a day and age that is advancing faster than I can download an iPhone app, it makes sense that people want immediate satisfaction," which pressures media "to evolve faster to meet the demands of the people."

She meant the market, that is, the electronic cash register, but I took her point. America is now about franchised fast food, not gourmandise. It's about Hollywood gossip more than it is about the films Hollywood makes, and there's no mystery as to why that is, given the quality of most big-studio films. And that, my students tell me, is indelibly connected to the terrible and "stupid" music.

Hold on, I thought: This sounds like something someone my age would say, not a twenty year-old. I remember sitting in the back seat of my father's Buick with my friend, both of us holding our stomachs and howling with laughter as Fats Domino or Jerry Lee Lewis came on the radio and my dad pleaded, "Can't we listen to pretty music? " Youth has always dismissed its elders' preferences, which is as it should be. How else does progress happen?

So what kind of American kid despises his own mainstream culture and popular music, as so many kids today seem to do? Does that suggest some kind of problem, perhaps?

< 231 >

One shouldn't exaggerate. There is plenty of good new music out there, and once you've found it, it's easier than ever to purchase and play it. Maybe a lot of the complaints amount to typical youth snobbery. Said one student, for example, "Great music is happening today in abundance and anyone who feels differently is not looking hard enough. The realness is out there, but most people don't want to find out and would rather brush their teeth with the garbage fed to them."

Yet this same student pointed out that the technology has allowed the proliferation of so many options that audiences have become hopelessly fragmented. There's no longer a general sense of what's good and what isn't. When Bruce Springsteen was asked to give the keynote address at the 2012 South by Southwest convention, he balked at the idea that there was such a thing as a "keynote" in music today. "There is no unified theory," he said. "You can take Kiss, Phish, the Beatles, or Springsteen himself, and make a case that each makes either the best of the worst music you ever heard."

Of course, youth tastes in pop music always divide into contending schools. Even in my day some people liked the California sound of the Beach Boys and Jan and Dean while others hated it; some loved the rumbling roughness of the Rolling Stones, and others loved Motown. Some couldn't get enough of Grace Slick and the Jefferson Airplane, while others couldn't switch it off fast enough. Some devoured Dylan's earnestness and the deliberate weirdness of the Velvet Underground and the Incredible String Band; others thought anyone who listened to that stuff needed a psychiatrist. But most of us listened to all, or nearly all, of whatever came on the radio. Now kids can carve out their own narrow niches with ease. "If you literally know only one song you like," one of my students pointed out, "you can type it into Pandora and instantly have thirty new bands of a similar ilk at your fingertips."

In other words, you can be unique in your musical tastes, just like everyone else. Still, the result is a far more individuated audience. One can have a little fun with this: if Fats Waller were writing "I've Got Rhythm," today he would have to call it "I've Got Rhythm and You Don't, Because It's Mine, Mine, Mine." (He was known to ad-lib lines like that.)

< 232 >

But it's not entirely funny that there is no more youth culture music solidarity, no more defining whole generations by sound—especially now that the impossible has happened, which is that lots of kids actually like the stuff their parents listened to at their age. My students say they listen regularly to, for example, The Beatles, The Band, Bob Dylan, The Zombies, Neil Young, Crosby, Stills, Nash, and Young, Eric Clapton, The Allman Brothers, Aretha Franklin, Cream, Jimi Hendrix, Dr. John, Fleetwood Mac, Carole King, Joni Mitchell, Simon & Garfunkel, Rod Stewart, Van Morrison, and The Doors, along with twenty others I wouldn't have suspected they even knew about.

And all of this music was written and recorded long before any of these kids were born.

At their age, all I knew about my parents' music was that I didn't like it. It made me feel as though I were at a skating rink; it was to ears what lime Jell-O with marshmallows at church socials was to my taste buds. Now the young people tell me that what they don't like is the mass-market music of their own era, and that the real action now is about the music trying to break away from itself. As pop becomes more electronic, indie musicians and the labels they record on are trying to pull music back to its acoustic beginnings. Then there's the whole lo-fi movement, which uses old-school technology to put out music that sounds homemade and under-produced. I am told that some big acts and big labels are using lo-fi cynically; as a result, as one student explained, "we are distancing ourselves from and purposefully obscuring what has already existed, appropriating previously developed material and transmogrifying it without offering any generational innovation of our own. We fetishize the past while simultaneously denying it."

The technology of recording now enables just about anyone, whether he or she knows how to play a musical instrument or not, to take pieces of old recordings—a drum track, a bass riff, dogs barking—and layer it over with other canned sounds to get a new "song." This is not about money as a barrier to artistic entry but about having any musical talent at all.

As to the former, it's worth pondering the fact that, in 1953, anyone with four dollars in his pocket could record two sides on an acetate disk at Sun Stu-

< 233 >

dios; that year, Elvis Presley cut a record there, purportedly as a Mother's Day present. Today, anyone can record an album on the CD Baby web site and have it distributed to iTunes, Amazon and other online services for a one-time setup fee of $49. In 1953 dollars, that's only slightly more than Elvis paid.

It's because of the question of talent—how much and what kind of talent is required these days to make music—that the new music cannot exist without the old. If you search YouTube for "Video explains the world's most important 6-sec drum loop", you'll learn of a short solo played by the drummer of a group called The Winstons that appeared in a song called "Amen, Brother." The song was the b-side to a 45 rpm record that appeared in 1969, but it has been used by group after group ever since. It's a "six-second clip that spawned several entire subcultures," as the notes to the video say. But the video's author, Nate Harrison, transcends his immediate subject to produce nothing less than, in his words, "a meditation on the ownership of culture" and "the nature of art and creativity." Perhaps that explains why more turntables and other electronic sound gadgets have been sold in recent years than guitars. There's a gloss on the nature of creativity for you.

Moreover, we have democratized the process of making commercially viable music (or what passes for it) just as the delivery system has also become more diffused, so that the entire business model of the music industry is now shaking, rattling and rolling. That helps to explain why, in another kind of individuation, there is hardly such a thing as an album, an ensemble of songs meant to relate to one another in a whole that is more than the sum of the parts. Songs are more often bought one by one. The future of solvency in the music business seems to lie in internet providers like iTunes and stations like Sirius/X M.

While clicking an order tab on the same computer I'm writing this chapter on isn't as satisfying as getting on my bike and peddling to a music store to get the latest 45 by the Everly Brothers, I can't do that any more. Ironically, the cost of a vinyl single in the mid-1950s is about the same as the purchase price for that same song online today, taking inflation into account.. And I can get every song I loved when I was ten years old, plus all the ones that have been recorded since, and I can dial up videos on YouTube for free and see amazing stuff by some of my favorites I never even knew existed.

< 234 >

This is just a little of what I mean when I say that the relationship between the music and its delivery system has changed to the point that old questions no longer make sense. Techno-culture has now almost completely fuzzed the distinction between the how the music is created and what it actually is. Now the question comes to be more like, did the reverb switch come before that wobbling D minor chord ("borrowed" from some Kinks song from 1969) or did the chord come before the reverb switch? And who exactly should get credit for this song anyway? The mixmaster lording over the assembly process, the technological innovators who made it all possible, or Ray Davies et al.? Davies also wrote a song about the music business back in 1970 called "The Money-Go-Round" that lamented the artist getting ripped off by the companies and the middlemen. He didn't realize how good he had it and how simple things were then.

In "Lola," Davies did say that it's a mixed-up, muddled-up, shook-up world. If only he had known then how right he would turn out to be. But all is not lost. Many kids these days understand the interactions between the music, the musicians, the audiences, the technology and business models better than we ever did, and it's vastly more complicated than anything we had to deal with in the 1960s and 1970s. The kids are all right—they'll figure it out.

One hopeful sign is rock-and-roll's resurrectionist movement. Sharon Jones and the Dap-Kings, Black Joe Lewis and the Honeybears, Eli "Paperboy" Reed, St. Paul and the Broken Bones, Ryan Shaw—they're all soul revivers. They make a living doing it, too. So does Bettye Lavette doing interpretations of the British Invasion music, and note the recent album of Buddy Holly songs performed by contemporaries as different as Cee Lo Green and Fiona Apple.

One group on that *Rave On Buddy Holly* album is The Black Keys. The Black Keys are as stripped down as you can get. It's two guys, one who sings and plays guitar and another who pounds the drums. Visually, they come across like the duo you'd see in a Holiday Inn lounge when you were traveling on business and went downstairs for a drink and found yourself tapping your foot to a pair you thought might make something of themselves someday if only they

< 235 >

could get a break. The Black Keys are really, really good, and not just because their roots are in fifty-year-old music whose rhythms and chord progressions are timeless. It's because they are excellent musicians.

So if NASA ever sends out another Voyager probe with a "golden record," I'm for keeping Bach, Beethoven, Mozart and Chuck Berry. But I'd definitely add the Black Keys.

< 236 >

Sources and Suggestions
for Further Readings

I'VE ALWAYS APPROACHED THE SUBJECTS of my writing from three angles. First, I read everything I can lay my hands on. Then I visit accessible sites; in music, these might include clubs or other concert venues, museums and birth places, and living artists' homes. Finally, I talk to everybody I can: curators, other writers, the artists themselves, their fans.

It should be obvious by now that fandom, mine and others, is the engine that drives my writing. Every one of these chapters was born out of my love for its subject, and most of my research consisted to listening to the music over and over again.

However, the books and essays of others both focus and deepen my passion. What follows are the ones I found most useful. In some cases, a mere handful of sources are mentioned because that is all there are, which is another reason for my writing this book.

EPIGRAPH

Remnick, David. "We Are Alive: Bruce Springsteen at Sixty-Two." *The New Yorker*, July 30, 2012, 46.

THE HOT POTATO THEORY

Cohn, Nik. *Awopbopaloobop Alopbamboom: The Golden Age of Rock*. New York: Grove Press, 2001.

Giraldi, William. "Jack My Heart: On Obsession and the Artist." *Oxford American*, Summer 2014, 88-96.

< 237 >

Lovell, John. *Black Song: The Forge and the Flame; The Story of How the Afro-American Spiritual Was Hammered Out*. New York: Macmillan, 1972.

Marcus, Greil. *The History of Rock 'n' Roll in Ten Songs*. New Haven, CT and London: Yale University Press, 2014.

Mould, Bob with Michael Azerrad. *See a Little Light: The Trail of Rage and Melody*. New York: Little, Brown, 2011.

Pareles, Jon. "Rock Through the Ages: The Glory of Disarray." *The New York Times*, April 3, 1994.

Stanley, Bob. *Yeah! Yeah! Yeah! The Story of Pop Music from Bill Haley to Beyoncé*. New York: Norton, 2014.

STEEL DRIVIN' MAN: THE STORY BEHIND "JOHN HENRY"

Marcus, Greil. *The History of Rock 'n' Roll in Ten Songs*. New Haven, CT and London: Yale University Press, 2014.

Nelson, Scott Reynolds and Mark Aronson. *Ain't Nothing but a Man: My Quest to Find the Real John Henry*. Des Moines, IA: National Geographic Children's Books, 2007.

---. *Steel Drivin' Man: John Henry, The Story of an American Legend*. New York and London: Oxford University Press, 2008.

Roberts, Chris. *Heavy Words Lightly Thrown: The Reason Behind the Rhyme*. New York: Gotham Books, 2005.

DID GEORGIA TURNER WRITE "THE HOUSE OF THE RISING SUN"?

Anthony, Ted. *Chasing the Sun: The Journey of an American Song*. New York: Simon & Schuster, 2007.

Holden, Stephen. "Absorbing Life's Lessons, Happy or Sad / Barbara Cook Performs at Feinstein's at Loew's Regency." *The New York Times*, April 26, 2012.

< 238 >

THE CHITLIN' CIRCUIT, OR IS HITLER THE FATHER OF ROCK 'N' ROLL?

Lauterbach, Preston. *The Chitlin' Circuit and the Road to Rock 'n' Roll.* New York: W. W. Norton, 2011.

Neal, Mark Anthony. *What the Music Said: Black Popular Music and Black Public Culture.* New York: Routledge, 1998.

Walking to New Orleans: The Man Behind the World's Most Popular Music

Coleman, Rick. *Blue Monday: Fats Domino and the Lost Dawn of Rock 'n' Roll.* Boston, MA: Da Capo, 2006.

Early, Gerald. *One Nation Under a Groove: Motown and American Culture.* New York: Ecco Press, 1995.

Roach, Joseph. *Cities of the Dead.* New York: Columbia University Press, 1996.

Roche, Jimmy. Interview, Tallahassee, FL, February 13, 2010.

THE GHOST IN ROCK MUSIC: BIG BILL BROONZY

Kirby, David. "Goin' Up the Country: Intrepid Brit Seeks Blind Willie McTell." *Georgia Music*, no. 19 (Winter 2010), 18-19.

Riesman, Bob. *I Feel So Good: The Life and Times of Big Bill Broonzy.* Chicago: University of Chicago Press, 2011.

SAM COOKE, YOU SEND ME, HONEST YOU DO

Guralnick, Peter. *Dream Boogie: The Triumph of Sam Cooke.* New York: Little, Brown, 2005.

Wolff, Daniel and S.R. Crain, Clifton White, and G. David Tenenbaum. *You Send Me: The Life and Times of Sam Cooke.* New York: William Morrow, 1995.

< 239 >

Our Other National Anthem: "Tutti Frutti" and the Integration of America

Cohn, Nik. *Awopbopaloobop Alopbamboom: The Golden Age of Rock*. New York: Grove Press, 2001.

Emerson, Ken. *Always Magic in the Air: The Bomp and Brilliance of the Brill Building Era*. New York: Viking, 2006.

Herbert, Bob. "Champagne and Tears." *The New York Times*, August 30, 2008.

Hodgkinson, Will. *Song Man: A Melodic Adventure, or, My Single-Minded Approach to Songwriting*. Boston, MA: Da Capo, 2008.

Little Richard: The Specialty Sessions. Los Angeles, CA: Specialty, 1990. 3-disc box set.

Marcus, Greil. *The Old, Weird America: The World of Bob Dylan's Basement Tapes*. New York: Picador, 2011.

Smith, Harry. *Anthology Of American Folk Music*. Washington, DC: Smithsonian Folkways, 1997. 6-disc box set.

Song of America. [No city given]: Split Rock Records/Thirty One Tigers, 2007. 3-disc set.

White, Charles. *The Life and Times of Little Richard*. Boston, MA: Da Capo, 1994.

The Joe Blow Version: Otis Redding as Torch Singer

Carey, Benedict. "A Dream Interpretation: Tuneups for the Brain." *The New York Times*, November 9, 2009.

Coldiron, Anne. Personal message to author.

Freud, Sigmund. *Beyond the Pleasure Principle*. New York: Basic Books, 2010.

---. *The Interpretation of Dreams*. New York: Bantam, 1967.

< 240 >

Mendelson, Edward. "Introduction" to *W. H. Auden: Selected Poems*. New York: Vintage, 2007.

Stanley, Bob. *Yeah! Yeah! Yeah!: The Story of Pop Music from Bill Haley to Beyoncé*. New York: Norton, 2014.

Stax Profiles: Otis Redding. Berkeley, CA: Stax Records, 2006

The Very Best of Otis Redding. Los Angeles, CA: Rhino Records, 1992.

THE DEVIL AND JERRY LEE LEWIS

Bonomo, Joe. *Jerry Lee Lewis: Lost and Found*. New York: Continuum, 2009.

Bragg, Rick. *All Over But the Shoutin'*. New York: Pantheon, 1997

---. . *Jerry Lee Lewis: His Own Story*. New York: HarperCollins, 2014.

THE ITALIAN-AMERICAN DECADE IN AMERICAN MUSIC

Dimucci, Dion with Davin Seay. *The Wanderer: Dion's Story*. New York: Quill, 1989.

Rotella, Mark. *Amore: The Story of Italian American Song*. New York: Farrar, Straus & Giroux,2010.

THE DANCER FROM THE DANCE: PEGGY LEE AND MARY WELLS

Banjaminson, Peter. *Mary Wells: The Tumultuous Life of Motown's First Superstar*. Chicago, IL: Chicago Review Press, 2012.

George, Nelson. *Where Did Our Love Go?: The Rise and Fall of the Motown Sound*. Champaign, IL: University of Illinois Press, 2007.

Richmond, Peter. *Fever: The Life and Music of Miss Peggy Lee*. New York: Henry Holt, 2007.

< 241 >

THE SAVAGE YOUNG BEATLES

MacDonald, Ian. *Revolution in the Head: The Beatles' Records and the Sixties.* Chicago: Chicago Review Press, 2007.

Spitz, Bob. *The Beatles: The Biography.* New York: Little, Brown, 2005.

Stark, Steven D. *Meet the Beatles: A Cultural History of the Band That Shook Youth, Gender, and the World.* New York: William Morrow, 2006.

GIRL GROUPS AND GO-GO DANCERS: ROCK 'N' ROLL COMES OF AGE

Austen, Jake. *TV a Go-Go: Rock on TV from American Bandstand to American Idol.* Chicago: Chicago Review Press, 2005.

Emerson, Ken. *Always Magic in the Air: The Bomp and Brilliance of the Brill Building Era.* New York: Viking, 2006.

Marcus, Greil. *The History of Rock 'n' Roll in Ten Songs.* New Haven, CT and London: Yale University Press, 2014.

Viertel, Jack. "Leiber's Second Act: Broadway's Pioneer." *The New York Times,* September 3, 2011.

Weiss, Mary. Quoted by Greil Marcus in "Real Life Top Ten," *Salon,* October 1, 2001.

Wilson, Daniel J. "Covenants of Work and Grace: Themes of Recovery and Redemption in Polio Narratives." *Literature and Medicine,* 13 (Spring 1994): 22-41.

A BIGGER WORLD: MARTHA AND THE VANDELLAS' "DANCING IN THE STREET"

Kurlansky, Mark. *Ready for a Brand New Beat: How "Dancing in the Street"*

< 242 >

Became the Anthem for a Changing America. New York: Riverhead, 2013.

"I Don't Play Guitar, I Play Amp": How Jimi Became Jimi

Roby, Steven and Brad Schreiber. *Becoming Jimi Hendrix: From Southern Crossroads to Psychedelic London, the Untold Story of a Musical Genius.* Boston, MA: Da Capo, 2010.

"Everybody's Audience Was Hipper Than Mine": The Jewish Elvis

Greene, Andy. "Neil Diamond, Rock and Roll Hall of Fame Inductee, Says He Feels 'Very Lucky.'" *Rolling Stone*, December 10, 2014.

Wild, David. *He Is . . . I Say: How I Learned to Stop Worrying and Love Neil Diamond.* Boston, MA: Da Capo , 2008.

Everybody Who Heard Them Started a Band: The Velvet Underground, The Doors

Marcus, Greil. *The Doors: A Lifetime of Listening to Five Mean Years.* New York: PublicAffairs, 2011.

Jovanovic, Rob. *Seeing the Light: Inside the Velvet Underground.* New York: St. Martin's, 2012.

The Very Best of the Velvet Underground. Music CD: Ume Imports, 2006

The Velvet Underground —Under Review. Documentary DVD: Sexy Intellectual, 2006.

< 243 >

Great Song. Who Wrote It? Doc Pomus and Townes Van Zandt

Halberstadt, Alex. *Lonely Avenue: The Unlikely Life and Times of Doc Pomus*. Boston, MA: Da Capo, 2007.

Kruth, John. *To Live's to Fly: The Ballad of the Late, Great Townes Van Zandt*. Boston, MA: Da Capo, 2008.

Song Man: Will Hodgkinson's Failed Quest and What We Can Learn From It

Allman, Gregg. *My Cross to Bear*. New York: William Morrow, 2012.

George-Warren, Holly. *A Man Called Destruction: The Life and Music of Alex Chilton, From Box Tops to Big Star to Backdoor Man*. New York: Viking, 2014.

Hodgkinson, Will. *Song Man: A Melodic Adventure, or, My Single-Minded Approach to Songwriting*. Boston, MA: Da Capo, 2008.

Komar & Melamid and Dave Soldier. *The Most Wanted Song / The Most Unwanted Song*. New York: Dia Center for the Arts, 1997.

Luscombe, Belinda. "Ten Questions for Sting." *Time*, November 21, 2011.

Marcus, Greil. *The History of Rock 'n' Roll in Ten Songs*. New Haven, CT and London: Yale University Press, 2014.

---. *The Shape of Things to Come: Prophecy and the American Voice*. New York: Farrar, Straus and Giroux, 2006.

Morris, Bill. "A Chiefest Pleasure: Discovering *The Sot-Weed Factor* on its 50th Birthday." *The Millions*, July 13, 2010.

Why There'll Never Be Another Willie Nelson

Gopnik, Adam. "The In-Law." *The New Yorker*, October 7 2002.

< 244 >

THE ROAD TO EXCESS: LED ZEPPELIN AND QUEEN

Doherty, Harry. *Forty Years of Queen*. New York: St. Martin's Press, 2011.

Hoskyns, Barney. *Led Zeppelin: The Oral History of the World's Greatest Rock Band*. Edison, NJ: Wylie, 2012.

Jones, Lesley-Ann. *Mercury: An Intimate Biography of Freddie Mercury*. New York: Touchstone, 2012.

Pareles, Jon. "In a Musical Pairing, Old Hands Guide a New Face: Queen + Adam Lambert Take On Madison Square Garden." *The New York Times*, July 18, 2014.

THE KIDS AREN'T ALL RIGHT: HUSKER DÜ
AND THE MEANING OF PUNK

Earles, Andrew. *Husker Du: The Story of the Noise-Pop Pioneers Who Launched Modern Rock*. Minneapolis, MN: 2010.

Mould, Bob and Michael Azerrad. *See a Little Light: The Trail of Rage and Melody*. New York: Little, Brown, 2011.

SKATEBOARDS, HEROIN, AND WHY GRUNGE MATTERS

Brannigan, Paul. *This is a Call: The Life and Times of Dave Grohl*. Boston, MA: Da Capo, 2011.

Dylan, Bob. *Chronicles, Volume 1*. New York: Simon & Schuster, 2004.

Stanley, Bob. *Yeah! Yeah! Yeah! The Story of Pop Music from Bill Haley to Beyoncé*. New York: Norton, 2014.

Yarm, Mark. *Everybody Loves Our Town: An Oral History of Grunge*. New York: Crown Archetype, 2011.

< 245 >

Anderson, Chris. *The Long Tail: Why the Future of Business is Selling Less of More.* New York: Hyperion, 2006.

Anthony, Ted. *Chasing the Sun: The Journey of an American Song.* New York: Simon & Schuster, 2007.

Bellamy, Edward. *Looking Backward: 2000-1887.* New York: Modern Library, 1951.

Brooks, David. "The Segmented Society." *The New York Times*, November 20, 2007.

Coleman, Rick. *Blue Monday: Fats Domino and the Lost Dawn of Rock 'n' Roll.* Boston, MA: Da Capo, 2006.

Early, Gerald. *One Nation Under a Groove: Motown and American Culture.* New York: Ecco Press, 1995.

Frere-Jones, Sasha. "A Paler Shade of White: How Indie Rock Lost Its Soul." *The New Yorker*, October 22, 2007.

George, Nelson. *Hip Hop America.* New York: Viking Penguin, 1998.

Guralnick, Peter. *Searching for Robert Johnson: The Life and Legend of the "King of the Delta Blues Singers."* New York: Dutton Adult, 1989.

Jay-Z. "Addicted to the Game, The *Rolling Stone* Interview." *Rolling Stone,* November 29, 2007.

MacFarquhar, Neil. "Muslim Singer With a Country Twang." *The New York Times*, November 13, 2007.

Sanneh, Kelefa. "The Shrinking Market Is Changing the Face of Hip-Hop." *The New York Times*, December 30, 2007.

< 246 >

Sharon Jones, or Why Soul Music is Forever

Borzykowski, Bryan. Personal message to author.

"A Fictitious Head of State From a Place Nobody Knows": Bob Dylan

Cott, Jonathan, ed. *Bob Dylan: The Essential Interviews*. New York: Wenner Books, 2006.

Marcus, Greil. Liner notes to *Bob Dylan—The Original Mono Recordings*. New York: Columbia/Legacy, 2010.

---. *The Old, Weird America: The World of Bob Dylan's Basement Tapes*. New York: Picador, 2011.

What Producers Do and Why We All Need One

Benjaminson, Peter. *Mary Wells: The Tumultuous Life of Motown's First Superstar*. Chicago, IL: Chicago Review Press, 2012.

Carlin, Peter Ames. *Catch a Wave: The Rise, Fall & Redemption of the Beach Boys' Brian Wilson*. Emmaus, PA: Rodale, 2007.

Davis, Clive and Anthony DeCurtis. *The Soundtrack of My Life*. New York: Simon & Schuster, 2013.

George, Nelson. *Thriller: The Musical Life of Michael Jackson*. Boston, MA: Da Capo, 2010.

Greenfield, Robert. *The Last Sultan: The Life and Times of Ahmet Ertegun*. New York: Simon & Schuster, 2011.

Lauper, Cyndi and Jancee Dunn. *Cyndi Lauper: A Memoir*. New York: Atria Books, 2012.

Miller, Steve. *Detroit Rock City: The Uncensored History of Rock 'n' Roll in America's Loudest City*. Boston, MA: Da Capo, 2013.

< 247 >

Sisario, Ben. "Jimmy Iovine, a Master of Beats, Lends Apple a Skilled Ear." *The New York Times*, May 28, 2014.

Stanley, Bob. *Yeah! Yeah! Yeah! The Story of Pop Music from Bill Haley to Beyoncé.* New York: Norton, 2014.

EPILOG: THE ATTACK OF THE KILLER TURNTABLES

Baltin, Steve. "Bruce Springsteen Delivers South By Southwest Keynote." *Rolling Stone*, March 15, 2012.

Bauman, Zygmunt. *Liquid Modernity.* Cambridge, England: Polity, 2000.

DeLillo, Don. "American Blood: A Journey through the Labyrinth of Dallas and JFK." *Rolling Stone*, December, 1983.

Sisario, Ben. "Electronic Dance Concerts Turn Up the Volume, Tempting Investors." *The New York Times,* April 4, 2012.

< 248 >

Acknowledgments

THE CHAPTERS IN THIS BOOK came from two distinct parts of my writing life. First, many of them began as book reviews that were written for various newspapers. I am grateful to the editors of *The Atlanta Journal-Constitution, The Chicago Tribune, The New York Times, Newsday, The Wall Street Journal*, and *The Washington Post* for giving me one of the best jobs in the world, one in which I get paid for writing about books I'd read for free.

That said, none of the chapters that began as reviews appear here as they did originally. Newspaper editors keep the writer to a strict word length, so if an editor wanted, say, 800 words, I'd write 2,000, send the editor the core 800, and save the longer version. Then I'd read three or four more books on the subject, make some phone calls, and, mainly, ride around and around in my car listening to the music; over time, the long version would get longer and eventually become a chapter in this book. This approach gave me the double advantage of trying my prose on some of the most gimlet-eyed editors in the business while also allowing me to develop ideas I had to treat succinctly in the original versions.

A second group of chapters consists of full-length essays, versions of which appeared first in these magazines: *American Interest* ("Attack of the Killer Turntables"and "Ebony vs. Ivory: The Re-Segregation of Rock 'n' Roll"), *The Christian Science Monitor* ("'A Fictitious Head of State From a Place Nobody Knows': Bob Dylan" and "Sharon Jones, or Why Soul Music is Forever"), and *TriQuarterly* ("Our Other National Anthem: 'Tutti Frutti' and the Integration of America"). "The Joe Blow Version" appeared in *The Poetics of American Song Lyrics (American Made Music)*,edited by Charlotte Pence, Lamar Alexander, Gordon Ball and Adam Bradley.

None of these pieces would have appeared anywhere were it not for the editors who often sought me out and sometimes were approached by me and

< 249 >

then not only said yes but saw my prose into print. They gently questioned a loose fact or a questionable word choice, offered kind words where appropriate or necessary, and put up with my queries about payment. Tom Beers, Peter Davis, Reid Davis, Dennis Drabelle, Jon Garelick, Adam Garfinkel, Dwight Garner, Margo Hammond, Marjorie Kehe, David Kelly, Laurie Muchnick, Robert Messenger, Elizabeth Taylor, Teresa Weaver, and Yvonne Zipp, you made me a better writer. To these names I add those of Okla Elliott and David Bowen of New American Press, than whom no publishers are more kind, encouraging, and quick to respond.

To my childhood friend Bill Bertrand and my colleagues John Corrigan, Thomas Joiner, Neil Jumonville, Jon Maner, Darrin McMahon, Mark Pietralunga, Dave Scott, and Mark Winegardner, I say thanks for your good will, good humor, and good sense of direction. Keep a bag packed, because there are more trips to come. To my truest friend, Barbara Hamby, thanks for always being there when I get home.

Crossroad is dedicated to Newton Collier, who played trombone with Grammy winners Sam and Dave from 1963 until their break-up in 1970. Then he worked freelance until 1973, when an unknown assailant shot him in the face, making it impossible for him to play his instrument. He had returned to his home town of Macon, Georgia, and was driving a cab when I met him during my research for a book on Little Richard. He became my guide and then my friend, and now, thanks to new technologies, he can play again.

Newt exemplifies the connection all artists have with the communities they come from and give back to. When I asked him recently how he knew so many ordinary people as well as titans of show biz, Newt said, "Well, you know me—I've got a smile on my face, and I'm always shooting the jive." That's why this book is dedicated to him.

< 250 >

Index

< 251 >

< 255 >

< 256 >

< 257 >

< 258 >

< 261 >

< 262 >

< 263 >

About the Author

DAVID KIRBY is the author or co-author of thirty books, including the poetry collections *The House on Boulevard St.: New and Selected Poems, The Ha-Ha, The House of Blue Light, and The Travelling Library*, in addition to the essay collection *Ultra-Talk: Johnny Cash, The Mafia, Shakespeare, Drum Music, St. Teresa Of Avila, and 17 Other Colossal Topics Of Conversation*. His awards include fellowships from the National Endowment of the Arts and the Guggenheim Foundation.

His *Little Richard: The Birth of Rock 'n' Roll* was named one of *Booklists*'s Top Ten Black History Non-Fiction Books of 2010 and was hailed by the *Times Literary Supplement* of London as a "hymn of praise to the emancipatory power of nonsense." Kirby is the Robert O. Lawton Distinguished Professor of English at Florida State University. For more information, see www.davidkirby.com.

CPSIA information can be obtained
at www.ICGtesting.com
Printed in the USA
FFOW03n1119250615
14628FF